A Sage's

LETTERS OF BAAL HASULAM

A Sage's Fruit

LETTERS OF BAAL HASULAM

Laitman
Kabbalah
Publishers

Yehuda Leib HaLevi Ashlag

A Sage's Fruit: letters of Baal HaSulam
Copyright © 2014 by Michael Laitman

All rights reserved
Published by Laitman Kabbalah Publishers
www.kabbalah.info   info@kabbalah.info
1057 Steeles Avenue West, Suite 532, Toronto, ON,
M2R 3X1, Canada
2009 85th Street #51, Brooklyn, New York, 11214, USA

Printed in Canada

ISBN - 978-1-897448-90-8

Library of Congress Control Number: 2014939501

Layout: Elinor Twena, Chaim Ratz
Cover Design: Inna Smirnova
Translation: Chaim Ratz
Editors: Michael R. Kellogg, Mary Pennock
Proofreading: Noga Burnot, Mary Miesem
Executive Editor: Chaim Ratz
Printing and Post Production: Uri Laitman

FIRST EDITION: DECEMBER 2014
First printing

Table of Contents

Introduction

Written by the Author's Son

Thank the Lord for His grace is everlasting. Our eyes shall see and our hearts shall rejoice with the revealing of the concealed—letters of my father and teacher that were hidden and concealed in his holy writings, and have now been printed, to open the eyes of the yearning and longing, who are thirsty for Your mercies, who crave to water and satiate their thirst from the river that comes out of Eden, to be perfumed by its light, and to be cleansed by the pleasantness of the Lord.

And once they have been rewarded, "Then shall Israel sing this song: Spring up, O well." "Spring up, O well" out of the stream to announce to Israel the wonders of the Lord upon the revelation of His mercy and kindness over they who fear Him.

Happy are they who are rewarded with clinging unto Him. It was said about them: "The secrets of Torah are revealed before him, and he becomes like an ever-flowing fountain and like a river that never stops..." This pertains to the spiritual attainment presented in this book and in the rest of his writings.

To understand even a little the meaning of spiritual attainment, I will now present an essay that I had heard from his holy mouth.

***

We discern many degrees and discernments in the worlds. We must know that everything that relates to discernments and degrees speaks of the attainment of the souls with regard to what they receive from the worlds. This adheres to the rule: **What we do not attain we do not know by name.** This is so because the word "name" indicates attainment, like a person who names some object after having attained something about it according to one's attainment.

Hence, reality in general is divided into three discernments with respect to spiritual attainment:

1. *Atzmuto* (His Essence)
2. *Ein Sof* (Infinity)
3. The Souls

1) We do not speak of **Atzmuto** at all. This is because the root and the place of the creatures begin in the Thought of Creation, where they are incorporated, as it is written, "The end of an act is in the preliminary thought."

2) **Ein Sof** pertains to the Thought of Creation, which is "His desire to do good to His creations." This is considered *Ein Sof*, and it is the connection existing between *Atzmuto* and the souls. We perceive this connection in the form of "desire to delight the creatures."

Ein Sof is the beginning. It is called "a light without a *Kli* [vessel]," yet there is the root of the creatures, meaning the connection between the Creator and the creatures, called "His desire to do good to His creations." This desire begins in the world of *Ein Sof* and extends through the world of *Assiya*.

3) The **Souls**, which are the receivers of the good that He wishes to do.

He is called *Ein Sof* because this is the connection between *Atzmuto* and the souls, which we perceive as "His desire to do good to His creations." We have no utterance except for that connection of desire to enjoy. This is the beginning of the engagement, and it is called "light without a *Kli*."

Yet, there begins the root of the creatures, meaning the connection between the Creator and the creatures, called "His desire to do good to His creations." This desire begins in the world of *Ein Sof* and extends through the world of *Assiya*.

All the worlds are, in themselves, considered light without a *Kli* where there is no utterance. They are discerned as *Atzmuto*, and there is no attainment in them.

Do not wonder that we discern many discernments there. This is because these discernments are there in potential. Afterward, when the souls come, these discernments will appear in the souls that receive the upper lights according to what they have corrected and arranged. Thus, the souls will be able to receive them, each according to its ability and qualification. And then these discernments appear in actual fact. However, while the souls do not attain the upper light, they, in themselves, are considered *Atzmuto*.

With respect to the souls that receive from the worlds, the worlds are considered *Ein Sof*. This is because this connection between the worlds and the souls, meaning what the worlds give to the souls, extends from the Thought of Creation, which is a correlation between the souls and *Atzmuto*.

This connection is called *Ein Sof*. When we pray to the Creator and ask of Him to help us and to give us what we want, we relate to the discernment of *Ein Sof*. There is the root of the creatures, which wants to impart them delight and pleasure, called "His desire to do good to His creations."

The prayer is to the Creator who created us, and His name is **"His desire to do good to His creations."** He is called *Ein Sof* because this speaks of prior to the restriction. And even after the restriction, no change occurs in Him as there is no change in the light, and He always remains with this name.

The proliferation of the names is only with respect to the receivers. Hence, the first name that appeared, that is, the root for the creatures, is called *Ein Sof* [Infinity]. And this name remains unchanged. All the restrictions and the changes are made only with regard to the receivers, and He always shines in the first name, "His desire to do good to His creations," endlessly.

This is why we pray to the Creator, called *Ein Sof*, who shines without restriction or end. The end, which appears subsequently, is corrections for the receivers so that they may receive His light.

The upper light consists of two discernments: attaining and attained. Everything we say regarding the upper light concerns only how the attaining is impressed by the attained. However, in themselves, meaning only the attaining, or only the attained, they are not called *Ein Sof*. Rather, the attained is called *Atzmuto*, and the attaining is called "souls," being a new discernment, which is a part of the whole. It is new in the sense that the will to receive is imprinted in it. And in that sense, creation is called "existence from absence."

For themselves, all the worlds are regarded as simple unity, and there is no change in Godliness. This is the meaning of "I the Lord do not change." There are no *Sefirot* and *Behinot* [discernments] in Godliness.

Even the subtlest appellations do not refer to the light itself, as this is a discernment of *Atzmuto* where there is no attainment. Rather, all the *Sefirot* and the discernments speak only of what a person attains in them. This is because the Creator wanted us to attain and understand the abundance as "His desire to do good to His creations."

In order for us to attain what He had wanted us to attain and understand as "His desire to do good to His creations," He created and imparted us with these senses, and these senses attain their impressions of the upper light.

Accordingly, we have been given many discernments, since the general sense is called "the will to receive," and is divided into many details, according to the measure that the receivers are able to receive. Thus, we find many divisions and details, called ascents and descents, expansion and departure, etc.

Since the will to receive is called "creature" and a "new discernment," the utterance begins precisely from the place where the will to receive begins to receive impressions. The speech is discernments, parts of impressions. For here there is already a correlation between the upper light and the will to receive.

This is called "light and *Kli*." However, there is no utterance in the light without a *Kli*, since a light that is not attained by the receiver is considered *Atzmuto*, where the utterance is forbidden since it is unattainable, and how can we name what we do not attain?

From this we learn that when we pray for the Creator to send us salvation, cure, and so on, there are two things we should distinguish: 1) the Creator, 2) that which extends from Him.

In the first discernment, considered *Atzmuto*, the utterance is forbidden, as we have said above. In the second discernment, that which extends from Him, which is considered the light that expands into our *Kelim*, meaning into our will to receive, that is what we call *Ein Sof*. This is the connection of the Creator with the creatures, being "His desire to do good to His creations." The will to receive is regarded as the expanding light that finally reaches the will to receive.

When the will to receive receives the expanding light, the expanding light is then called *Ein Sof*. It comes to the receivers through many covers so that the lower one will be able to receive them.

It turns out that all the discernments and the changes are made specifically in the receiver, with relation to how the receiver is impressed by them. However, we should make a discernment in the topic of discussion. When we speak of discernments in the worlds, these are potential discernments. And when the receiver attains these discernments, they are called "actual."

Spiritual attainment is when the attaining and the attained come together, as without an attaining there is no form to the attained, since there is no one to obtain the form of the attained. Hence, this discernment is considered *Atzmuto*, where there is no room for any utterance. Therefore, how can we say that the attained has its own form?

We can only speak from where our senses are impressed by the expanding light, which is "His desire to do good to His creations," which comes into the hands of the receivers in actual fact.

Similarly, when we examine a table, our sense of touch feels it as something hard. We also discern its length and width, all according to our senses. However, that does not necessitate that the table will appear so to one who has other senses. For example, in the eyes of an angel, when it examines the table, it will see it according to *its* senses. Hence, we cannot determine any form with regard to an angel, since we do not know its senses.

Thus, since we have no attainment in the Creator, we cannot say which form the worlds have from His perspective. We only attain the worlds according to our senses and sensations, as it was His will for us to attain Him so.

This is the meaning of "There is no change in the light." Rather, all the changes are in the *Kelim*, meaning in our senses. We measure everything according to our imagination. From this it follows that if many people examine one spiritual thing, each will attain according to his imagination and senses, thereby seeing a different form.

In addition, the form itself will change in a person according to his ups and downs, as we have said above that the light is simple light and all the changes are only in the receivers.

May we be granted with His light and follow in the ways of the Creator and serve Him not in order to be rewarded, but to give contentment to the Creator and raise Divinity from the dust. May we be granted adhesion with the Creator and the revelation of His Godliness to His creatures.

Baruch Shalom, son of my teacher and father,
Yehuda Leib HaLevi Ashlag, of blessed memory

Letter No. 1

1920

To my friend.

It is now noon and I have received his letter from the eighth of the first month, and your beggar's complaints against me are an accepted prayer, as it is written in *The Zohar*.

I have already proven to you in my previous letters that while you reproach me for not writing, it is your own languor you should be reproaching. Note, that since the seventh of *Shevat* [Hebrew month around February] to the eighth of *Nissan*, meaning more than two months, you have not written a word to me in more than two months, while I wrote you four letters in that time.

And if this wisp still satiates the lion, it is as it is written, "for one higher than the high watches, and high ones are atop them." And as for the answer he firmly demands, I shall reply that everyone believes in private providence, but do not adhere to it at all.

The reason is that an alien and foul thought cannot be ascribed to the Creator, who is the epitome of the "good that does good." However, only to the true workers of God does the knowledge of private providence open, that He caused all the reasons that preceded it, both good and bad. Then they are cohesive with private providence, for all who are connected to the pure, are pure.

Since the Guardian is united with its guarded, there is no apparent division between bad and good. They are all loved and all clear, for they are all carriers of God's vessels, ready to glorify the revelation of His uniqueness. It is known by instinct, and to that extent they have knowledge from the end that all the actions and the thoughts, both good and bad, are the carriers of God's vessels. He has prepared them, from His mouth they've come, and at the end of correction it will be known to all.

However, in between it is a long and threatening exile. The main problem is that when one sees some wrongful action, he falls from his degree (and clings to the famous lie and forgets that he is like an ax in the hand of the cutter). Instead, one thinks of oneself as the owner of this act and forgets the reason for all consequences from whom everything comes, and that there is no other operator in the world but Him.

This is the lesson. Although one knows it at first, still, in a time of need, one does not control this awareness and unites everything with the cause, which sentences to a scale of merit. This is the entire reply to his letter.

I have already told you face to face a true parable about these two concepts, where one teaches of the other. Yet, the force of concealment overpowers in between, as our sages said about those two jokers before the rabbi, who were amusing all those who were sad.

There is a parable about a king who grew fond of his servant until he wanted to raise him above all the ministers, for he had recognized true and unwavering love in his heart.

However, it is not royal comportment to raise one to the highest level all at once without an apparent reason. Rather, the royal comportment is to reveal the reasons for all with great wisdom.

What did he do? He appointed the servant a guard at the city gate, and told a minister who was a clever joker to pretend to rebel against the kingship and wage war to conquer the house while the guard is unprepared.

The minister did as the king had commanded, and with great wisdom and craftiness pretended to fight against the king's house. The servant risked his life and saved the king, fighting devotedly and bravely against the minister, until his great love for the king was evident to all.

Then the minister took off his clothes, and there was great laughter (for he had fought so fiercely and now realized that there was only fiction here, not reality). They laughed most when the minister told of the depth of the imaginations of his cruelty and the fear he had envisioned. Every single item in this terrible war became a round of laughter and great joy.

However, he is still a servant; he is not scholarly. How can he be raised above all the ministers and the king's servants?

Then the king thought in his heart, and said to that minister that he must disguise himself as a robber and a murderer, and wage fierce war against him. The king knew that in the second war he would display wondrous wisdom and merit standing at the head of all the ministers.

Hence, he appointed the servant in charge of the kingdom's treasure. The minister now dressed as a ruthless killer and came to loot the king's treasures.

The poor appointee fought fearlessly and devotedly until the cup was filled. Then the minister took off his clothes and there was great joy and laughter in the king's palace, even more than before.

The details of the minister's tricks aroused great laughter, since now the minister had to be smarter than before because now it is evidently known that no one is cruel in the king's domain, and all the cruel ones are but jokers. Therefore, the minister used great craftiness to acquire clothes of evil.

Yet, in the meantime, the servant inherited "wisdom" from after-knowledge, and "love" from fore-knowledge, and then has been erected for eternity.

It is true, that all the wars in that exile are a wondrous sight, and everyone knows in their kind interior that it is all a kind of wit and joy that brings only good. Still, there is no tactic to ease the weight of the war and the threat on oneself.

I have spoken of that at length to you face to face, and now you have knowledge of one end of this parable, and with God's help you will also understand it on its other end.

The thing you most want to hear me speak of is one to which I cannot answer anything. I have also told you a parable about this face to face, for "the kingdom of the earth is as the kingdom of the heaven," and the true guidance is given to the ministers.

Yet, everything is done according to the king's counsel and his signature. The king himself does no more than sign the plan that the ministers devised. If he finds a flaw in the plan, he does not correct it, but places another minister in his place, and the first resigns from office.

So is man: a small world behaving according to the letters imprinted in him, since kings rule the seventy nations in him. This is the meaning of what is written in the *Sefer Yetzira* [*Book of Creation*]: "He crowned a certain letter."

Each letter is a minister for the time being, making evaluations, and the King of the world sings them. When the letter errs in some plan, it immediately resigns from office, and He crowns another letter in its place.

This is the meaning of, "Each generation and its judges." At the end of correction, that letter called Messiah will rule. It will complement and tie all the generations to a crown of glory in the hand of God.

Now you can understand how I can interfere with your business of state, that have already ...kings and judges, and each must uncover what he has been assigned to uncover. The ferry of unification ... he does not want to correct them; I will correct them nonetheless. And yet, all will become clear through incarnations.

Because of it, I yearn to hear all your decisions in their every detail. This is because there is profound wisdom in every detail, and if I had heard some fixed orders from you, I would have been able to fulfill them and delight your heart.

Know that it is very difficult for me to hear your language, for you have no permanence in the names and their meaning. Hence, I will open a door for you in the meaning of the appellations, and you will measure for me the sentence of your wisdom. In this way, I will be able to follow your intention through.

Therefore, I will set the appellations as I have seen from all your letters, to establish between us permanently, and to know all that you write without any scrutiny, like signs on wine-jars.

We shall begin from the root of all roots, and reach the very end. Five degrees are marked in general: *Yechida, Haya, Neshama, Ruach,* and *Nefesh.* All these are put together in the corrected body.

Yechida, Haya, and *Neshama* are above time, and though found in a creature's heart, they are as considered surrounding from afar. They do not come in a body during its correction, for in the hidden source, too, there is a root discerned: *Rosh, Toch, Sof* [respectively: Head, Interior, End].

The *Rosh* is the root for the *Yechida*; it is *Ein Sof* [Infinity]. There, even in its own place, its light is undisclosed and everything is nullified as a candle before a torch.

Afterward, the root of the *Toch*, and it is the root for *Haya*. This is the meaning of the light of *Ein Sof*, meaning the appearance of His complete light. While in time, this light is attained only as its sustenance, it is called "root for *Haya*."

After that, the root for the *Sof*, and it is the root for the souls. It is just as in the beginning, *Ein Sof*. Here, an Upper Veil spreads, and the time begins in the form of "six thousand years the world exists, and one is ruined." This is called *Ruach*, *Nefesh*, and their root is cleaved to the *Neshama*.

However, they also expand below as Torah, which is a spirit of life, and commandment, which is the *Nefesh*. This *Nefesh* is the permanence, stillness, the embracing force that strengthens the body in a permanent state by the force of females imprinted in this *Nefesh*.

This *Ruach* blows the spirit of life and the light of Torah in the image of the female. Its root explains the meaning of "and breathed into his nostrils the breath of life; and man became a living soul." This pertains to the spirit that rises to the soul and receives life from it, in the light of the king's face, bringing this life to the soul, which at this time it is called "living soul."

This is also the order in all the *Zivugim* [couplings] of the seven females of the *Rosh*, and the two below in the *Nefesh*. This is the meaning of "God places the lone ones in the house," meaning when the force of the females appears, by "All glorious is the king's daughter within the palace."

The primary corrections and the work are to reveal the forces of the soul, which *The Zohar* calls "The Upper World." This, too, belongs to the hidden source, as the root of the end, and any mating is for the appearance of one light in the reality of the Upper World. This is the meaning of "We whose sons are as plants grown up in their youth," meaning the conception in the

Upper World. By the coupling ... to the lower ones ... so it came upon His thought, and the end of the beginning of the hidden source will be completed with all the lights ... a continuation from the book, *Treasure of Knowledge*.

The mind is the essence of man's soul, and the whole man. This is because in it he is entirely defined, and what comes out of it is its clothes and those who serve it. Some are its branches, and some are considered alien to it.

This force, though it is in his soul, he will still not see it; it is concealed from any living thing. Do not wonder about that, for the eye controls and is the most important among all senses. Yet, one never sees oneself, but only feels one's existence. Vision would have added no knowledge to them at all, and hence, nothing was created in vain, for they are sensations to them, and there is no need to add to the sensation.

There is also the mental power, which is the essence of man. It is not given in any discernment in the senses, for the sensation of one's existence is quite sufficient, and no person will not suffice in one's own existence and demand testimony to his senses.

(The reason is that there is no feeling without movement, meaning that sometimes the sensation stops and there is no movement in Him, so it is more like absolute awareness.) It is a grave mistake to resemble the form of the essence of the mind to a form of concept gripped in diminution by the mind's eye. This is utter falsehood, for this concept is like a light that emerges and operates. Its light is felt as long as it is active, until it ends its actions, and then its light vanishes.

From this you learn that the concept, sensed while active, is but a small and feeble branch of it. (The essential sensation is considered knowledge, for the power to sense is also a sense, a consequence, and does not need the essential feeling).

It is not at all like the essence, neither in quantity, nor in quality, like the beaten stone that shows sparkles of light that are renewed by the general embracing force in the stone, although in the form of the embracing force in it there is no light at all. Also, the mind's essence is the general force in man, and various branches stem from it, as in heroism and power, heat and light, according to the laws of the operated action.

Although we refer to it as the "mind's soul," or the "essence of the soul," it is because the mind is also a branch of it, the most important one, since "One is praised according to one's mind."

Since one does not give that which he does not have, we thus define it as mind, meaning at least not less than the felt sensed mind, as it is a branch and a part of it. It reigns over all her branches and swallows them, as a candle before a torch. The mind does not connect in any action, but the various actions connect and become fixed in the mind.

One discerns that all of reality is but its servants, both in discipline, and in order to improve it, for they are all lost, while the mind in general evolves. Hence, all our dealings are only in the ways of the mind and its ambitions, and more than that is not necessary.

Letter No. 2

1920

To my flesh and blood ... the exalted and glorified.

Now I have come to reply to your letter from the 33rd of the *Omer* Count [*Lag BaOmer*], along with your letter from the 15th of *Sivan*, which I received yesterday, and for which I refrained from replying to your letter from *Lag BaOmer*, as I had hoped you would inform me of the order of fixed names between us by which to disclose the thoughts in our hearts. However, I received the argument, "I do not know" ... and for which now, too, I will not be able to elaborate due to my fear that you would misunderstand. I will therefore await a third letter; perhaps I will be able to discern a clear way by which to let you know that which is in my heart and I will not miss the target.

I regret the long time that I had disappointedly spent in vain in three long letters—the first from the 22nd of *Shevat*, in which I wrote a good poem for the work, which begins:

Indeed, let my tongue stick to the roof of my mouth; all my bones are dried of oil.

And from the work of the Lord is every potion.

And the life of all, in Him shall it be believed.

Another letter from the 10th of *Adar*, in which I interpreted a bewildering Midrash [commentary]: "A hegemon asked one of the members of the house of Selini. He said to him: 'Who will take the kingship after us?' He brought a clean piece of paper, took a pen and wrote on it, 'And after that came out his brother,' etc. They said, 'Look, old words from the mouth of a new one, who is old.'" I had explained the wondrous truth in these words.

A third letter was from the third day of [the Torah portion] *VaYikrah*, in which I explained the dispute between the House of Shammai and the House of Hillel considering how to dance before the bride, as well as a truthful and pertinent poem that begins:

Please see, whose is the signature?

It is a question for all the people of the world.

And for the burning fire/As a wrongdoing man or as a rebellious woman.

I find no flaw in them that should have caused their loss, except that you might have misunderstood them due to lack of clarity between us. Therefore, it is a great commandment to break this iron wall that stands between us, where one does not understand the language of the other, as in the generation of Babylon.

And what you have proven lengthily in your letter, to evidently show that the foundations of our love are based on "concealed love," and concluded from it what you consider a clear conclusion that there is no fear at all regarding all the questions I had asked you. These are your words, verbatim: "However, I have no fear at all for your question of me regarding you, or of you regarding me. They are all annulled and nullified, and you, too, should not fear at all or look at the façade, but rather at the internal revealing of the heart, as a lover who hides the myriad thoughts rushing through his heart, and makes a loaf, good and strong, to repel all the pickles, piquant foods, garlic, and onion.

By that request I do not mean to increase the love or revoke it, for the love stands in its place, perfect and whole, completely unchanged, on which there is nothing to add or subtract.

"However, to not make you sorry needlessly—and why and what for, for by your sorrow you will add to mine, and you certainly do not want me to be sad—I have therefore hinted those two hints for you, for they are true and simple," thus far your words.

What shall I do if I cannot lie even when the truth is bitter? Therefore, I shall tell you the truth: I am still uncomfortable with all your lofty words. If that pains you, truth is still my most beloved. It is written, "Love your friend as yourself," and "That which you hate, do not do to your friend," so how can I leave you with a "sweet thing" if it is not real? This is truly loathed by me and I shall vomit it and utterly repel it.

Especially, regarding the most important matter, called "love," which is the spiritual connection between Israel and their Father in heaven, as it is written, "And You shall bring us, Our King, to Your great name, Selah, in truth and love," and as it is written, "Who chooses His people, Israel, with love." This is the beginning of salvation and the end of correction when the Creator reveals to His creations—which He has created—all the love that was previously hidden in His heart, as you well know.

This is why I must disclose to you the flaws that I had tasted in your two dainties: the first reason from the threefold string that is far more valuable than worldly love of friends. You were very wrong in this parable, comparing and equating rudimentary, spiritual love with love of friends that is conditional—revoked when the matter is revoked. In the other reason, you added insult to injury to support our love by the natural love of equivalence that is present with us to a great extent.

I do wonder, "Abraham's master, you have supported the lesson without a source," that our love is rudimentary and everlasting, dependent on the love of natural equivalence, which can be nullified, and "When the supporter fails, the supported falls."

But I am at one, and who can turn me? And I shall tell you, if you are a storyteller, do not compare the "rudimentary, spiritual" love to love of friends that is dependent on any reason that is to be ultimately cancelled, but rather to the love between father and son, which is also rudimentary, unconditional.

Come and see a wondrous custom in this love. It seems that if the child is an only child to his father and mother, the child must love his father and mother even more, for they display toward him more love than parents who have many children.

However, in reality, it is not so. On the contrary, if the parents become extremely attached to their children by their love, the children's love is then greatly decreased and diminished. Sometimes it even becomes apparent among children of this sort of love that "The feeling of love has been quenched entirely in their hearts." This is a custom that is of the laws of Nature and is applied in the world.

The reason for it is simple: The father's love for his son is rudimentary and natural. As the father wishes for his son to love him, the son also wishes for his father to love him. That craving in their hearts causes them constant, incessant fear. That is, the father is very much afraid that his son will hate him in any extent, even the slightest of the slightest, and the son, too, fears that his father might hate him in any extent, the slightest of the slightest.

This "constant fear" causes them to display good deeds between each other. The father always exerts to show his love in actuality to his son, and the son, too, constantly exerts to show his love in actuality to his father, as much as he can. In this way, the feelings of love multiply in both their hearts, always, until one prevails over the other in good deeds to a great and complete extent. In other words, the fatherly love of the father appears to the son in full, such as to which there cannot be addition or subtraction.

Upon reaching that state, the son sees "absolute love" in his father's heart. I wish to say that the son has no fear whatsoever that his love will diminish, nor has he hope that his love will grow. This is called "absolute love."

Then, slowly, the son grows idle in displaying good deeds before his father. To the extent of the diminution of good deeds and displays of love in the son's heart toward his father, to that very extent the sparks of "rudimentary love" that has been engraved in the son's heart by Nature quench. A second nature is made in him, close to hatred, for all the good deeds that his father does with him are low and little in his eyes compared to the obligation of "absolute love" that has been stamped in his organs. This is the meaning of the words, "I am not worthy of all the mercies, and of all the truth," and delve deeply in it, for it is profound and long.

And since it is always my conduct to praise Nature's systems, which the Creator has imprinted and set up in our favor all the days, I will tell you the reason for instilling that boundary. It is not that He has ill will, God forbid. On the contrary, it is all the multiplication in spirituality, for the main thing desired of the servants of the Creator is *Dvekut* [adhesion], and there is no *Dvekut* unless from love and pleasure, as it is written, "And bring us closer, our King, to Your great name, Selah, in truth and love." With what love did they say? With complete love, since the complete cannot be on the deficient, and complete love is "absolute love," as said above.

Therefore, how can there be multiplication in the desired *Dvekut* that rises and is obtained by all the adventures that have come upon them? This is the meaning of the Creator clothing a soul in the body and in the murky matter, which finally found out that it needs to actually display love, and the deficiency of the display of love in his own heart, for the nature of the substance is to promptly quench any feelings of love that it has already acquired.

In this manner, "The complete is over the complete," and there is absolute knowing in complete and absolute love on the part of the intellect. And yet, more love can be added, and if he does not add love, he will certainly subtract and all the possessions he has already acquired will certainly quench. This is the meaning of "And the land shall not be sold forever." These are all sincere and true words, and you should treasure them for the end of days.

Now you will understand my thoughts about you, as I see that you do not fear that my love for you will cool and that my love for you is absolute love. You wrote explicitly that our love will always stand, "without additions or subtractions." But in the end, our spirituality is clothed in matter, and the nature of matter is to cool because of absolute love. This is an unbreakable law.

Therefore, moreover, if you feel our love as complete, you must now begin to perform actual actions, "to display love," due to the fear of cooling that rises out of the feeling of **absolute love**, negating any fear. In this way the desire and the love increase twofold. This is called "multiplication."

My words are said by seeing, and "A judge has only what his eyes see," and no scrutiny and doubt will repeal my words. If you do not feel my words in your heart, it is due to being troubled with your own loss. But when you find the loss and the trouble is removed, then look into your heart and you will find it vacant from any feeling of love, due to the lack of actual actions to display the love, and this is clear. Even now, the shackles of our love are being very slightly shaken due to "lack of fear" **because of the knowing that is in absolute love.**

But hear me out and you will always be happy, for there is none so wise as the experienced. Therefore, I shall advise you to evoke within you fear of the coolness of the love between us. And although the intellect denies this depiction, think for yourself—if there is a tactic by which to increase love and one does not increase it, that, too, is considered a flaw.

It is like a person who gives a great gift to his friend. The love that appears in his heart during the act is unlike the love that remains in the heart after the fact. Rather, it gradually wanes each day until the blessing of the love can be entirely forgotten. Thus, the receiver of the gift must find a tactic every day to make it new in his eyes each day.

This is all our work—to display love between us, each and every day, just as upon receiving, meaning to increase and multiply the intellect with many additions to the core, until the additional blessings of now will be touching our senses like the essential gift at first. This requires great tactics, set up for the time of need.

This is the meaning of the words, "In those days they shall say no more, '**The fathers have eaten a sour grape, and the children's teeth are made blunt.**' ... Any man who eats the sour grapes, his teeth shall become blunt." That is, as long as they did not come to know it—that a display of love is required—they could not correct their father's sin, which is why they said, "The fathers have eaten a sour grape, and the children's teeth are made blunt."

But once they have come to that awareness, they were promptly rewarded with correcting their father's sin, and any flaw that they find, they will know that they will sin with displaying love, as was said above. Therefore, each day will be as new in their eyes, as on the first time. To the extent of the display of love on that day, they will draw the light until it is sensed. And should they feel only a little, it is due to eating the unripe fruit of that day, for on that day they did not display love sufficiently and ate prematurely. This is why it lessened in their senses, for it is not as on the first time.

The words are primarily a law for the Messiah, but it also applies to this world, since by strengthening the heart to display love between him and his Maker, the Creator instills His Divinity in him in remembrance, as in, "In every place where I mention My name, I will come to you and bless you."

When the remembrance increases by the actual work, the desire and longing increase, as in, "And spirit draws spirit and brings spirit," and so forth. Finally, the remembrance increases and grows by the craving, and ascends in good deeds, for "All the pennies join into a great amount," and this is the meaning of "Behold, this one comes and His reward is with Him, and His work is before Him."

I have been lengthy about it although the intellect is short in studying. However, it takes a long time to acquire this concept until it is absorbed in the organs.

And yet, this is all the awakening from below—that the speed of the correction during the corrections, and the measure of multiplication after the end of correction during the work on the desirable side, depend on the extent to which it is possessed.

You should not doubt my words, for otherwise "The proselyte is above and the citizen is below," for the measure of love is volitional, dependent on the heart; it is not intellectual. Therefore, how can it be displayed at the top of all the intellectual degrees, as I have elaborated on?

But all who taste and see that the Lord is good witness all those things, since we are dealing with *Dvekut* [adhesion] with the Creator here, and His uniqueness includes all the discernments in the world. Still, there is no doubt that there is nothing corporeal about His uniqueness, and therefore no step outside of an intellectual object.

For this reason, all who are rewarded with cleaving unto Him grow wiser, as they adhere with simple intellect. During the *Dvekut*, the worshipper is adhered to the worshipped by the mere strength of displaying his will and love. But in Him, the will, intellect, and knowing are in simple unity, without any difference of form, as in the laws of corporeality, and this is simple. Therefore, obtainment of the disclosure of His love is the very blessing of the intellect.

Come and learn from the complete worker (complete even in awakening from above). Ask your elders and they will tell you that the complete one is complete in everything, and has complete knowledge in the "blessing in his future." And yet, it does not weaken him at all because of it—from the labor in Torah and the searching.

On the contrary, none exert in the Torah and in searching as much as he. It is for a simple reason: His labor is not so much to bring the good future to himself. Rather, all his labor is in the form of displaying love between him and his Maker. This is why the feelings of love grow and multiply each day until the love is complete, in the form of "absolute love." Afterward, it leads him to double his wholeness in the form of awakening from below.

And by the way, I will clarify for you the meaning of the charity for the poor, which is so praised in *The Zohar*, the *Tikkunim*, and by our sages: There is an organ in man with which it is forbidden to work. Even if the smallest of the small desires to work with it still exists in man, that organ remains afflicted and stricken by the Creator. It is called "poor," for its entire sustenance and provision are by others working for it and pitying it. This is the meaning of the words, "Anyone who sustains a single soul from Israel, it is as though he sustains an entire world." Since the organ depends on others, it has no more than its own sustenance.

And still, the Creator regards it as though he sustained an entire world, that this itself is the entire blessing of the world and everything in it, multiplied and completed solely by the force of that poor soul, which is sustained by the work of other organs.

This is the meaning of "And He took him outside and said, 'Now look toward the heavens ...' and he believed in the Lord and reckoned it to him as righteousness." That is, by taking him outside, there was some desire to work with this organ; this is why He forbade him the work.

It was said, "Now look toward the heavens." At the same time, he was given the promise of the blessing of the seed. These are tantamount to two opposites in the same subjects, since all his seed, which is to be blessed, necessarily comes from this organ. Thus, when he is not working, how will he find a seed?

This is the meaning of "And he believed in the Lord," meaning that he accepted those two receptions as they were, both the complete prohibition on the work, and the promise of the blessing of the seed.

And how did he receive them? This is why he concludes, "And [he] reckoned it to him as righteousness," meaning as the form of charity [*Tzedakah* means both "charity" and "righteousness"] for a poor [person] who is sustained by the work of others.

This is the meaning of the two sayings of our sages: One [person] thought that the Creator would treat him with righteousness, meaning keep and sustain him without work, and one thought that Abraham would act with righteousness toward the Creator. Both are the words of the loving God, for prior to the correction, that organ is in heaven, and the charity is counted for the lower one. At the end of his correction it is achievable, and then the giving of the charity is counted for the upper one. Know and sanctify for it is true.

Yehuda Leib

Letter No. 3

.

"Four entered a PARDESS,"[1] etc.. Before the world was created, there was He is One and His name One, because the souls were not considered souls, since the issue of name refers to when one turns one's face away from one's friend, and the friend calls upon him, so he would turn his face back.

And since prior to creation, the souls were completely attached to Him, and He placed upon them crowns and wreaths, glory, majesty, and splendor, even what they did not evoke, since He knows their wish and grants them. Hence, it is certainly irrelevant to state a name that relates to an awakening from below of some side. Hence, it is considered "simple light," since everything is utter simplicity, and this light was understood to every simple person, even to those who had never seen any wisdom.

This is why sages and the wise called it *Pshat* [literal], since the *Pshat* is the root of everything. Authors and books do not discuss it, as it is one, simple, and famous concept. And although in the lower worlds, two divisions are detected in the *Reshimo* of this simple light, it is because of the division in their own hearts, by way of "And I am a smooth man."[2]

---

1   Translator's note: In Hebrew, a *Pardess* means grove, as in orange grove. But in Kabbalah, this word is an acronym for *Pshat* (the literal Torah), *Remez* (intimation), *Drush* (interpretations), and *Sod* (secret).

2   Translator's note: In Hebrew, *Halak* means both 'smooth' and 'part.'

Yet, the abovementioned place has no changes in any depiction you might make. It is like a king who took his darling son and put him in his grand and wondrous grove. And when the king's son opened his eyes, he did not look at the place where he stood, since due to the great light in the grove, his eyes wandered far away, as the east is far from the west. And he cast his eyes only at the buildings and palaces far to his west. Thus, he walked for days and months, wandering and wondering at the glory and the grandeur he was seeing to the west.

After some months, his spirit rested and his desire was fulfilled, and he was satiated from looking to the west. He reconsidered and thought, "What can be found along the way I have traversed?" He turned his face eastwards, the side through which he'd come, and he was startled. All the grandeur and all the beauty were right beside him. He could not understand how he had failed to notice it thus far, and clung only to the light that was shining to the west. Then he became attached solely to the light that shines to the east, and he was wandering eastwards until he returned right to the entrance.

Now do consider and tell me the difference between the early days and the latter days. All that he had seen in the latter months, he'd seen in the early months, as well. But in the beginning, it was not inspiring, since his eyes and heart were taken by the light that shines westwards. And after he was satiated, he turned his face eastward and noticed the light that shines toward the east. But how had it changed?

But being near the entrance, there is room for disclosing the second manner, which the sages call *Remez* [intimation], as in, "What do your eyes imply?" It is like a king who hints to his darling son and frightens him with a wink of his eye. And although the king's son does not understand a thing, and does not see the fear that is hidden in the hint, still, due to his devout adherence of his father, he promptly jumps from there to another side.

This is why the second manner is called *Remez*, since the two manners, *Pshat* and *Remez*, are registered in the lower ones as one root, as the meticulous ones write, that there is not a word that does not have a two-letter root, called the "origin of the word." This is so because no meaning can be deduced from a single letter; hence, the acronym for *Pshat* and *Remez* is PR [pronounced *Par*], which is the root of *Par Ben Bakar* [young bull] in this world. And *Pria* and *Revia* [multiplication] comes from that root, as well.

Afterward, the third manner appears, which the sages call *Drush* [interpretation]. Hence, there was no *Drisha* [demand] for anything, as in, "He is One and His name One." But in this manner, there is subtraction, addition, interpretation [studying], and finding, as in, "I labored and found," as you evidently know. This is why this place is ascribed to the lower ones, since there is an awakening from below there, unlike the awakening of the face of the east Upward, which was by way of "Before they call, I will answer." This is because here there was a powerful call, and even exertion and craving, and this is the meaning of "the graves of lust."

Afterward begins the fourth manner, which the sages call *Sod* [secret]. In truth, it is similar to *Remez*, but in the *Remez*, there was no perception whatsoever; it was rather like a shadow following a person. Moreover, the third manner, the *Drush*, has already clothed it.

Yet, here it is like a whisper, like a pregnant woman ... you whisper in her ear that today is *Yom Kippur* [Day of Atonement], so the fetus would not rock and fall. And we might say, "Moreover, it is the concealment of the face, and not the face!" For this is the meaning of the words, "The counsel of the Lord is with them that fear Him; and His covenant, to make them know it." This is why he made several circles until a whispering tongue said this to him: "He has given *Teref* [food/prey] unto them that fear Him," and not *Trefa* [non-kosher food], as that soldier sneered.

You understood by yourself, and you wrote me in your letter, though timidly, that you are a bachelor, and hence, naturally polite.

Since this verse came into your hands, I shall clarify it for you, as this is also the poet's question: "The counsel of the Lord is with them that fear Him." And why did he say so? It is as our sages' question, where we find that the text wastes (eight) twelve letters, to speak with a clean tongue, as it is written, "and of the beasts that are not clean," etc.

But your reason does not suffice the poet, for He could have given abundance to the souls, and with a clean tongue, as Laban said to Jacob, "Why did you flee secretly and outwit me, and did not tell me, that I might have sent you away with mirth and with songs, with a drum and with a harp." The poet's answer to that is, "and His covenant, to make them know it."

This is the meaning of the cutting, the removal, and the drop of blood, meaning the individual thirteen covenants. Had the secret not been in this manner, but in another tongue, four corrections from the thirteen corrections of *Dikna* would have been missing, and only the nine corrections of *Dikna* in ZA would remain. Thus, ZA would be clothing AA, as it is known to those who know God's secret. This is the meaning of "and His covenant, to make them know it," and this is the meaning of "Ancestral merit has ended, but ancestral covenant has not ended."

Let us get back to our issue, which is PR [pronounced *Par*], PRD [pronounced *Pered*], and PRDS [pronounced *Pardess*]. This is their order and combination from above downwards. Now you will understand these four sages that entered the *Pardess*, meaning the fourth manner, called *Sod*, since the lower one contains the Upper Ones that preceded it. Hence, all four manners are included in the fourth manner, and they are to the right, left, front, and back.

The first two manners are the right and the left, meaning *PR*. (This is the meaning of his words on the step at the Temple Mount: "All of Israel's sages are worthless in my eyes.") These are Ben Azai and Ben Zuma, as these souls nurtured off the two *PR* manners. And the last two manners are the *Panim* [front] and *Achor* [back], which is Rabbi Akiva, who entered in peace and came out in peace. They correctly stated, "It indicates that for every thistle, mountains of laws can be learned."

Achor is Elisha Ben Avoia, who went astray [became heretical]. Our sages said about that, "One shall not raise an evil dog within one's home," for it is going astray. Everything that was said about them—"peeped and died," "peeped and was hurt," "went astray"—is said of that generation when they have gathered closely together, but were all thoroughly corrected, one by one, as it is known to those who know the secret of reincarnation.

Yet, after he saw the tongue of Hutzpit, the translator, he said, "Return, O backsliding children," except for the other, and Rabbi Meir, Rabbi Akiva's disciple, will take his place. It is true that the Gemarah, too, finds it difficult; how did Rabbi Meir learn Torah from another? And they said, "He had found a pomegranate, ate its content, and threw its shell (another)." And some say that he corrected the *Klipa* [shell], too, as in raising smoke over its grave.

Now you can understand Elisha Ben Avoia's words: "He who teaches a child, what is he like? Like ink, written on a new paper," meaning the soul of Rabbi Akiva. "And he who teaches an old one, what is he like? Like ink, written on used paper," he said of himself. This is the meaning of his warning to Rabbi Meir, "Thus far the Shabbat zone," for he understood and estimated his horse's steps, since he had never come off from his horse. .

This is the meaning of "the transgressors of Israel, the fire of Hell does not govern them, and they are as filled with *Mitzvot* [good deeds] as a pomegranate." He says that it is all the more so with the golden altar, which is merely as thick as a golden coin. It stood for some years, and the light did not govern it, etc., "The vain among you are as filled with *Mitzvot* as a pomegranate, all the more so," as he says, that the *Klipa*, too, is corrected.

Know that the great Rabbi Eliezer and Rabbi Yehosha are from the souls of *PR*, as are Ben Azai and Ben Zuma. But Ben Azai and Ben Zuma were in the generation of Rabbi Akiva, and were his students, among the 24,000. But Rabbi Eliezer and Rabbi Yehosha were his teachers.

This is why it is said that instead of Rabbi Eliezer, they were purifying the purifications (*Pshat*) that they had done over Achnai's oven, since they cut it into slices (eighteen slices) and placed sand between each two slices. In other words, the third manner is as the sand between the first slice, which is the second manner, and the second slice, which is the fourth manner. And naturally, the sister and the awareness are conjoined as one. And Rabbi Tarfon and Rabbi Yehosha as one are disciples of the great Rabbi Eliezer, and Rabbi Akiva is seemingly included in them. This is because a second good day, with respect to the first good day, is like a weekday [*Chol* means both "sand" and "weekday"] in the eyes of our sages, since the *Drush*, compared to the *Remez*, is like a candle at noon.

But the sages of his generation defiled all those purifications and burned them, and the great Rabbi Eliezer proved with the aqueduct whose water rose that Rabbi Yehosha was a great sage, and the walls of the Temple will prove. And they began to fall before the glory of Rabbi Eliezer, and they did not fall before the glory of Rabbi Yehosha. This is a complete proof that there is no place for any doubt that he is pure.

But the sages took Rabbi Yehosha for himself, and they did not wish to rule as with Rabbi Eliezer, his teacher, until a voice came down, that Rabbi Yehosha was really his disciple. But Rabbi Yehosha did not connect to his place and said that you do not pay heed to a voice: "It is not in heaven," etc. Then sages blessed him, for the light of *Awzen* [ear] was cancelled from them, since they did not follow the rules of the great Rabbi Eliezer. And Rabbi Akiva, his favorite disciple, told him that his 24,000 disciples had died during the count, and the world was sickened, a third in olives, etc.

Elisha Ben Avoia and Rabbi Tarfon came from the same root. But Elisha Ben Avoia is the *Achoraim* [posterior] itself, and Rabbi Tarfon is the *Panim* [face] *de Achoraim* [of the posterior]. To what is this likened? In one house, lay bitter olives that are good for nothing, and in another house, lies the beam of the oil-press, which is good for nothing. Then a man comes and connects the two. He places the beam over the olives and produces a wealth of oil.

It follows that the good oil that appears is the *Panim*, and the beam is the *Achoraim*. And the plain wooden tools are thrown away after they have completed their work.

Understand that this custom is in the expansion of the roots to the branches in worlds lower than itself. But at their root, they both appear at once, like a person who suddenly enters the oil-press and sees the beam, and under it, a large pile of olives with oil flowing abundantly from them. This is so because at the root, all is seen at once. This is why one is called "another," and the other is called "Tarfon"; one is "a beam" and the other is "oil," which immediately flows by means of it.

This is also the meaning of going astray. After the desire has emerged, which is the soul of Rabbi Tarfon, the soul of "another" remained as "bad manners" in one's home. This is the meaning of the letter combination, *Sod: Samech* is the head of the word *Sod* itself, the soul of "another," and *Dalet* is the head of the word *Drush*, the soul of Rabbi Akiva, because they act. And the *Vav* in the middle is Rabbi Tarfon.

Letter No. 4

1920

To my friend,

Indeed, I see your hardships with simplicity, that you are embarrassed to speak straightforwardly. Yet, in all my dealings with you, in words and in letters, I did not affect your spirit whatsoever, as it is the way most people behave on such matters: They are ashamed as thieves of every organ they sin with or behave with it as do beasts. They cover it with seven covers, as with the circumcision organ, the hind part, and other such organs that do as beasts do.

Hence, I must be lenient with you regarding this change and speak to you as ... under a cover of allegories, for I have grown tired of waiting for solutions to this question, which we both need, and especially for the glory of Heaven, for this is all I need.

I shall speak to you cunningly, in a language that the ministering angels do not need. And therefore, I shall request of you to thoroughly clarify to me the words of the holy *Zohar* in three places. And even the things you clearly see that are considered an advantage, or even a sin to disclose such secrets, especially before those who know and understand, or even with the most ordinary matters, which are so light that they fly like birds in the sky, I need it all. And although they are not needed for themselves, it is a need in general.

See in *The Zohar*, from the portion *Shemot* [Exodus] unto the words of the break after Passover and onward, to thoroughly clarify. Afterward, delve in the pages preceding the holiday of *Shavuot* [Feast of Weeks], from nearly there through *Elul* of that year when they had crossed onto the land of Israel. Thus you have two places, and afterward, from the pages of the virtues of the land of Israel through its end.

First, clarify every kind of change and action from this place to that place, meaning with the fulfilling of the degrees, and understand the issue as much as you can. Then, clarify every good thing in the steps of its body and its parts, which is necessary and which is redundant, and what it is necessary for, in what way it is redundant, and what the world would lack without it, as well as depicting the lines of hope in each place.

And most of all, the drawings should bring out the features with its shades and lights, with a terrible face or beautiful face, or a laughing face or a welcoming face. On such a living bulge, even simple and redundant and known things must be registered, so that all the drawings are included in one collection in each picture, arranged clearly.

And do not repeat the mistake of interpreting the commentary that you have found in the drawings, and the drawings themselves are hidden in your commentary. Moreover, it is the drawings themselves that I need, and to interpret them myself with aptitude such as yours, and especially, as though they have fallen from above, prior to your interpretation that you gave them from below.

And because I still fear your idleness, which is only a *Klipa* [shell], or hunts clean and innocent souls, I myself will write to you some novelties in these forms that I request. And after you explain to me all the abovementioned drawings, as much as you can, simply, and without commentaries, as though they had fallen from the sky, then you will interpret in your own words what I interpret here in the language of translation [Aramaic]. In this way I will know how well you understand my writing and my thoughts.

And after you interpret what is in my mind, review my words and add to them, subtract from them, or both. And for God's sake, follow my request and do not skip any of your studies or prayers, even for several weeks, until you have completed my request, and until your words reach me with a clear answer. After all, my fingers are tied by fear and I cannot correspond with you under the canopy of the Torah and Higher Love.

Come and see: There is a holy language for the Upper Ones and there is a holy language for the lower ones. It is after them that all those sages of the truth are called "God's mouth." What is the reason? It is because the holy Divinity speaks from their mouths, and all that they speak, their palates taste, and no other's. Hence, the way of these sages of the truth is to convey wisdom to their friends mouth to mouth.

And what is the reason it is mouth to mouth and not mouth to ear? It is because what the palate tastes is not given to the ears; they are separate. It is written about that: "With him do I speak mouth to mouth, even manifestly, and not in riddles." "Manifestly" means by people's vision, and "in riddles" means by people's hearing.

But these are not at all the ways of the wisdom of truth, which is (the wisdom of truth) given only in the palate, as it is written, "For who will eat, or who will enjoy, if not I?" By this rule the sages know the judgment in the judgment, each kind with (what is not) its kind, its flavor, since each kind has its own flavor.

And since these wicked have seven abominations in their hearts, their hearts are divided and their flavors are not the same, for "the Lord confused their language," "that they may not understand one another's speech."

But with the sages, no lie comes to their palates. Hence, all that they eat is true, and all their awakenings are for the truth. Therefore, all the sages are as one man, understanding each other's language, since their palate is one. Thus, they necessarily have the power to disclose secrets to each other **mouth to mouth**.

It is in that regard that the loyal shepherd prayed for Judah, "and brings him in unto his people." Our sages explained that he could stand among the righteous and discuss rules with them, meaning, as it is said, he understood their language.

This is so because one who is flawed—who did not properly correct the sin of the generation of Babel—is under the dominion of the gods of Babel, called *Ball*. "And there confound their language," and he did not know what our sages said. Woe onto him and woe unto his soul. "And what does Divinity say? It is lighter than my head, lighter than my arm."

And should you say, "How can such a great sin be corrected?" After all, it is written, "For God is in heaven and you upon earth; therefore, let your words be few." And it is also written, "Why should God be angry with your voice?" This is undoubtedly true.

But as it is here, it is the force of Moses that we need, the loyal shepherd, who testifies about himself: "It is not in heaven ... it is in your mouth and in your heart to do it." It is known that by the great power of the loyal shepherd, the Torah has already come down to earth, as though in the combinations of the letters in the names of the Torah.

And in all those deeds that he has set up before us and for the whole world, as in, "from the permitted which is in your mouth," now they are actually in the earth, as it is written, "It is in your mouth and in your heart to do it." That is, by the cleaving of spirit and mind to all the intelligence and reason that there is in the sayings of the fathers and the sayings of the fathers' servants, and in the 613 commandments. In each act, one combination becomes known to the eyes, in the manners of the ways of the Master of the world, manners within which all the upper light is deposited. One who cleaves to one discernment in complete reason did not work in vain, for here is one part of the 613 parts of the soul. Subsequently, he multiplies all those degrees until he finds all the organs of his soul.

If he is rewarded with the wholeness of his soul, he will be confident that he has won everything, for nothing is absent in the king's palace, and there is no poverty in a place of wealth.

Woe unto those fools, destructors of the world. They know full well that it would be better for them had they not been born. There is only one thing that they say, that they had better days than now, meaning before they were born. The Creator does this to them to display their flaw before people. It is written, "Do not say, 'What was it, that the days before were better than these, for it is not out of wisdom that you ask this.'" In other words, the text has mercy on them and notifies them to cover this thing in their hearts, as it is a sign of the flaw of folly that is in them.

The faithful prophet, Malachi, admonished them over it: "You offer soiled bread upon my altar and say, 'With what have we soiled you?' By your saying, 'The table of the Lord is contemptible.'" So is the manner of all the fools of the world. Since their palates taste the sweet as bitter, they say that it is bitter and despise the bread of the holy king.

This is why he curses them and says, "But cursed be the swindler who has a male in his flock," showing them that this swindling is them swindling against their master. What is the reason? It is because there is a male in their flock and they are idle in their work and do not exert to find him. This is why the holy prophet curses them, since they can bring a pure male to the king's palace, yet they bring a lame and blind one.

Woe unto they who show disgrace in the king's palace. This is why they are shown, with much cleverness, their flaw, as in, "Offer it to your governor; would he be pleased with you?" "Your governor" is an inclination to a place that has been made lower, where they flawed, meaning in the upper lip, a place that according to us is a flaw, and according to them is not a flaw. But that place is not filled by their twisting of their lips and the Creator shows their wickedness in their faces, as I had said to you when I was with you, as it is written, "The clean and the righteous do not kill." The mind is called "clean," and the heart is called "righteous." Woe unto one who changes his name, who lies in the name of the Creator and reverses the meaning. The text testifies about them and before them: "I will not justify the wicked."

Therefore, you, the love of my life, will not follow in the footsteps of the destructors of the world, the fools, sons of fools, as they are worthless compared to you, whether in trunk, branch, and all the more so in the fruits. In your trunk, you are unique in this generation. In the cleanness of that trunk, you are better than me, as I told you when I was with you. You lack nothing except to go out to a field that the Lord has blessed, and collect all those flaccid organs that have drooped from your soul, and join them into a single body.

In that complete body, the Creator will instill His Divinity incessantly, and the high streams of light will be as a never ending fountain. Then, each place on which you cast your eye will be blessed, and all will be blessed because of you, for they will be constantly blessing you, and all the chariots of impurity will be on them ... forever because it is their wish to curse you. At that time, the blessing of the grandfather, "Those who bless you are blessed," will come true.

Let us return to the issue that we dealt with first: the Lord's mouth. There is an upper lip, and there is a lower lip. Those crowns came down equal to each other, but to add to all those worthy ones, good upon good, and light upon light, four high and holy corrections of the *Dikna* were made on them. Happy is he who has been rewarded with inheriting them, and happy also is he who has been rewarded with cleaving to the worthy one who has already inherited them.

It is written in relation to those four corrections: "My thoughts are not your thoughts, nor are your ways My ways." The high and holy thoughts are not as the thoughts of an uneducated one. The high and holy ways are not as the ways of the uneducated. The thought is the *Rosh* [head/mind], and a way is the path by which the *Rosh* spreads and by which it multiplies.

Come and see. There is an upper *Rosh* and an upper path on the upper lip, and there is a lower *Rosh* and a lower path on the lower lip. This is why the mustache hair was established over the upper lip, which is the similitude of the upper *Rosh* that I have said.

This correction is called "merciful" (see *Idra Rabah, Nasso*). When one is rewarded with seeing that vision with the eye, it is full of mercies on all sides, for there is no place in it ... which is why it is indeed "merciful."

Afterward, they are rewarded with seeing the upper path, the path of those who ascend, who are male goats. This is why it is seen by all those lower worlds, like the precious correction of the *Rosh*, called "merciful," which is the praise of all the praises that appear to them.

In this way, there is a stop on those hairs in the middle, and that cessation of this path is seen to the lower ones by the two holes in the nose. There that path spread and was imprinted

47

in the middle of the upper lip. This correction is called "and gracious," and all those who know the secrets certainly see it.

Now that you have been rewarded with those two names ... lower ones, and we will see what it is before us in that place where we find a lip ... under the lower lip. There ... meaning a *Rosh* [head/mind] to the lower ones, and all those worthy ones were awarded kisses ... although the kisses ... lower one as one.

Thus, we should ask, "Why did they cling to the *Rosh* of the bottom lip?" ... good reason ... and a holy mouth ... of that path that was imprinted in the upper lip, and shows them that place like ... a path of no flesh ... as it should be with love. ... And then ... they grew stronger in the bottom lip. At that time, "Love is as strong as death." Their soul comes out with upper and lower love together, and when their soul ... lower one.

This is why that place is called "the bottom *Rosh*." What is the reason? It is because it is completely similar to the upper *Rosh*, and everyone knows that one begot the other. This is called "lengthy," since the *Panim* [face] of the upper *Rosh* grew longer ... is not in everyone for one another. And as they were integrated as one, they are eyes for everyone.

It is in that regard that the sages asserted, "A voice, a vision, and a scent are not considered fraud." What is the reason? It is because in those three, all the ... are seen. And since we have been rewarded with this bottom *Rosh*, it was doubled at its conclusion and came in three praises. ... As the upper *Rosh* came to us, there is certainly no fraud in them, and there is no flaw in those precious corrections that were extended ... theirs, and everyone knows that one begot the other, except for the court's clowns who would say, "Sarah conceived from Abimelech, king of Gerar."

This is why the verse, "'As for Me, this is My covenant with them,' says the Lord: 'My Spirit which is upon you,'" came true in this holy seedling of the seed of Israel. It follows that this correction is certainly the *Rosh* of the lower ones, as it is for the lower ones to keep them and connect them to the bundle of life, as we have said.

But the sages have established, "There is no admission to the *Azarah* [a special section in the Temple], except for the kings from the House of David." What is the reason? It is because they are in the *Rosh*. But for the rest of the generation, that place was made only to pass by it. Were it not so, that rest would have been an easygoing stroll, which is why it was established and extended from that *Rosh* through the lower one.

It is similar to the upper path, but it appears and comes like an old man, weary from the many days, and "There is no reason in the elderly." It is like Barzillai the Gileadite, for because the shape of that bottom path is completely similar in everything, as the upper path that expanded from the upper *Rosh*, for this reason he sees that the *Guf* is below, and is in the bottom path, similar to the upper one as a monkey to a human. And what he saw, he saw well.

This is why that correction is called "face," to show that not all faces are the same, and all the falls of people should be on the face, as in, "And they bowed down with faces to the earth."

This is why that path was registered in the bottom lip, directly opposite the path on the upper lip, like the faces of the cherubim "facing one another." Because their shape resembles one another's, they were strengthened by one another and were registered in the lips more deeply. This is also the meaning of "face," meaning that until now it was not known at all that there were faces above and faces below, and that not all faces are the same.

And when I hear of that wise disciple who said that he is laughing at the whole world by merit of "The image of the Lord does he behold," and he rejoiced and boasted his degrees, that he, Anah, "found the springs in the desert while pasturing the donkeys of his father Zibeon," and the first iniquity was erased, I say to myself that it is from our sages, who was found on the bottom path and calls it "the lower path": Anah, the shepherd of his father, Zibeon. He also calls that lower *Rosh*, Zibeon, which is something I had never heard of in earlier writings.

I exert to find these words sufficiently interpreted, 1) to know what these "springs" do, meaning all the *Reshimot* [imprints/ recollections] in their faces, to the length, to the width, in sound, vision, and in scent. Also, what is their question, and what is their answer—whether it is a new question or hidden in their ears from the shepherd of his father, Zibeon, of that Anah? And what was Zibeon thinking about this wise son if he had told him, "My son, if your heart is wise, my heart, too, will rejoice"?

In general, was there joy over the question? And how many days did it last, or was it joy for a few hours? All of this is clearly interpreted and explained in that clarification of the bottom *Rosh* and the bottom path that I have said. And if it is not so for you, but some other way, tell me how the actual work was done.

And now that we are relieved regarding the bottom *Rosh* and the bottom path, and the holy names for those who have been rewarded with their faces with corrections of the hairs under the bottom lip—"long face" indeed, we will descend further, to below the holy curtain. In it, a good reward for the righteous is bundled, concealed, and revealed, as well as bitter and harsh punishments for the wicked. That curtain is called "very merciful," as it was established, as he leans toward *Hesed* [mercy]. It has all the merits and all the bounty of the Master of the world.

Woe unto one who displays incest. He severs his soul in this world, and it is severed for the next world. He is in the form of "You will give truth to Jacob," which is why his hand held Esau's heel. He found all this mercy that we mentioned because in his perfection, that seventh correction—called "and truth"—was revealed and came, since truth and mercy were included here in one another, as in, "You will give truth to Jacob, mercy to Abraham."

Come, see, and understand the order I had said to you thus far in all the degrees that you have seen thus far, and look upon their depictions properly. You will find them as a depiction of a garden-bed in which plantings have been sown, two opposite two, and one comes out the tail. That is, above is a *Rosh* and a path, and below, directly opposite them, is a *Rosh*, a path, and that one of now, which is called "very merciful," which is in the middle toward everyone and below everyone.

There is also a garden-bed where these plantings are depicted in a different combination—three plantings above, considered *Rosh, Toch, Sof.* The upper *Rosh* is called *Rosh,* the upper path is called *Toch,* and the bottom *Rosh* is called *Sof.*

What is the reason that this is their combination? It is because the taste, appearance, and smell of these three plantings are the same. By that, the three conjoin as one, and all three of them are regarded as superior, as in *Rosh, Toch, Sof.*

That lower path, and that unification of "very merciful" are called "two branches of the willow." What is the reason? It is because they exist simultaneously, and the children of the exile that are among the nations and have mingled with them say about those two branches of the willow that they have neither taste nor smell. Thus, there are three above and two below in the garden-bed that I have mentioned.

In those five letters that we said [*Elokim*], there are 120 combinations. But I said those two in order to show one combination in "remember," and one combination in "keep." The rest are included in those two sides that I mentioned, and these orders are called "the five letters of the name *Elokim.*"

51

What is the reason? It is because they were set up along their emanation path, one below the other. However, there is measuring to the width, and thus far I have not heard from you an interpretation from the text, and so I cannot speak of it at all until I hear that you are in it yourself.

When I said, "above" and "below," I was not implying to places, for the spirits have no place. However, they certainly do have a time in which to become known in the world. What I called "above" was because it was seen first, and I call "below" what appeared subsequently.

And I ask more of you: When you interpret, in your own words, all those five chapters that I showed you, in an order of above and below, interpret for me each time, when is it the first chapter, and when is it the following, and likewise for all of them, as meticulously as your memory allows, or an approximate calculation, and the duration of each chapter.

And most of all, I long to hear the duration of those two branches of willow that I mentioned regarding the bottom path, called correction of the "face," and the holy curtain, called "very merciful," and their beginning is "truth."

And although it is a small thing for you, it is great for me. I believe you already implied in another letter that you have forgotten their times, but remember it, for it is as though I am in prison, and I cannot labor and discuss the matter with you for an important reason, which is in my heart.

Therefore, try hard to remember their times, more or less, their durations as well as their beginnings. And please, have mercy on the time that was regrettably lost in vain, and send me a clear letter with complete explanations of all the questions I have asked of you, so I will not need to correspond with you thereafter.

Now, my dear, come and see how you can furnish me with your true answers. And because I carry the burden with you,

I have nothing more than gloom now. Yet, I have no doubts about you, since the answers precede the questions—if he does not spare his life, etc.

Yet, let bygones be bygones, and henceforth count the moments lest you lose even one of them, for there is a herald upon us from above each and every day. It is not authority that I have given you. Rather, it is servitude that I have given you. And who is he and where is he who leads an evil, foreign *Klipa* [shell] of idleness here among the king's children? It is certainly insolence toward heaven, and "The door turns on its hinges, and the idle is in his bed." The holy Divinity is cast to the dust under the feet of her mistress, who regularly walks and tramples over her head and arm, with great insolence, as foreign mistresses do, wishing only to spit impure spit in their mistress' face, arising contempt and wrath.

For all those who have the power to remove this insolence, yet stand and see all this insolence, you call them "idle"? Idle is not their name. Rather, they have no perception of the preciousness and glory of the Master of the heaven [the Creator] who is before them.

Likewise, we should announce that there is no labor in extending time, but in studying, for that filthy substance is appeased and desires to work twenty-four hours a day, but not a single hour in the exertion of the study.

And the main labor is in finding all the secrets of the Torah and its reasoning, for there is no other slavery in this exile. This filthy substance would want anything, but not to exert in the reasons for the *Mitzvot* [commandments]. And even if some reasons are found, it is shown that it is tiring, and that one novelty is not so different from the other, and then he grows tired and can no longer exert.

This is the heart of the matter. It should be uprooted and taken out from the yards of the Lord's house, and one should assume labor to find the reasons of Torah and the meanings of the *Mitzvot* in the words of the Torah. And then the Maker will be brought back to His throne.

Yesterday evening I received your letter from the fourteenth of *Heshvan*. Now, early in the morning, my letter is complete and ready to be sent. I wanted to know how you know that this man who comes and goes into your house without a son is a true sage and a holy man, as you had said to me ... for the proper order of your body. Let me know in detail in what way is he opposite, for I need to know it, but clarify it thoroughly, and if he is not that bookbinder or bookseller that I saw in your house, and if he looks in letters ... and what he says about them. But most important, do not be frugal with those words that seem redundant to you, for upon increasing such depictions, the perceptions between us will increase, and I do need it now.

Your friend,
Yehuda

Letter No. 5

To my soul mate, may his candle burn forever:

... What you implied in your last letter, that I hide my face from you and regard you as an enemy, your intention is as one who hears his disgrace but keeps silent, and that I am not sharing the burden with my friends or care at all for my friends' pains. I admit that you are right about that; I do not feel those pains that you feel whatsoever. On the contrary, I rejoice in those revealed corruptions and the ones that are being revealed.

I do, however, regret and complain about the corruptions that have not appeared, but which are destined to appear, for a hidden corruption is hopeless, and its surfacing is a great salvation from heaven. The rule is that one does not give what he does not have. So if it appears now, there is no doubt that it was here to begin with, but was hidden. This is why I'm happy when they come out of their holes because when you cast your eye on them, they become a pile of bones.

But I do not settle for it even for a moment because I know that those who are with us are more than those who are with them. But weakness stretches time, and those contemptible ants are hidden and their place is unknown. The sage says about it, "The fool folds his hands and eats his own flesh." Moses let down his hands, but when Moses lifts his hands of faith, all that should appear promptly appears, and then Israel triumphs "in all the mighty hand, and in all the great terror."

This is the meaning of "Whatsoever you find that you can do by your strength, that do." When the cup is full, the verse, "The wicked are overthrown," comes true. And when the wicked are lost, light and gladness come to the world, and then they are gone.

I remember discussing similarly with you on the first day of *Rosh Hashanah* [the first day of the Jewish year], TARPA [September 13, 1920], upon our return from the house of A.M. You shared with me very sad things that you saw that morning during the morning service [prayer]. I was filled with joy before you and you asked me, "Why the joy?" I replied to you the same then, that when buried wicked appear, although they have not been fully conquered, their very appearance is regarded as great salvation and causes the sanctity of the day.

And what you wrote me, that you cannot prefer the son of the loved one over the firstborn son of the hated one, I spoke to you about it often face to face, that the place of faith is called *Bor* [pit/hole], and the filling of faith is called *Be'er* [well] of living waters, or succinctly, "life." It is not as the nature of ordinary water, that when some water is missing, the well still stands. Rather, this well has the nature of animals, and moreover, all its parts are organs on which the soul depends. Puncturing them in any way causes the entire animate level to die and disappear. This is the meaning of "They have forsaken Me, the source of living waters, to hew them out cisterns, broken cisterns that can hold no water."

Although there is no deficiency in the water, there is some deficiency in the well, so it is completely broken, certainly, beyond any doubt that it will not hold the water in it. This is what the prophet implies in the name of the Creator, and this is true Kabbalah for anyone who is wise and understands with his own mind. If you do not understand, go forth and examine, and then you, too, will be wise and understanding with your own mind.

What you wrote me at the end of your letter, that you'd like me to voice my pleasant voice to you, since for me it is no labor at all to delight a bitter soul from its hardships, for a heart full of love sweetens them at their root, the root of all pleasantness.

I will reply to you in brief, that there is a time for everything. You evidently saw that in my first letter, I wrote you and inscribed a very nice thing for its time, rejoicing the heart of God and men, interpreting the true meaning of "They will be satiated and delighted by Your kindness," for it is true, and its end will be pleasant for every palate that longs for true words.

You see how I can exert and delight you with words of truth at this time. God forbid that I should sin in delighting you with falsehood, like the false prophets during the time of the ruin, for there is no falsehood in my domain at all. You already know what I say about those who draw their students to the truth with a network of falsehood and lies, or with luxuries. I have never been defiled by their idols, and not in those is Jacob's lot. Therefore, all my words are said in truth, and where I can't disclose the truth, I keep completely silent.

Do not think that if I were close to you I would be saying more than in writing. If I knew that this was so, I would not have left you in the first place. What I said to you is the complete truth, that judging by our preparation, you do not need me, and so it is. Do not suspect me that I fabricated untrustworthy words for my own pleasure. When the Creator helps to be rewarded with the end of correction, you will need me very much, and may the Creator grant us this within twelve months, because the day is still long and you are not as fast as I am. Still, I hope that within twelve months from this day forth you will finish the work, and then you will see with all your efforts that we will be together for some years, because the depth of the work begins primarily at its end.

I have elaborated on all that for you because of thoughts that I detected between the lines of your letter. You have forgotten the pure truth that is always in my heart and mouth. But let me promise you that more than you have witnessed the truthfulness of my words thus far, you will evidently witness that all my words are forever true, and will not change even as a hairsbreadth. Also, all the words I wrote you carry a true meaning that will not suffer change, but require attention because the time is a time for brevity.

Believe that I could not write to you until now the words that are revealed in this letter, for reasons that I keep to myself. My gaze is fixed on the goal, to make it succeed the most, and this is what surrounds me with the finest guarding for every single word. I know that in time, all my words and conducts toward you will become clear, as it is written, "Happy are you, vessels, who entered in impurity and came out in purity," for this is the path of Torah.

I have grown tired of asking you to write more, and to promise you that in return I would write you often. Each day I sit and wait, perhaps a word about you—either from your spiritual life, or from your corporeal life—will come my way. But there is not a sound. What can you say to justify it? There are no answers here with strong words or with faint words, only answers with dry words uttered in a florid style, as though for being overburdened, but you probably do not even understand yourself.

... And yet, I know that times will be better, and then, to the extent that they improve, their open love will grow, as well. We have yet to be satiated with eternal love together, as a never-ending fountain, satiated and delighted together, for the pleasantness of the Lord is for the complete receiver who feels no satiation. This is why He is called "Almighty," since for those who do His will appears an old light and a new light in one unification.

This is acquired by keeping Sabbaths and remissions for the world of *Yovel* [fifty-year anniversary, as well as jubilee]. This is also the meaning of "They left it until morning," etc., "And it did not rot, nor was there any worm in it." It is written, "They will be satiated and delighted by Your kindness," as corporeal eating fills the belly by the corporeal measure. Moreover, it lifts up smoke to the brain due to the cooking in the stomach, and one grows tired and falls asleep.

This is the meaning of Pinhas stabbing the spear into her belly while they were attached. "Then Pinhas stood and prayed, and the plague stopped." This is why he was rewarded with the anointing oil although he was not from Aaron's sons, since Moses himself told him, "Behold, I give to him My covenant of peace." First it was with a cut Vav, but through the light of Torah, it grew long, and "My covenant was with him, the life and the peace" together, and "By the light of the king's face is life."

Yehuda Leib

Letter No. 6

1921, Warsaw

To my soul mate ... may his candle burn forever:

I have already written you two letters but did not have the time to send them to you. In truth, I would like to see you prior to my leaving on the 22nd of *Av*. Now I would like to offer you a taste of the honey from my honeycomb.

It is written, "You destroy those who speak falsehood; the Lord abhors the man of bloodshed and deceit." There is an allegory about a king who took it on himself to teach his son tactics of kingship. He showed him the land, his enemies, and his friends.

The king also gave his son a sword from his hidden treasures. The sword possessed a wonderful power: When he showed it to the enemies, they would promptly fall before him as dung on the earth.

The king's son went ahead and conquered many countries, took much spoil and succeeded greatly.

In time, the king said to his son, "Now I will go up to the tower and hide myself there. You sit in my place and lead the whole earth with wisdom and might. And here is also this shield, which until now has been hidden in the treasury of the

61

kingdom. No enemy or harm-doer will be able to hurt you when you have this shield with you."

The king took the sword, tied it to the shield, gave them to his son, and the king himself went up to the tower and hid there.

The king's son did not know that the sword and the shield were tied to each other, and since he had no regard at all for the shield, he did not watch it. Thus, the shield was stolen from him, and with it, the sword.

When the news spread through the land that the sword and the shield had been stolen from the king's son, the ruler of the earth, they immediately became impudent, and his enemies waged war on him until they took him captive, he and all his many possessions. With their enemy in their hands, they poured out their vengeance on him, and avenged him for all his abuse of them in the days of his father's leadership. Each day they would beat him ferociously.

The son was embarrassed before his father because his father's plight hurt him more than his own, so he resolved to make a sword and a shield just like the first ones, to appease his father and to show him his wisdom and might.

With tactics, he made a sword that was similar to the first, and made a shield similar to the first shield.

With his arms in hand, he called on his father at the top of the tower: "Be proud of me, for a wise son makes a father glad." And while he was calling his father, his enemies were bruising his brain and liver. And the more they beat him, the more he overcame in order to appease his father, yelling, "I am afraid of nothing, now, and who can fight me when I have my sword and shield in hand?"

And the more he boasted, the more his enemies beat and hurt him, stones and sticks landing on his head, and blood running down his face. And all the while he tried to keep upright, proudly, like a hero, to show his father that now he is afraid of nothing, that compared to his might they are as the dust on the balance, since the sword helps him, or the shield helps him.

This is what the poet implied, "You destroy those who speak falsehood," meaning those whose faces are as the face of a monkey before the face of a man, who make by their own strength a sword such as the Creator has made. And moreover, they wish to boast of their work as the Creator boasts. It is said about them, "The Lord abhors the man of bloodshed and deceit," for he makes a manmade shield and boasts that he feels no pain, etc., and this, too, the Creator abhors—one who shows false pretense saying that he is wise and strong and fearless, yet he is full of deceit and seeks cunning tactics. This the Creator abhors.

However, all the wholeness is in the holy name, God of my righteousness, whose every organ and tendon knows that the place of instilling of Divinity is in the place of justice, meaning in the absolute knowledge that all His thoughts are just, and never has a man anywhere in the world taken a bad step, just as one will not make a good step by himself.

And although everyone believes it, it is knowing that they need—so it may settle in the heart. It is like a first concept, where the pouring out of a truly faithful heart to the Creator can disclose this concept in the world, like any simple and acceptable thing settles in the heart sufficiently.

This is the meaning of "And you will seek 'from there' the Lord your God and you shall find." This is also the meaning of the blessing, "Good and does good," who does good to others, for His attainment is truly on the good, as this is why He is called "good." This name is easily attainable by any person, and it is also called "God of my mercy." But because it is so easily acceptable, due to the ease of accepting it, the individual does not remain over all the people.

This is why the work in exile and keeping Torah in poverty is evidently revealed to the eye of all the organs of a servant of the Creator—the holy name, "God of my righteousness." That is, it was not at all bad in reality even for the slightest moment, which is the meaning of "and does good," meaning that it does not appear on the "good," but only on the "good to others," as in, that, too, is for the best. This is a very deep and important matter, and that unification leaves no room even for ... at that time, other than him.

This is also the meaning of "The Lord is one and His name is 'One,'" which is attained as simple to the ones who are whole.

Yehuda Leib

Letter No. 7

1922, Jerusalem

To my friend, my heart, and my point, the glory of his name is my glory, may his candle burn and shine for all eternity, Amen, may it be so:

Since the ninth of *Elul* [Hebrew month in the summer] to the second day of *Hanukah*, some four months, I have been anticipating the joy of your written word. But in the end, a long letter is lying before me, full of poetic phrases and intimations, like the dust that a fox raises when stepping in a tilled field. What fault have you found in me to make me unworthy of knowing anything about your situations, although you know how much I care about them?

I am also surprised that you did not pay attention to what we said, that you would not write me anything that is covered with poetic phrases, in which I flee endlessly, so much so that I cannot find you in even one of them.

I ask of you, for God's sake, that from now on you will write me some information, and make certain that you interpret it simply, as a person speaks to his friend, who is not a prophet, making certain he will not stray or even contemplate, nor note the eloquence, but rather the ease of explanation. And most important, to not mix in his words poetic phrases or intimations, for there is no fear of any foreign eyes ... and in my house there is no entrance to foreigners.

When you write me novelties in the Torah, clarify them to me without any names or *Partzufim* that are common in the books, but in ordinary people's language. For myself, I also take notice to explain my points in ordinary style, and it falls under my senses in complete simplicity, through and through, for it is a near and true way to clarify something to the fullest.

While I clothe the matters in the names of the books, at that time appears in me the desire to know the thoughts of the books, so my mind strays from the goal of my way, and this I have tried and tested. Moreover, when I obtain some direction in the poetic phrases in the books for my way, the joy even increases, to mingle falsehood with truth.

Therefore, when I come to scrutinize something that I must, I keep myself carefully from looking into books, before and after. And it is likewise in writing; I do not use poetic phrases with them, so as to always be ready in purity to find a word of truth with admixtures or assistance from something external to it. Only then does the palate taste...

Yehuda Leib

Letter No. 8

1922, Jerusalem

To my honorable friend...

I must comment on your slacking in your work of writing, to approach me every once in a while with information of your points. It would have added a few benches at the seminary, and I have already proven to you in my previous letter from the first of *Nissan* [Hebrew month in the spring].

See in Midrash Rabah, *Yitro* [Jethro]: "Rabbi Yirmiah [Jeremiah] said, 'What if when He gives life to the world, the earth will quake? When He comes to avenge the wicked who breached the words of Torah, it will be even more so, as it is said, 'Who can face His wrath, and who can calculate the day of His arrival?' When He desires, no being can face His might. When He rises in His anger, who will stand before Him? Whoa, who will not fear You, King of the nations?'" Although the words of Rabbi Yirmiah make inherent sense, concerning the Torah, as long as you engage in it, you find flavor [reason] in it.

Let me illuminate them for you.

You find in the poem, "You are more terrible than all terrors, prouder than all who are proud; You surround everything and fill everything." Interpretation: We see dreadful terrors and pains that are worse than death. Who is the one doing all that?

... This is His name, "You are more terrible than all terrors," who is removed from them!

Also, we see how many people have—for generations—tormented themselves with afflictions and self-torment, all in order to find some rhyme or reason in the work of God, or to know who was the owner of the capital.

Yet, they have all wasted their lives away and left the world as they came, without finding any relief. Why did the Creator not answer all their prayers? Why was He so haughty over them, so unforgiving? And what is His name? "Prouder than all who are proud." This is His name (see my poem, attached to this mail, which asks for whom the field was sown, for I have the right answer). But they who suffer the terrors and perceive that removed pride know for certain that the Creator is removed from them, although they do not know *why* He is removed.

What do poets say about it? They say that there is a sublime purpose for all that happens in this world, and it is called "the drop of unification." When those dwellers of clay houses go through all those terrors, through all that totality, in His pride, which is removed from them, a vent opens in the walls of their hearts, which are tightly sealed by the nature of Creation itself, and they become fit for instilling that drop of unification in their hearts. Then they are inverted like an imprinted substance, and they will evidently see that it is to the contrary—that it was precisely in those dreadful terrors that they perceive the totality, which is removed by foreign pride. There, and only there, is the Creator Himself clung, and there He can instill them with the drop of unification.

He turned everything around for them in such a way that the master of unification knew He had found ransom and an open vent for instilling Him.

This is what is written in the poem, "You surround everything and fill everything." During the attainment, abundance is felt. It appears and sits precisely on all those contradictions. This is the meaning of "more terrible than all terrors, prouder than all who are proud," and naturally, "fill everything." The poet knew that He fills them abundantly, and none else perceived the pleasantness of unification with Him until it seemed to him, at the time of his wholeness, that the afflictions they had suffered had some merit, to value the savor and pleasantness of unification with Him. His every organ and tendon will say and testify that each and every person in the world would chop off his hands and legs seven times a day for a single moment in their entire life, of tasting such a savor.

This is the law of the leprous on the day
of his purification;
he was brought unto the priest for all his fault.

It is a judgment for every good deed;
thus you will meet its operator in a land of duty.

Every passerby shall have it;
it is known how ... [unclear in Hebrew] and He will dwell.

What is His conversing at that time,
while strolling among great beasts?

There, an ear is lent to very pleasant words;
rivers of persimmon are extended, dents over dents.

They see what is heard—that it is only for their fault
that it is pleasant.

Their stench goes as far from them
as the east is far from the west.

He laughs at them because He has known
their souls forever.
The ransom will not be limited at all in their eyes,
when He gives Himself to them for ransom,
and every stranger will be ears for fine words.

It is a hand for every vessel of purification.
He will grip it to disclose the light,
to create, and to sustain the light on it,
in the sentence of redemption and in the sentence
of transformation.

And although all these do not elude you, I wish to fill with
them the words of Rabbi Yirmiah. This is his sublime meaning
with his allegoric words, "What, etc., ... When He desires, no
being can face His might. When He rises in His anger, who will
stand before Him? Whoa, who will not fear You, oh King of the
nations?" That is, "more terrible than all terrors, prouder than
all who are proud," and all in order to sound "the words of the
living God."

In other words, the sublime terrors were established only
to see the voices, which the eye cannot see nor the heart think
and contemplate. Until He came to that quality, the Creator was
operating without any grievance for the operation, as it is sensed
that the operation still did not exist. For this reason, throughout
this terrible and long process, He desired and consented to His
operation, to disclose it for the destined time.

This is what Rabbi Yirmiah said, "When He desires, etc.,"
meaning that His intention is only to prove to worshippers of

the Creator that that sublime side will always be before them once the act has been sufficiently revealed.

Therefore, who is to be held accountable that His honor will not be desecrated, for what fool would say that the Creator is lenient? He brings the verse, "Who can stand in the day of His wrath, and who can calculate the day of His arrival," from the long and sublime past? The day of His wrath is the one that calculates the day of His arrival; they are weighed together as though on scales.

By that you will understand the words of Rabbi Tarfon, who maintains that they say, "Enough." He proves from the verse, "And her father indeed spat [Hebrew: spat, spat] in her face, she will be disgraced for seven days," much less for Divinity to have at least two weeks. And still he concludes, "She shall be closed up seven days," meaning just as before the action and Divinity were exposed, and there was only "Her father indeed spat in her face," meaning exposing her face.

It is considered two spits—one is considered the heart, and one is considered the mind, as in, "more terrible than all terrors, prouder than all who are proud." Saying "enough" before Divinity to begin with, if you are pure-hearted you will understand through your heart the meaning of the words that after being closed up for seven days they went on their way in the systems of Torah, unlike prior to the completion of the quarantine.

Even if my mouth was filled with singing like a sea, my lips with florid praise as its numerous waves, it would not be enough to detail the righteousness of the Creator, who has done, is doing, and will do before His creations, which He has created, is creating, and will create. I have thoroughly learned that a great mass were, and are yelling in the world at the top of their lungs, but they remain unanswered. They come alone, and they leave alone. As they began, so they end, myriad subtract, but do not add, and woe to that shame, woe to that disgrace.

It is a precise law that sanctity increases and does not decrease, but the uniqueness of the Creator—who takes pride over the bodies, which are devoid of any desirables—does not wane at all. Rather, He even prides over "the elect men of the assembly, men of renown," and they, too, unless they carefully watch over themselves not to waste their time, He will be able to rid them of their world like the first, since the Glory of the World is strong and does not change for fear of His creations, of course.

Many great people have erred about it because they said that they were certain their hearts were awake. And the writing says, "And Er [Hebrew: awake], the firstborn of Judah, was bad in the eyes of the Lord, and the Lord put him to death." The sages say, "Even one who is slacking in his work is brother to one who destroys," for the most important is to pay attention and be mindful, and "Anything that you find you are able to do by your strength, that do," to extol and to sanctify His great and blessed name.

And precisely in a mindful manner, not as the cry of the fools, who know how to utter words without a wise heart. But the wise one, his eyes are in his head, and he knows no bodily forces. He is not Er or Onan, but rather, "The words of sages are heard in contentment, with fervent scrutiny for the Creator alone.

It is written in *The Zohar*, "Everything is clarified in thought." There are no outcries here, no self-tormenting or any illness or mishap whatsoever. Rather, "Her ways are ways of pleasantness, and all her paths are of peace," "All who is greedy is angry," and "All who is angry, it is as though he is idol-worshipping," and his soul departs from him.

But we should do much scrutiny and think with all our aim and strength, and "All day and all night they will never keep silent. You who remind the Lord, take no rest for yourselves, and give Him no rest until He establishes and makes Jerusalem a praise in the earth."

Let me tell you the truth: When I see the most vain ones wasting their lives away, it does not pain me whatsoever because in the end, no spiritual misfortune happens to them, only a body of flesh and bones that is tortured, and for which it was made, as has been detailed above. The fate of every beast is the slaughter, and being mindless, they are all as beasts.

All of Nature's orders do not sadden the pure-hearted. Rather, they rejoice the hearts of the understanding. But when I see the fallen ones, the men of renown, it is as though a blazing, fiery sword pierces my heart, for they torture the holy Divinity with their follies that they lie and fabricate.

Woe unto this beauty that withers in this dust, the holy, faithful drop. All the prolonged guidance is turning so as to reveal the face of the truth, and upon its revealing, returns and throws pure, faithful water on every corner of the guidance and reality. Then, all who are empty, fill up, and all the afflicted are bestowed upon, and there is neither an iron-web nor a cobweb here. Rather, there is great glory here, and faithful love returning and coming back from the Creator to His creatures, and every place where He lays his eyes heals.

Happy is the ear that has never heard slander, and happy is the eye that has never seen a false thing. All that He curses is utterly cursed, and all that He blesses is utterly blessed. Every thing that comes out of His mouth has neither doubt nor surplus in it. Rather, this is the thing which the Creator commanded, "Cleave unto Him."

Dust, dust, how obstinate you are. All that is beautiful to the eye withers in you; how insolent you are. That eye that blesses wherever you may turn, how has it become strangeness, and every place He looks burns and becomes consumed? How will those most desperate people be comforted "with a comfort of vanity and joy of the flesh"? What shall they answer in the day of calling? It evokes contempt and wrath.

Therefore, I have spoken at length against those people with whom you are face to face, and of the words they fabricate, such as the expansion of corporeality. As they, so are their works, "All who trust them," and "Cursed is the man who trusts man and makes flesh his arm," and "Blessed is the man who trusts in the Lord." "Happy is the man who did not follow the counsel of the wicked, ... but delights in the law of the Lord, and on His law does he reflect day and night," as our sages said, "I have created the evil inclination, I have created for it the Torah as a spice," and "If you encounter that villain, draw him to the seminary." How man does not fear or feel that his master is assisting him.

This is what I told you face to face at a time of joy, that the primary sin of the generation of knowledge [generation of the desert] was as according to the verse, "Our fathers in Egypt did not perceive Your wonders ... and were rebellious at sea, in the Red Sea." I interpreted that the value of a gift is as the value of the giver. They were the first to blemish it, when they "did not perceive Your wonders," but merely "wonders." Thus, the gist is missing from the book, which caused them to turn back at the time of the reception of the Torah, saying, "You speak with us and we will hear." Although the Torah does not attribute them sin in the matter, for it is said, "May this heart of theirs were given to fear Me all the days," it is because the sin preceded the giving of the Torah and was not written in the Torah, and it is known that the Torah engages in the path of correction and not in the path of sins.

You asked me, "What should I do with it?" I replied that you should exert and give many thanks for the benefit, for it is natural that when the giver sees that the receiver is not grateful, his future giving wanes.

You replied to me that the thanks for His blessings does not appear in the words of a corporeal mouth, but through exertion and broadening the heart in the benefit of the merit of unification, by which the enemies are stopped on the right and on the left, that this is called "gratitude for His blessings," and not the words of a corporeal mouth.

But come and see how lovely is faithful water from the never-ending fountain, of which it was said, "Let them be satisfied and delighted by Your goodness." The satiation does not cancel the pleasure because he has perceived "Your wonders," and not wonders and tokens, as to whom will he answer? Even he himself does not need it, and he never said to them or to the like of them, "Give Me, offer a bribe for Me from your strength." Their father has come to loathe going with his flock's dog for inferior guarding, "and the helper shall stumble, and he that is helped shall fall," and "The Almighty, whom we cannot find, is excellent in power."

It all came upon him since the time he forgot the quality of "lofty and exalted, very, very high," and began to engage by measuring of flesh and blood, and from there to measuring the trees, and also wishing to build himself on calculations. He was calculating calculations of others, but it is already written, "And you have found."

Ravnai said, "Until it comes into his hand. This means that he does not purchase just by seeing; this is the simpletons' phrasing: 'He does not buy until he holds it in his hand.'" Therefore, the Tanah teaches of two gates, one in finding, and one in negotiating, to understand and to instruct until he actually holds it in his hand.

It seems that at the end of days he will discover ... our sages: "When he sees from whom he took the coins?" They explain that he took from two people (which implies another thing that will be revealed at the end of days), from one—voluntarily— and from another—involuntarily, and we did not know with whom it was voluntary, and with whom, involuntary. This is the meaning of the verse, "What shall we do to our sister on the day when she shall be spoken for?" She will appear and be seen at the end of the right, for we will extend in the law for the Messiah.

Let us return to our topic, which is primarily to learn more about the giver of the gift, His greatness, His worth, and then he will be rewarded with true *Dvekut* [adhesion] and will obtain the flavors of Torah, for there is no other remedy in our world but that.

I shall recite a fine and pleasant poem about it, which brings joy to a true heart, and which is tried and tested in ten trials.

My drop, my drop, you are so fine, all the expanses of my
life, all my mornings, all my nights.

The face of the curtain, you raise the cover, in the
expanses of my futures, all my grieving, all my comfort.

The wasteland, the multitudes shall carry you with
branches that I added, all my ruin, all my filling.

You penetrate my heart, and all of your reward is in my
hand, from all my banners, I love, all my gold,
all my merchandise.

A good guest, what does he say? All the troubles that the landlord has troubled himself, he has troubled himself only for me, according to the verse, "One must say, 'The world was created for me.'" So it is, as the world was created for him, all the elements in his reality were also created for him.

One element—because of the unification—the general and the particular are equal to it, and everything that all the people in the world will attain at the end of correction, they attain the complete elements in each generation. This is why each one finds the elements of his organs in the Torah, for because it is generally set up for the whole collective, it is also generally set up for an individual. Moreover, in the collective, there is not more than there is in an individual, and this is a true and complete measure in great scrutiny.

This is why it is written, "With her love you will ravish always," and "You shall contemplate it day and night," and "The Torah, the Creator, and Israel are one." It is a measure completely adapted, for everything is one, and the spiritual cannot be divided into parts. One must sanctify and purify himself in mind and heart, and when you bless with the blessings of the Torah as before, you will attain the distinguished verse, "See now that I am I, and there is no other God with Me."

I ask that for your benefit and delight; do send me frequent information of your situation in the Torah, for it will save much time. Know that prolonging the time of correction diminishes the value of the correction, and anything spiritual improves and ascends when it takes less time. If you knew, as I know, that prolonging the stay on the paths of light is harmful, you would certainly be quicker in your work.

Although I neither wish nor am permitted to study for you, it is permitted and a great *Mitzva* to delight and perfume those loved ones that you find in a field which the Lord has blessed. Our whole engagement in life is only to raise Divinity from the dust, to delight her, to sing before her with all our might, to always praise the Creator with your mouth with what is permitted, and especially where we know that you will certainly succeed. For this reason, I urgently need information of you, and we shall be satiated with love together, to uproot the thorns, and we shall see the high rose soon in our days, Amen.

Yehuda

Letter No. 9

1923, Jerusalem

To my friend, may his candle burn:

I can no longer restrain myself regarding all that is between us, so I shall attempt open and sincere admonition. I need to know the value of a word of truth in our land, for so is always my way—to study all the workings of creation in utter precision and to know its merit, whether it is good or bad. This is the only place my fathers left for me as a boundary, and I have already found precious things and secrets in these passing, trifle images. It is with good reason that this lot has been set up before me, and they are lovely letters for the sentence of every wisdom and every knowledge, and were created only for combinations of wisdom.

First, we shall judge the quality of laziness in this world. ... On the whole, it is not such a negative and contemptible quality. The evidence is that our sages already said, "Sit and do nothing—better." And although common sense and several writings contradict this rule, still, to make the proper precision I shall show that "Both are words of the living God," and all will be settled peacefully.

It is clarified beyond any doubt that there is no other work in the world but His work, and all the other works besides His—even for the souls, if it concerns only oneself—would be better if they did not come into the world, as they turn matters upside down, for a receiver does not become a giver. This is an unbreakable law, and "If he had been there, he would not have been redeemed."

Thus, we should not discuss a work or a worker whose doer is in the form of reception, since this is utter vanity, and there is no doubt that it would be better to "Sit and do nothing," for he is doing harm by his work, either to himself or to others. Its benefit is utterly absent, as we said above.

I do not care at all if part of you finds this ruling uncomfortable, and even openly protesting my words, for so is the nature of every truth—it does not require the consent of any woman-born, great or small, and anyone who has been rewarded with thorough knowledge of the Torah is very opinionated.

Therefore, following this great and famous truth—that one who curses in his work "is a friend of a destroyer"—I feel no mercy or concern for the idle, to seek advice for them, due to the great rule: "Sit and do nothing—better." In any case, if they cherish the word of God and truly wish to worship their maker, to glorify His works, there is no doubt that the spirit of idleness will not be with them, since the spirit of the Creator robes with strength and might, from which idleness is blown as straw by the wind. However, if it turns out that they have unity along with this spirit of idleness, there is no doubt that at that time their minds are not dedicated only to the Creator, and then "Sit and do nothing" is certainly better.

I have much to say about this matter, but what can I do that time causes you to misunderstand my words, for you are not accustomed to my novelties in the Torah, which are said in utter simplicity. It requires a very high level to be able to lower one's level so much, and to elevate them. And yet, I cannot change my way, as I see in it the will of God.

Although you have heard from me many words of Torah said in simplicity, and I also troubled myself extensively to make you understand all my ways and all my wishes in the work of the Creator, I wish to say—regarding that profession—that with the Creator's help, I added to my teachers in the generation before me, and the Creator permitted me, and you are my witness.

And yet, our study of this matter had been short, approximately ... from the second day of the portion, *BeHaalotcha* [When You Mount], to the portion, *Shemot* [Exodus], since your situation during the week ... did not permit me to speak with you more of my novelties in the Torah. Also, I stopped entirely the way that I teach for reasons that I keep to myself, and even prior to that, I let you know about it with some explanation.

But since the time was very short, you have not become accustomed to my way, hence my ways were not immersed in you at all. For this reason, you have inserted many changes in my teaching ... for which you have lost much time. ...

You said explicitly that you would help me with all your might and power to scrutinize the ways of my teaching and its expansion in the world, but you sit and wait for the right time to come when you can partake with me in this matter. You promised it wholeheartedly, resolutely, and ceremoniously, without a shred of doubt, that who knows if you will be rewarded with the above-said.

And now what can you say of all your promises to me ... and I know your tactic and ploy, which you have devised, to wash your whole body all at once in endless water.

I also know the answer that is readily available for you regarding my question—that you are still unfit to display knowledge and to ruin or build, much less bond with me in work, while you yourself have insufficient grip on it.

And yet, it is the inclination in you, and you inherently contradict yourself. That is, you answer another question without humility, but to the contrary. Thus, how can you grip both ends of the rope?

... I say to you that there is no shame here whatsoever, no smallness, and no greatness, only the work of the devil that has succeeded in interfering with every good thing that appears in his way. After all, why should you mind if I perceive your smallness too much? Is it my praise that you crave? I rather know that your heart is purer than such litter.

Also, why should you mind if I understand the exact measure of your greatness as it is within your heart? Do you not fear my mocking you for your obstinacy?

And why this shame to speak before a friend such as me with boasting words? And also, all our sages have traversed this road, disclosing their secrets either to a special teacher or to a special and true friend, whether high or low, just as they came in their hearts.

The ways of the path of truth are not impressed at all by the truth, be it bitter or sweet. And most important, each scrutiny is as though accepted at the time, for the mind must be "clean," and under no circumstances biased due to one's bitterness. And the heart, too, must be righteous in its place, justifying the Creator even if He is not depicted.

And as there is no measure to the Creator's merit and Almightiness, there is no measure to the lowliness of a woman-born (and to his weakness), unless that creation, for all its lowliness, is willing to accept a word of truth without any biasness, for its afflicted body. Instead, it is always as in the verse, "The clean and the righteous do not slay," so it marches on the rungs of sanctity and purity until ... "What is this work for you?"

I evidently see that you will fall in this pit, whether less or more. This is the final Satan, which I find in my fruitful work for my generation. With God's blessing, I have been found agreeable in the eyes of my Creator, to reveal to me the full lowliness of the generation, and all sorts of easy and faithful corrections, to bring each soul back to its root as quickly as possible.

But what can I do in the day of calling, for you will have to answer the wicked's question, "What is this work for you?" Although the answer is clarified in the *Haggadah* [Passover story], "If he had been there, he would not have been redeemed," as there is no need for fools, worshippers of vanity. Still, no one is chosen for His work unless his heart is wholly with the Creator, to work the work of the burden devotedly, all day and all night, always, endlessly, only to bring a shred of contentment to one's Maker. Thus, why should this wicked one mingle and deliberate with such lovers of the Creator?

And yet, my brother, this is not an intellectual question. It is clear and it is true, and no reflection or doubt is left in the matter. But precisely because of it, it is a question to which there is no answer, for it is the question of a murky and turbid matter, and it is only a demand on the part of the material body to return to the idols of his father, in whose work he shares, or even truer—he is the worker and all the pleasure is his. And since the asker is but a mindless matter and body, the power of the mind is weak in answering any answers to it, for it has no ears and it is "like the deaf asp that stops its ear."

I know the great advantage with which the Creator has granted me over my contemporaries, for I have searched a long, long time why I have been chosen by God's will. And after all the lowliness emitted from the wicked son, which is the *Klipa* [shell] that rules in my time, and after I have witnessed its true measure, I realize the Creator's kindness with me, to distract my heart today and always from hearing the abovementioned question of the wicked.

I find myself committed and obligated, as today and as always, to be as an ox to the burden and as a donkey to the load, all day and all night. I will not rest from searching for some place where I can bring some contentment to my Maker. Even in this day that I am in, I am pleased to work under a great burden even seventy years, without any knowledge of its success (even my whole life), except that it is certainly the way that I have been commanded walk in all His ways and to cleave unto Him, which I have heard initially.

At the same time, I cannot excuse myself at all by any notion or contemplation from doing any work for His sake because of my lowliness. I crave and think all day about the sublimity of the work of God, in such sublimity that I cannot even write about it.

It is true that as I discussed these matters with my contemporaries, I saw that they have a sort of code of law in which they delve to find their measure of the work of God for all their needs. But I have never seen that code of law, that it allots conditions and amount to the Creator's wish from His creations, which He has created, concerning the rungs of *Dvekut* [adhesion] with Him.

By and large, I have received face to face that small and great are equal before Him, and all creations are ready for the instilling of His Divinity in their hearts, and the measure of instilling depends on the Creator's will, and not on him, at all. I therefore wonder—it is a grave disgrace for a woman-born, whoever he may be, to place a limit, or a seeming limit, on the quality of the Creator's will.

My words are utterly simple, yet I have yet to see in my generation anyone who is—in his own eyes—such a simple man as to understand the value of my words as they are, for they cannot lower their bodies so.

And once I have come to this, I will reveal to you all their secrets in the chambers of their figures. If you understand ... that it all came to them because of the question of a wicked man, "What is this work for you?" for they always need blindness toward that wicked man.

... But they are people, and why did they not turn their work nonetheless to that profession? What does the owner of the vineyard receive from his vineyard? And still, they were worshipping their Creator intellectually, whether He would pour upon them spirit from on high to see fruits in their work, or not. But they would not be excluded from among the worshippers of the Creator nonetheless.

When they are compared to beasts, carrying the material emotions, such as worshipping God with their will, without wanting to understand that they will lose all the substance along with anything they can acquire, and their memory shall be severed from the earth forever.

And yet, my brother, I have spoken to you at length regarding these matters face to face when we were together, and it is impossible to elaborate so in writing. Yet, I am certain that if you properly scrutinize these words that I have written in this letter, you are certain to find many issues with which you will be displeased, and which I wrote for you deliberately, as I believe that perhaps you *will* understand henceforth.

Do let me know every detail and every root where you do not completely agree with me, for my heart is wholly with yours, and you ... and the Creator is my witness that if I could feed you of heaven's milk above, I would not spare labor or exertion.

Yehuda Leib

Letter No. 10

1925, Warsaw

To the disciples, may the Lord be upon them:

... I terribly regret the dwindling organs that external circumstances overcame them from joining you. May the Creator give them strength so they can join us, and the Creator will be with them.

I understand that you are not engaged in unifications of mind and heart as I would like you to be. Still, do what you can and the salvation of the Lord is as the blink of an eye. The most important thing before you today is the unity of friends. Exert in that more and more, for it can recompense for all the faults.

It is said, "An exiled disciple, his rav [teacher] is exiled with him." This was perplexing to our sages, for how can there be slandering in the Torah and work of the disciple to the point of expelling him from the Creator's domain, especially once he has clung to a true teacher? They explained that when the disciple descends, it seems to him that the rav has descended, too. And because it is so, it really is so, meaning that he can enjoy his rav only to the extent that he assumes in his heart. Therefore, all he has is a low and inferior rav, as much as he gauges him. Thus, his rav is exiled with him.

The exile and enslavement in Egypt begin with the words, "And a new king arose over Egypt, who did not know Joseph." That is, a new ruling appeared in the minds of each and every one, a newly made ruling, since they fell from their previous degree. We have said that "an exiled disciple, his rav [teacher] is exiled with him," so clearly, they did not know Joseph. In other words, they attained him according to what they gauged in their hearts.

Therefore, they depicted the image of Joseph as they themselves were. Because of it, they did not know Joseph and the enslavement began. Otherwise, the righteous would certainly protect them and exile or enslavement would not be depicted to them at all.

Their enslavement in *Homer* [mortar/plaster] and *Levenim* ["bricks," as well as "white"] is explained: Mortar is the iniquity of the *Hamor* [donkey] by which one is sentenced for the thought. The bricks [white] are the repentance, when they are granted upper mercies and temporarily obtain upper light from the faith of the holy fathers, and are whitened from their iniquities. However, it was not permanent, so they were incarnating and coming into every work of the field, meaning continuation of hard work that concerns the rest of the *Mitzvot* [commandments, corrections].

Our sages said, "The intermediate, both judge them." This is why that *Klipa* is called Pharaoh, with the letters *Peh-Hey Reish-Ayin* [initials of *Peh Ra* (bad mouth)]. That is, the *Malchut* in *Mochin* is called *Peh* [mouth], meaning it is a resolution and consent not to break His word, and all that comes out of His mouth will be done.

In the exile in Egypt, the ruling was that of the abovementioned bad mouth, and they reverted back to evil. Thus, although they were rewarded with some upper illumination from the first nine, it could not be absorbed in the *Guf* [body] because of the bad mouth, the opposite of "*Peh* of *Kedusha* [holiness]." That is, the back of the neck was blocking the abundance that comes down from the *Rosh* [head], and sucked out all the abundance that began to come down for Israel. This is why no slave could escape Egypt, since Pharaoh put a great charm over the openings of Egypt, as our sages said.

By that we understand the verse, "And I know that the king of Egypt will not give you leave to go, except by a mighty hand." Through Moses, His servant, the Creator announced that no mighty hand or powers in the world would help with this evil *Klipa* because it surrenders only to the Creator. This is the meaning of "I and not a messenger," and the meaning of "And I will put forth My hand, and strike Egypt ... And I will grant this people favor in the eyes of the Egyptians..."

Now we shall interpret the enunciation of redemption and Moses' mission. It is written, "And Moses answered and said, 'But they will not believe me' ... for they will say, 'The Lord did not appear to you.'" Interpretation: Because the mouth of *Kedusha* was in exile, as in, "for I am slow of speech and slow of tongue," Moses, the faithful shepherd, argued before the Creator, "But they will not believe me." Even if I tie Israel to me and bring down some bestowal for them, the *Klipa* of Pharaoh sucks it out and robs it from them. And although they are attached to me, they will still not listen to me. That is, while the Pharaoh *Klipa* has dominion, and a mouth and speech in the exile, still, if they believed in the faithful shepherd properly, the children of Israel would be able to listen to Moses, who is above the mouth and speech. If they strengthened themselves in that, they would certainly be saved from the Pharaoh *Klipa*.

This is what Moses, the faithful shepherd, complained about to the Creator, "They will say, 'The Lord did not appear to you,'" as explained above, "And a new king arose over Egypt, who did

89

not know Joseph." Upon their descent into matter [substance], they will also deny the greatness of Moses, the faithful shepherd, so how was it possible for Moses to redeem them from that evil and strong *Klipa*?

Therefore, the Creator gave three signs for Moses to show before the children of Israel, and taught him to arrange these signs before them one at a time. The Creator also promised him that He would help him from heaven, so he can show it to them, after which the children of Israel will accept these signs from him and come to listen to Moses, and then he will be able to redeem them from that bitter exile.

Now I will explain the three signs. The first sign is the turning of the scepter into a serpent, and the serpent into a scepter. The second sign is that by taking out his hand not from his bosom, it was as leprous as snow. And when he took out his hand from his bosom, it returned to being as his flesh. The third sign is that by spilling the water of the Nile on the land it turned into blood.

Now I will interpret how He showed them to Israel. In the hand of the redeemer was a scepter, which is the faithful shepherd. He is holding the scepter to steer the white of Israel to their father in heaven. If he throws it to the ground, it means that the children of Israel are taking His scepter to do with it as they wish (*Artza* [to the ground] is like *Ratzon* [desire]). "And it turned into a serpent" means that their sin seemed to them like animals.

Before they approached his scepter, their sin was considered still. After they brought themselves to his scepter, it became an actual serpent until "And Moses fled from it" (according to what Israel gauged in themselves, as in "Who did not know Joseph").

Subsequently, when Moses came to save them from the serpent's bite, he gripped the serpent by its tail and not by its head because when a false redeemer comes to save Israel, he grips the serpent by its head, to break the serpent's head, as so is the way of all snake-catchers.

But a real redeemer actually grabs it by its tail (according to the secret that that serpent bends its head and strikes with its tail, which I already interpreted for you), "And it became a scepter in his hand," for then it really works in their hearts to turn them to a scale of merit. And once the children of Israel receive that sign, the Creator gives him permission and authority to show them the second sign.

I have already interpreted for you the words of our sages, "Will sacrifice him to His will." How "to His will? He is forced until he says, 'I do.'" This is so because when discussing the thought, the filth of the serpent will be corrected through the offering that atones for the thought.

And yet, making the offering should be with love and fear, and one who needs a sacrifice can toil out of fear, but not out of love, so the offering is disqualified for lack of love. Our sages say about that that He—the Creator—is forced, as in, "My sons defeated Me," for the *Zivug* of one who works out of fear is called "forced." "Until he says" means the Creator. Finally, the Creator says, and reveals to him His desire and will say, "I do want," in this work, and it becomes apparent that there was no coercion to begin with, but an actual *Zivug* with love and friendship.

This is the meaning of "She opens her mouth in wisdom, and the teaching of kindness is on her tongue." In the opening of the mouth, upper *Hochma* appears because at that time, when the *Klipa* of "bad mouth" parts from the *Kedusha*, the "mouth of *Kedusha*" comes out. This is the meaning of opening the mouth wide, and there are no more evil occurrences to break his word because "He who knows the mysteries will testify about him that he will not return to folly." Promptly, he is rewarded with upper

Hochma because the disclosure of law and judgment always come together. This is the meaning of "She opens her mouth in wisdom."

And once he has reached the disclosure of *Hochma*, with which he was rewarded only through his prior labor in his *Zivugim* [couplings], coercively, it turned out that were it not for the tongue of *Nukva*, in which there is the quality of labor, he would not have been rewarded with anything. Thus, it becomes apparent that to begin with, even the forced *Zivugim* were really *Zivugim* of love and embrace. This is the meaning of "and the teaching of kindness is on her tongue," specifically "on her tongue," and not on another's tongue.

Let us return to our topic that the first sign—that by Moses' grip by its tail it turned into a scepter in his hand. This is the meaning of "repentance from fear," as in, "She opens her mouth in wisdom," that from the time it is established below—and the *Klipa* is sent out and does not return—begins the root of disclosure of upper *Hochma*.

The meaning of the second sign is a root for repentance from love. When he brought his hand into his bosom, with upper faith, the law of *Hesed* appears on her tongue, and not on another's.

Scrutinize the words because indeed he must take his hand out of his bosom, as "bosom" is "I, and you will not have." The taking out of the hand is the expansion of knowledge [*Daat*]. If—when he takes out a hand for expansion of flavors [also reasons] of Torah and secrets of Torah—he remembers his root well, to not change its flavor [also reason], and knows the benefit of taking his hand out of his bosom.

It follows that law and judgment are tied to one another as two friends that won't separate. At that time the expansion flows in its ways properly.

By that you will understand the meaning of "And he put his hand into his bosom," which is the acceptance of the law, "and took it out," that he came to extend the expansion of *Daat* without strengthening to be adhered to the root, as well, which is the bosom. Then, "Behold, his hand was as leprous as snow." It is translated in Yonatan Ben Uziel, "His hands were closed," meaning that the fountains of bounty had closed, and there was no correction except to be strengthened once again. "And he put his hand back into his bosom," accepting the law, and then, "when he took it out of his bosom, it returned to being as his flesh." That is, the law accompanies and connects to the taking out of the hand, and law and judgment are connected. At that time, the flow of life and abundance returns to its place.

This is the meaning of "And if it comes to pass that they do not believe ... to the voice of the first sign," he will take out his hand not from his bosom. "And they will believe the voice of the latter sign," since he will see that by taking his hand out of his bosom it regained its health.

The third sign is a profound matter. The Nile is the god of Egypt, and Pharaoh is the god of the Nile, as he said, "My Nile is to me, and I have made it." We have already said that Pharaoh robbed to himself all the abundance that came down from the *Rosh* for Israel.

However, he gave to Israel the extract of the abundance that he robbed, and the extract given by Pharaoh is called "Nile." This is what waters all who dwell in Egypt. It is called "bread of idleness," for it does not require labor. This is why there was fear that the children of Israel would be blemished after the redemption of Egypt with the bread of the mighty, as it happened in the desert when they said, "We remember the fish that we ate in Egypt for free." This is the correction, "And the water ... become blood upon the dry land," for everyone will see that they were disqualified from the drink of Israel. Afterward, the blood of Passover and the circumcision blood came to them from that.

This is also the meaning of "She looks well to the ways of her household." It means that the water of the Nile became blood upon the land, and then, "and does not eat the bread of idleness." This is a very deep subject, to be elaborated on elsewhere.

Yehuda Leib

Letter No. 11

To the one who is tied to my heart, may his candle burn:

I received your words, and concerning the traveling of ... I can inform you that God willing, I will bring him together with me to Jerusalem. I think I will issue a visa to Beirut for him, and from there to Jerusalem on my permit, for I have no other way at the moment. I have already informed this to my family in a letter.

... Concerning the words of Torah you ask of me, you should have written what it is you're lacking without them, for you should accept everything with love. Indeed, so is the path of truth, but you should feel the love, and it is felt only in a place of deficiency. This is the meaning of "He who shares the suffering of the public is rewarded with seeing the comfort of the public," and "To the extent that a person allots, he is allotted."

You have often heard that all the good of the awakening from below concerns only our learning how to feel the deficiency, as it is set before us by the Creator. This is the meaning of "A prayer makes half," because as long as one does not feel half the deficiency—the part that was cut off from the whole, and the part does not feel as it should—one is incapable of complete *Dvekut* [adhesion]. It is so because this will not be considered advantageous for him, and one does not keep or sustain a needless thing.

Our sages told us that there is a remedy for this feeling by the power of the prayer. When one is persistent in praying and craving to cleave unto Him perpetually, the prayer can do half, meaning that he will recognize that it is half. When the sparks multiply and become absorbed in the organs, he will certainly be rewarded with complete salvation, and the part will cling to the whole forever.

This is the meaning of "There is only a hairsbreadth between the upper and lower waters," as our sages said, "A thread [or hair] was tied to him," as in, "mountains that hang on a thread." This thread needs a filling, and this is the reason for the division of the lower waters from the upper ones.

This is the meaning of the words, "The head of its mouth was inside of it." That is, as long as the blocked was not opened, meaning the mouth in the head [Peh de Rosh], it is fed through its navel [Tabur], and the blocked must be open. It turns out that "The head of its mouth was inside of it; it will be a lip around his mouth," means he will not settle for little because "If we permit our share, who will permit the share of the altar?" This is why he will feel the heaviness in the head.

That feeling will circle for him a lip for the mouth, since he will pour out his heart to the Creator extensively, to purify the lower lip. This is the meaning of the verse, "It will be a lip around his mouth, a weaving," meaning that the sparks of craving gather side by side and unite together "like the opening of a coat."

In other words, the reasons that cause the sensation of pain and pouring out of the heart will not be cancelled whatsoever, but will gather together and become a mouth, as our sages said, "His sins became to him as merits." It follows that he has two mouths, for "around" (in Aramaic) means *Sehor, Sehor* [circling, as well as merchandise].

Thus, the face is a complete *Partzuf*, and the *Achoraim* is a complete *Partzuf*. If he is rewarded with it, he acquires "the opening of a coat," and then "That man is guaranteed that he will not be torn because his name is Yinon for all eternity." Observe carefully and find, for this is the meaning of "They shall inherit doubly in their land."

There is great depth in my words, but I haven't the strength to interpret them now. But if you understand my words you will certainly be rewarded with coming and going without permission. As the portion ends, "And its sound is heard when he enters the holy place and when he goes out," may it be so.

On the whole, you do not understand the merit of attaining the Torah. If you did, you would certainly devote yourself to it and you would be rewarded with it. You see the verse, "A candle is a commandment; the Torah is light." If you have a house full of candles but no light, the candles will be taking up room in vain. The name, "Torah," comes from the word, *Horaah* [instruction], and from the words, *Mar'eh* and *Re'iah* ["vision" and "sight" respectively], meaning complete recognition that leaves no thread behind it. May the Creator make you understand my words henceforth...

I will also ask that you make great efforts in love of friends, to devise tactics that can increase the love among the friends and revoke the lust for bodily matters from among you, as this is what casts hate, and between those who give contentment to their Maker there shall be no hatred. Rather, there are great compassion and love between them.

I ask that each will show his letter to his friends because the matters are said from one to another, and there is one law for you in enslaving the body and sanctifying the soul. But do not change, God forbid, as do those with bodies. You should henceforth heed my words, for it is your life and the length of your days.

It is not for my own favor that I ask, but what can a fine general do when soldiers change his orders to them?

Yehuda

Letter No. 12

1925, Warsaw

To the honorable students, may the Lord be upon them:

... You must grow stronger in what concerns our prime wish. You know what I interpreted about the verse, "And the Lord your God will bless you in all that you will do." The lower man must do all he can do, and only then is there room for the instilling of Divinity. However, it is folly to think that this makes the Creator obliged to instill the blessing precisely in the place of one's work.

On the contrary, for the most part, the work is in one place and the blessing is in another, in such a place where one made no work at all, since he did not know or could not do anything there himself. In the real blessing, it is an unbreakable law, and this is the meaning of the finding, as in, "I labored and found," and I have already elaborated on that.

As for me, I enjoy my labor; hence, "They who seek the Lord will not lack abundance," and as it is written, "My salvation is near to come, and my righteousness to be revealed." But what I ask most of all is that you brace yourselves and be strong, and the Creator will be with you. Do speak to the sagging friends to join us, and the foreign fears will depart from them at once, and if they make the house vacant, there will be room for idols. Do not fear the blazing sword that is turning on the way of the tree of life.

And if you wish to know, I will inform you that I do not find myself distant from you at all. Rather, one who feels remoteness, it is because of himself.

There is no more news.

The words of the one who longs to be with you in perfect unification.

Yehuda Leib

Letter No. 13

1925, Warsaw

To my dear ... may his candle burn forever:

I received your words with a heart full of longing, for you hide yourself from me. Still, you could speak to me in writing.

What you wrote, letting me know the exile in Egypt, I wonder; it is common knowledge. "They cried, and their cry went up to God from the work." Then "And God knew." If there is no knowledge of the Creator in the exile, redemption is impossible. And knowing the exile is itself the reason for redemption, so why do you let me know at the time of redemption?

Truth will show its way, that one who regrets makes his regret known. He cannot withhold himself or hide. Indeed, I feel all of you together, that today has been replaced for you with tomorrow, and instead of "now," you say "later." There is no cure for that but to exert to understand that mistake and distortion—that one who is saved by the Creator is saved only if he needs the salvation today. One who can wait for tomorrow will obtain his salvation after his years, God forbid.

This happened to you due to negligence in my request to exert in love of friends, as I have explained to you in every possible way that *this cure is enough to recompense for all your faults.*

And if you cannot rise to heaven, then I have given you moves on earth. So why have you not added anything in that work?

Besides the great cure that lies within it, which I cannot interpret, you should know that there are many sparks of holiness in each one in the group. When you assemble all the sparks of holiness into one place, as brothers, with love and friendship, you will certainly have a very high level of holiness for a while, from the light of life, and I have already elaborated on that in all my letters to the friends.

I also ask that each one will show his letter to his friend, and so should you. Test me from this day forth to understand and to hear me, at least with what you can do, for then "The Lord will open to you His good treasure."

To ... say that he should think for himself. What would he lose by corresponding with me? Why is he hiding himself from me? I do ask of him to strain to see the merits of the friends and not their faults at all, and connect in true love, together, until "love covers all transgressions." Have him look in all the letters I am sending to the friends, so as to learn, "And let him eat no more the bread of idleness."

Where are ... and ... ? I have not heard a word from them so far. Do tell them to nevertheless hold on to their friends' gowns and read their letters as much as they need, and not to forget that the first question is, "Did you expect salvation?"

If they expect salvation, can it be that they will say, "Is this the work that the Creator desires of them?" And if I had to save the lives of one of them, of the friends, I would certainly toil and labor more than you, much less the life of the king, so to speak.

Therefore, give much dowry and gifts to the king of the world, and you will be rewarded with the king's daughter, and the salvation of the Lord is as the blink of an eye.

Yehuda

Letter No. 14

1925, Warsaw

To... may his candle burn:

... And scrutinize well in a thousand weekdays, for they are the paths of the river of knowledge. It is as Samuel said, "The paths of the heaven are clear to me," as the Sabbath, as the paths of the river of knowledge, the weekdays. That is, "One who did not labor before the Sabbath, from where will he eat on the Sabbath?" Thus, all the lights of the Sabbath are set up in lights that are gained during the weekdays. This is the meaning of "a thousand weekdays."

By that you can understand the verse, "Come to Pharaoh." It is the holy Divinity in disclosure, from the words, "and let the hair of the woman's head go loose," as it is written in *The Zohar*. The thing is that to the extent that the children of Israel thought that Egypt were enslaving them and impeding them from worshipping the Creator, they truly were in the exile in Egypt. Hence, the redeemer's only work was to reveal to them that there was no other force involved here, that "I and not a messenger," for there is no other force but Him. This was indeed the light of redemption, as explained in the Passover *Haggadah* [story].

This is what the Creator gave to Moses in the verse, "Come to Pharaoh," meaning unite the truth, for the entire approaching the king of Egypt is only to Pharaoh, to disclose the holy Divinity. This is why He said, "For I have hardened his heart," etc., "that I may place these signs of Mine within him."

In spirituality, there are no letters, as I have already elaborated on before. All the multiplication in spirituality relies on the letters that are sucked from the materiality of this world, as in, "And creator of darkness." There are no additions or novelties here, but the creation of darkness, the *Merkava* [chariot/structure] that is suited to disclose that the light is good. It follows that the Creator Himself hardened his heart. Why? Because I need letters.

This is the meaning of "that I may place these signs of Mine within him, and that you may tell ... that you may know that I am the Lord." Explanation: Once the letters were accepted, meaning when you understand that I gave and troubled for you, as in, do not move from "behind" Me, for you will thoroughly keep the *Achoraim* [posterior side] for Me, for My name, then she will make her abundance and fill the letters. The qualities will become *Sefirot*, since before the filling, they are called "qualities," and upon their fulfillment for the best, they are called *Sefirot*, sapphire, illuminating the world *from one end to the other*.

This is the meaning of "that you may tell." I need all that for the explanation, meaning "And you shall know that I am the Lord" "and not a messenger." This is the meaning of the fiftieth gate, which cannot appear unless the forty-nine faces of pure and impure appear, one opposite the other, in which the righteous falls [also forty-nine] before the wicked.

This is the meaning of the words, "Let not a wise man boast of his wisdom, and let not the mighty man boast of his might ... but let him who boasts boast of this, that he understands and knows Me." That is, as it is written, "There shall be no one miscarrying or barren in your land." Miscarrying or barren are the same thing, except "barren" means the deficiency and the letter itself, and "miscarrying" is the filling that the *Sitra Achra* gives to fill that deficiency, which is unsustainable, short-lived, and full of anger. At the time of correction, it becomes revealed that that miscarrying becomes understanding, and that barren becomes "Know Me."

This is what the prophet instructs us: "Let not a wise man boast of his wisdom, and let not the mighty man boast of his might," since all the being and presence that a person feels in himself holds no spirit, neither for the upper ones nor for the lower ones. It is so because there are no novelties in any being or lights. This is the meaning of "Maker of light," meaning that there are no novelties in the light, but the making, when one can affect moves over those letters and disclose the shapes of the upper ones.

However, "and creator of darkness," for created means elicitation existence from absence, as Nahmanides wrote. There is no novelty here, but darkness, like the ink for a book of Torah. By the exertion of the worshipper of the Creator to bring contentment to his Maker and to complement the Creator's will, the miscarrying and the barren appear. By assuming the burden of the kingdom of heaven in full, which is the meaning of "this," he is rewarded with seeing the real forms of "Maker of light, through questions and troubles. Then he is rewarded with boasting of the knowledge, and it is known that this is a true gain, praised and desirable in the initial thought.

By that we understand the verse, "And he said to them, 'May it be so, the Lord is with you' ... and He drove them out from Pharaoh's presence." The entire strengthening of Pharaoh, king of Egypt, was only in the "little ones" who did not know Joseph, who fed them with bread according to the "little ones." The "little ones" means abundance that is restricted at the time of *Katnut* [smallness/infancy], as in what our sages said, "Why do infants come? To give reward to they who bring them."

This is why he demonstrated his strength on the little ones and said, "See that evil is before your faces. Not so, go now, you who are men," since one should thank for the sparks of *Gevurot* [pl. of *Gevura*] in the work of the Creator, and which come through the Creator. But for the sparks of evil before your faces, it cannot be said that it is coming from the Creator.

This is why he said, "For it is her that you seek," meaning that your whole intention is to enhance the sparks of *Gevura* and enhance the sparks of evil, and how can you unite the evil sparks with the Creator? By that they were driven out from Pharaoh's presence [face].

By that we will understand the plague of the locust, as it was said, "And it covered the eye of the earth, etc., and ate that which remained." That is, because the Creator saw that all the gripping of the king of Egypt (until he expelled them) was in sorting the men and repelling the infants (as in, "For that is what you desire"), the plague robbed them of the men, as well, and they lost all the sparks of *Gevura*, as well.

By that you will understand the verse of redemption: "This month to you is the beginning of the months." In Egypt, the month was called *Nissan*, as they said about Mount Sinai, that *Sinaa* [hatred] came down from there, like the hard labor in Egypt being called, in general, *Sivan*, like *Shanaan*, meaning *Sinaa Shelanu* [our hate], as in, "For it is her that you seek," and all their efforts were only to delete the letters because they hated them.

And by the light of redemption, when they were rewarded with *Alphey* [thousands of] *Shanaan*, that *Hidush* [novelty (sounding similar to *Hodesh*—month)] was made the very first. Then, instead of *Sivan*, the letters joined to form *Nissan*, meaning *Nissim she Imanu* [miracles that are with us]. This is what RASHI interpreted about this verse: "'This month' indicates that the Creator showed to Moses the moon in its beginning," and the words are ancient.

Yehuda Leib

Letter No. 15

February 12, 1925, Warsaw

To my friend ... may his candle burn forever.

A reply to your letter from the sixth day of [the portion] *Bo* [come], which I received along with your letter from the fourth day of [the portion] *BeShalach* [When Pharaoh Sent]: Concerning the argument, your last interpretation seems the most proper. But let me fill up your words a little: "I shall open the doors of my heart to a high guest," such as the promise to raise himself to the high path, devoid of any attainments of the lower ones.

"The hooks of the pillars of glory shall pronounce," for in this manner of ascent, the pillars of the heart connect in certain ties called "hooks," (as in, "You will connect in hooks") into a real *Dvekut* [adhesion], and then the upper light pours on him.

"I shall send free all my permitted ones," as though abandoning his entire fortune, meaning all that he has attained, since the permissions of the heart are the attainments of the body.

But he is not interested in sending them out free, so they will have the strength to cling to him in arguments. Rather, he will surely drive you out from his home, so they will have no contact and connection with him whatsoever.

To fully execute it comes the closing utterance and says, "Let them announce on what were her foundations established." It is like a question that he asks the permitted ones. He argues and says, "Perhaps you have small or great foundations in the earth, or some pillars, foundations upon which some intellectual construction is supported?" By that, he is telling them to let them know it if they know how to reply to him regarding the rhymes that extend onward, on which there is no human answer. By that he expels them, to announce that the earth hangs on nothing.

And regarding your letter from the fourth day of *BeShalach*, and what you wrote, that you do not understand my words, I am surprised. It must be that it is only due to idleness in the work, and what can I do? Especially now, receive this thing nevertheless, to have between you a steadfast bond in love, as I have cautioned you prior to my departure from you.

I have already written several letters about it, and my heart tells me that you will be slacking in this, for I sense negligence among you in general.

May the Lord have mercy on us and we will be rewarded with salvation soon...

Yehuda Leib

Letter No. 16

1925, Warsaw

To my soul mate, may his candle burn forever:

I received your letter yesterday and I enjoyed it because I saw that you want to do as I wish, after all. Regarding your first question, your words are very confused. It is a profound matter, and I am preoccupied now, but I will nevertheless elaborate a little on the matter; perhaps you will understand and accept it from now on.

I have already said in the name of the Baal Shem Tov that prior to making a *Mitzva* [commandment], one must not consider private Providence at all. On the contrary, one should say, "If I am not for me, who is for me?" But after the fact, a person must reconsider and believe that it was not by "My power and the might of my hand" that I made the *Mitzva*, but only by the power of the Creator, who contemplated so about me in advance, and so I had to do.

It is likewise in worldly matters because spirituality and corporeality are equal. Therefore, before one goes out to make one's daily bread, he should remove his thoughts from private Providence and say, "If I am not for me, who is for me?" He should do all the tactics applied in corporality to earn his living as do others.

But in the evening, when he returns home with his earnings, he must never think that he has earned this profit by his own novelties, but rather that even if he stayed all day in the basement of his home, he would still have earned his pay, for so the Creator contemplated for him in advance, and so it had to be.

And although the matters look the contrary on the surface, and are unreasonable, a person must believe that so the Creator has determined for him in His law, from authors and from books.

This is the meaning of the unification of *HaVaYaH Elokim*. *HaVaYaH* means private Providence, where the Creator is everything, and He does not need dwellers of material houses to help Him. *Elokim* in *Gematria* is *HaTeva* [the Nature], where man behaves according to the nature that He instilled in the systems of the corporeal heaven and earth, and he keeps those rules as do the rest of the corporeal beings. And yet, he also believes in *HaVaYaH*, meaning in private Providence.

By that he unites them with one another, and "they became as one in his hand," and thus he brings great contentment to his Maker, and brings illumination to all the worlds.

This is the meaning of the three discernments—commandment, transgression, and permission. The commandment is the place of holiness, the transgression is the place of the *Sitra Achra*, and permission is neither a commandment nor a transgression. Rather, it is the place over which the holiness and the *Sitra Achra* fight.

When a person does permitted things but does not dedicate them to the holiness, that entire place falls into the domain of the *Sitra Achra*. And when a person grows stronger and engages in permitted things to make unifications as much as he can, he returns the permission into the domain of holiness.

Thus, I have interpreted what our sages said, "It follows that the physician has been given permission to heal." That is, although the healing is certainly in the hands of the Creator, and human tactics will not move Him from His place, the holy Torah still informs us, "and shall cause him to be thoroughly healed," to let you know that it is permitted, that this is the place of the campaign between commandment and transgression.

It follows that we ourselves are obliged to conquer that "permission" under the holiness. But how is it conquered? When a person goes to a doctor, and the doctor prescribes him a medication that has been tried and tested a thousand times, and after he has taken the medication he is cured, he must believe that without the doctor, the Creator would still cure him, for his life has been entirely preordained. Thus, instead of singing and praising the human doctor, he thanks and praises the Creator, and by so doing *conquers the permitted under the domain of holiness.*

It is likewise in the rest of the matters of "permission." By that he expands the boundaries of holiness so that the holiness expands to its fullest measure, and he suddenly sees himself and his full stature standing and living in the palace of holiness. Indeed, the boundaries of holiness have so expanded that it reached his own place.

I have explained all the above-said to you several times already because this issue is an obstacle to several people who have no clear perception of private Providence, and "a slave feels comfortable with a life without a master." Instead of work, he wishes to trust even more, and desires even more to revoke the questions from his faith and acquire supernatural proofs.

This is why they are punished and put themselves to death, for since the sin of *Adam HaRishon* onward, the Creator has devised a correction to this sin in the form of unification of *HaVaYaH* and *Elokim*, as I have explained.

This is the meaning of "By the sweat of your brow you shall eat bread." It is human nature that what one obtains through one's own efforts, it is very hard for him to say that it is the Creator's gift. Thus, he has room for work, to exert in complete faith in private Providence, and decide that he would come to it even without his work. By that, that transgression is mitigated.

Therefore, once you knew and wrote that Nature is a condition from the Creator, why do you settle once more for occasionally breaching the condition of "it came to pass" in favor of "it will come to pass"? One who breaches the Creator's requisite will certainly fail because he does not unite *HaVaYaH* and *Elokim*, and "One who says, 'I will sin and repent,' is not permitted to repent."

Also, why the experiments when there are practical actions? I also understand how you come to think that there is no need to establish private Providence, and I have already warned you about it many times.

And what you wrote about the sentence, to regret the continuation of the flesh, it is certainly a must. If you are a strong man, throughout the day and always, you will not find stains during the examination. That is, you, too, helped a little to this completion.

It is all the more so at a time of anger, as well as during envy and feelings of pride and so forth. All these are stains that come from the creation of ideas that there are my power and the might of my hand in my possessions and property. However, it takes great craftsmanship to avoid falling into negligence in the work because of it, for he will not be able to move the good inclination over the evil inclination and say, "If I am not for me, who is for me," etc., as it is written, "And the fool is boasting and confident." However, as I have written above in the name of the Baal Shem Tov, all the above are fixed, irrevocable laws; they are eternal.

We need to understand that His thoughts are not our thoughts. When it comes to the Creator, there is no issue of oppositeness in reality; it is all an evaluation of our five senses.

We should also understand that all the letters and the combinations are desired by us, but in the upper one, everything includes two forms—contentment and anger—which surround every incident in the world. Contentment includes rest and all its pleasures, and anger includes all the power of movement. Every ... and every movement ... renewal of creation, which is the meaning of "Maker of light and creator of darkness"...

Yehuda Leib

Letter No. 17

1926

Dear...

... Yet, let me write to you with regard to the middle pillar in the work of God, so as to always be a target for you between right and left. This is because there is he who walks, who is worse than he who sits idly. It is he who deflects from the road, for the path of truth is a very thin line that one walks until one comes to the king's palace.

One who begins to walk at the beginning of the line needs great care so as not to deviate to the right or to the left of the line even as much as a hair's breadth. This is so because if at first the deviation is as a hair's breadth, even if one continues completely straight, it is certain that he will no longer come to the king's palace, as he is not stepping on the true line, such as this:

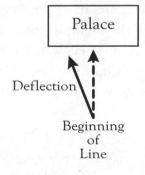

This is a true comparison.

Let me explain to you the meaning of the middle pillar, which is the meaning of "The Torah, the Creator, and Israel are one." The purpose of the soul when it comes in the body is to attain returning to its root and to cleave unto Him, while clothed in the body, as it is written, "To love the Lord your God, to walk in all His ways, to keep His commandments, and to cleave unto Him." You see that the matter ends in "to cleave unto Him," meaning as it was prior to clothing in the body.

However, great preparation is required – which is to walk in all His ways. Yet, who knows the ways of the Creator? Indeed, this is the meaning of "Torah that has 613 ways." He who walks by them will finally be purified until his body will no longer be an iron partition between him and his Maker, as it is written, "And I will take away the stony heart out of your flesh." Then he shall cleave to his Maker just as he was before the clothing of the soul in the body.

It turns out that there are three aspects: 1) **Israel** is one who strains oneself to return to one's root; 2) The **Creator**, namely the root one longs for; 3) The **613 ways of the Torah** by which one purifies one's soul and body. This is the **spice**, as it is written, "I have created the evil inclination; I have created for it the Torah as a spice."

However, these three are actually one and the same. In the end, any servant of the Creator attains them as single, united and unified. They only appear to be divided into three because of one's incompleteness in the work of the Creator.

Let me clarify something to you: You shall see its tip, but not its entirety, except when He delivers you. It is known that the soul is a part of God above. Before it comes in a body, it is as cohesive as a branch to the root. See in the beginning of *Tree of Life*, that He had created the worlds because He wanted to manifest His holy names, "Merciful" and "Gracious," etc., for if there are no creatures to have mercy on, etc. These words are very profound indeed.

However, as much as the pen permits, as "The whole Torah is but the names of the Creator," as they said. The meaning of attainment is, "That which we do not attain, we do not define by a name." It is written in the books that all these names are the reward of the souls, compelled to come into the body, for it is precisely through the body that it can attain the names of the Creator.

Its stature is according to its attainment. There is a rule: **The sustenance of any spiritual thing is according to the merit of knowing it.** A corporeal animal feels itself because it consists of mind and matter.

Thus, a spiritual sensation is a certain lore, and the spiritual stature is measured by the value of the lore, as it is written, "One is praised according to one's mind." However, **the animal knows, it does not feel at all.** Delve in this thoroughly.

Understand the reward of the souls: Before a soul comes into the body, it is but a tiny dot, though attached to the root as a branch to a tree. This dot is called the root of the soul and its world. Had it not entered into this world in a body, it would only have had its own world, meaning its own part in the root.

However, the more it comes to walk in the paths of the Creator, which are the 613 ways of the Torah that return to being the actual names of the Creator, the more its stature grows, according to the level of the names it has attained. This is the meaning of the words, "The Creator imparts each and every righteous 310 worlds."

Interpretation: The soul consists of two righteous: Upper Righteous, and Lower Righteous, as the body is divided from the *Tabur* [navel] upward and from the *Tabur* downward. Thus it acquires the written Torah and the oral Torah, which are two times 310, being 620 in *Gematria*. These are the 613 *Mitzvot* of the Torah and the seven *Mitzvot de Rabanan* [of our great Rabbis].

It is written in *Tree of Life*, "The worlds were created only to disclose the names of the Creator." Thus, you see that since the soul came down to clothe this filthy substance, it could no longer cleave to its root, to its own world, as before it came to this world. Rather, it must increase its stature 620 times more than how it previously was in the root. This is the meaning of the entire perfection, the entire *NRNHY* up to *Yechida*, for which *Yechida* is called *Keter*, implying the number 620.

Thus, you see that the meaning of the 620 names, being the 613 *Mitzvot* of the Torah and the seven *Mitzvot de Rabanan*, are, in fact, the five properties of the soul, meaning *NRNHY*. This is because the vessels of the *NRNHY* are from the above 620 *Mitzvot*, and the lights of *NRNHY* are the very light of the Torah in each and every *Mitzvah*. It follows, that the Torah and the soul are one.

However, the Creator is the light of *Ein Sof*, clothed in the light of the Torah, which is found in the above 620 *Mitzvot*. Understand that thoroughly, for this is the meaning of their words, "The whole Torah is the names of the Creator." It means that the Creator is the whole, and the 620 names are parts and items. These items are according to degrees and steps of the soul that does not acquire its light all at once, but slowly, one after the other.

From all the above, you find that the soul is destined to acquire all 620 holy names, its entire stature, which is 620 more than it had before it came. Its stature appears in the 620 *Mitzvot* where the light of the Torah is clothed, and the Creator in the collective light of the Torah. Thus you see that "the Torah, the Creator, and Israel" are indeed one.

Examine these words carefully, as they require only a simple explanation. It is about that that they said, "I shall not explain the literal," and you shall be happy if you perceive what is before you.

Let us return to the issue that before the completeness in the work of the Creator, the Torah, the Creator and Israel appear as three discernments. At times, one wishes to complete one's soul and return it to its root, which is considered Israel. At times, one wishes to perceive the ways of the Creator and the secrets of Torah, "for if he who does not know the commandments of the Upper One, how will he serve Him?" This is considered Torah.

Sometimes one wishes to attain the Creator, meaning to cleave unto Him with complete cognizance. One essentially regrets only that and does not agonize over attaining the secrets of the Torah. Also, one does not agonize over returning one's soul to its origin, as it was prior to clothing in a body.

Hence, one who walks upon the true line of preparing for the work of God must always test himself to see if he wants the three above aspects equally, as the end of the act equalizes with its beginning. If one wants one of them more than the second or the third, then one deflects from the path of truth, and understands this.

Thus, you'd better hold on to the goal of yearning for the commandment from the Upper One, for "He who does not know the ways of the Upper One and the commandments of the Upper One, which are the secrets of Torah, how will he serve Him?" Among all three, this is what guarantees the middle line most.

This is the meaning of "Open for me one aperture of repentance, such as the eye of a needle, and I will open for you gates where carts and coaches enter." Interpretation: The aperture is not for entrance and exit, but to insert the thread for sewing and for work.

Similarly, you are to crave only the commandment of the Upper One, to work, and then I will open for you a door such as an entrance to a hall. This is the meaning of the explicit name in the verse, "but in very deed [spelled like Hall in Hebrew] as I live and all the earth shall be filled with the glory of the Lord."

Yehuda Leib

Letter No. 18

To my soul mate, may his candle burn:

... However, keep away from suffering a man's jolt prematurely, for "where one thinks is where one is." Therefore, when a person is certain that he will not lack abundance, he can focus his efforts on words of Torah because "the blessed cling to the blessed."

But lack of confidence behooves labor, and any labor is from the *Sitra Achra*, and "the cursed does not cling to the blessed," for he will not be able to focus all his efforts only on words of Torah. And yet, if he wishes to travel overseas, he shouldn't contemplate these things at all, but just as quickly as he can, as though he is haunted, and will return to normalcy, so as not to scatter his sparks in times and places that apart from that are still not sufficiently united.

Know that no flaw comes from the lower ones except in the permitted time and place, as it is now. I wish to say that whether helpful or regretful, or God forbid despairs at the present moment, it is "rushing the end in all the times and in all the places in the world." This is the meaning of "a moment of His fury" and "How much is His fury? A moment."

Therefore, one has no choice but to direct all the present and future moments to be offered and presented to His great name. One who rejects a moment before Him, for it is difficult, displays his folly openly, for all the worlds and all the times are not worthwhile for him because the light of His countenance is not clothed in the changing times and occasions, although a person's work certainly changes because of them. This is why the faith and confidence above reason have been prepared for us by our holy fathers, and one can use them in the tougher times effortlessly and tirelessly.

This is the meaning of "By this comes lightly, ready for all His works on those six days." The letter *Hey*, which is the root of Creation, is a light letter, and laboring to enhance its level does not help at all, for it is thrown, as in, "no reason and no end." Therefore, one who assumes the complete burden of the kingdom of heaven finds no labor in worshipping the Creator, and can therefore be attached to the Creator day and night, in light and in darkness. The rain—which is created in coming and going, changes and exchanges—will not stop him because the *Keter*, which is *Ein Sof*, illuminates to all completely equally. The fool—who walks under a flood of preventions that pour on him from before and from behind—says to all that he does not feel the cessation and the lack of *Dvekut* [adhesion] as a corruption or iniquity on his part.

Had he sensed it, he would certainly have strained to find some tactic to at least be saved from the cessation of *Dvekut*, whether more or less. This tactic has never been prevented from anyone who sought it, either as in "the thought of faith" or as in "confidence," or as in "pleas of his prayer," which are suitable for a person specifically in the narrow and stressed places, for even a thief in hiding calls upon the Creator. For this reason, it does not require *Mochin de Gadlut* to keep the branch from cutting from its root.

"If he does not do these three for her," she shall "go out" into the public domain, under the enslavement of people, "free, without money," to this master, because he will not be given anything for his labor in idle things. It is as it is written, "They that make them shall be like them," etc., and what will one who was created by the worshipped—who bows to his own work—ask of them? Therefore, *anyone who says he has preventions from above, I say about him that he lies in the name of his Maker.* He maliciously pretends to be unable because he does not have the real desire to be adhered to the Creator due to his strong ties to the *Ketarim* of impurity. That is, he does not wish wholeheartedly to part from them forever.

This is the meaning of the words, "And you who have no money come, buy and eat. Come, buy wine and milk without money and without cost." In other words, our only prayer to the Creator to give us of His wisdom and splendor is because He desires us to adorn ourselves before Him with these desires, as in, "Spirit draws spirit and brings spirit."

For example, because it is impolite to come before the king without some request ... but in truth, we have no business with the gift itself, but in being granted with *Dvekut* with Him, whether less or more.

Thus, a slave who wants to cling to the king out of the craving in his heart begins to practice royal manners, and sets up for him some request. But the king rejects him. If he is clever, he will say to the king the sincerity of the point in his heart—that he desires no gifts, but for the king to assign him any service, the least of the least, in whatever way, as long as he is even slightly attached to the king in a connection that will not be stopped. Instantaneously, the king has revealed it to us in the form of *Dvekut* [adhesion], which is contemptible in the eyes of the lowly and its value is always according to the measure of desire of the point in the heart, meaning the prayer, faith, and confidence that he will never be wanting, even for a moment during the twenty-four hours of the day.

But the lowly—in their point in the heart—do not crave *Dvekut* with the King Himself, with the king's body, but with

His numerous gifts, who distributes property and strength with wonderful delights, sparks flow from the bottom of the heart toward His immense gifts. For this reason, they find *Dvekut* with Him laborious, for what will they get out of it and other forms of "so what?"

However, "apples of gold..." for which anyone who understands will laugh at those worshippers whose heart is deficient, who are saying to all that they are fools because they say they have preventions.

But "The covenant of the fathers did not end," and "He who comes to purify is aided." First thing in the morning, when he rises from his sleep, he should sanctify the first moment with *Dvekut* with Him, pour out his heart to the Creator to keep him throughout the twenty-four hours of the day so that no idle thought will come into his mind, and he will not consider it impossible or above nature.

Indeed, it is the image of nature that makes an iron partition, and one should cancel nature's partitions that he feels, and must first believe that nature's partitions do not cut off from Him. Afterward, he should pray from the bottom of his heart, even for something that is above his natural will.

Understand that always, even when forms that are not of *Kedusha* [holiness] traverse you, and they will instantly stop when you remember. See that you pour out your heart with all your might that henceforth the Creator will save you from cessations in *Dvekut* with Him. Gradually, your heart will grow accustomed to the Creator and will crave to adhere to Him in truth, and the Lord's desire will succeed by you.

Yehuda Leib

Letter No. 19

1927

My dear soul mate and disciple, and all the friends.

I have received all your letters, and may they please the Almighty. However, "Know thou the God of thy father and serve Him." **Know** means **recognition**, because a soul that does not know is not good. This means that if a person does not know his master, even though he has a soul and yearns and longs to serve Him, it is not good.

Even though one has a soul, he is not ready to know Him, "until the spirit be poured upon him from on high." However, one must lend an ear and listen to the words of the sages, and believe in them wholeheartedly.

It has already been written: "Surely goodness and mercy shall follow me all the days of my life." The Baal Shem Tov interprets: "The Lord is thy shade." Like the shade that follows one's movements, its inclinations lean every way the person does, so does man according to the Creator. It means that when love for the Creator awakens, one must see that the Creator has awakened toward him with intense longing, etc. This is the meaning of the words of Rabbi Akiva: "Happy are you Israel before whom you purify, and who purifies you."

Thus, in the beginning of one's nearing, he is given a soul that is like a circle. This means that the Creator awakens to him any time there is a prospect on one's part to cling to one with longing and yearning. This is what the poet writes: "Surely goodness and mercy shall follow me all the days of my life." King David is the collective soul of the whole of Israel. Hence, he always longed, yearned, and craved for true adhesion with Him.

However, one must know in one's heart that the Creator chases him just as much as he chases the Creator. One must never forget that, even through the greatest longing. When remembering that the Creator misses and chases one to cling to him as intensely as one wishes for it himself, he then always goes from strength to strength, with yearning and longing, in a never-ending coupling, the complete perfection of the soul. At last, one is endowed with repentance out of love, meaning the return of the *Vav* to the *Hey*, being the unification of the Creator with Divinity.

However, a soul without knowledge and recognition of the Master is in great decline, when the longing increases to a certain measure. It is so because one thinks that the Creator now dislikes him; woe to that shame and disgrace. Not only does he not complete his yearning and longing to be filled with eternal love, he is even in a state of "A whisperer separates from the champion," since he thinks that only he wishes and longs and yearns for the Creator. He does not believe our sages that to the very same extent the Creator wishes, longs, and yearns for him.

What are we to do to benefit those whose heart has not been fixed with faith in the sages? "From my flesh shall I see God?" I have already proven to you several times that the conducts of this world are *Otiot* [letters] that one must copy to their actual place in spirituality, for spirituality has no *Otiot*.

However, because of the breaking of the vessels, all the *Otiot* were ejected to corporeal conducts and people. When one corrects oneself and reaches one's root, he must collect them by himself, one by one, and bring them back to the root, to holiness. This is the meaning of "to sentence oneself and the entire world to a scale of merit."

The matter of the unification of the Creator and Divinity that one induces when he has had his fill of yearning and longing is precisely like the underside coupling, applying in the birth of a corporeal body. It, too, extends necessarily by cause and effect, meaning the hardening that is a certain measure of longing and yearning, called hardness in the corporeal tongue. Then, one's seed is also blessed, for it shoots like an arrow *Nefesh* [soul], *Shanah* [year], *Olam* [world]. This is the meaning of, how is there repentance? In the same place, at the same time, with the same woman, since *Hey Tata'a* [the Lower *Hey*] consists of *Nefesh*, *Shanah*, *Olam*.

Nefesh is the measure of the longing and the yearning. *Shanah* is the changing stimulations, as complete coitus bears the complete measure to restore past glory, meaning, as they were cohesive before they were separated in the corporeal world. However, one cannot be ready for this sublime mating, called complete coitus, all at once. Rather, "Surely goodness and mercy."

Hence, the stimulus, which is the beginning of the coitus, is the meaning of "a righteous who suffers." The Creator has no wish for his adhesion, so he does not taste love in the longing and yearning that needs "the same thing," and "the same place." Thus, one is found in a state of sorrow, which is *Nega* [affliction] that is destined to become *Oneg* [delight]. [The words are spelt with the same letters in reverse order.]

However, "time will do what the mind does not do." The Creator counts all the stimuli and collects them into the complete measure, which is the measure of hardness for the intended day. This is what the poet means by "Awaken and sound to sever any should." "Sticking" is orgasm, as it is said, "stuck in his brother's wife," which is the mating of the Creator with Divinity from above downward before the soul clothed in incarnation of this world.

After that, when a person prepares to return to his root, he does not induce the complete mating at one time, but creates stimuli, which is the degree of *Nefesh*, by way of cycles, chasing the holy Divinity with all his might, quivering and sweating, until he mounts this extremity all day and all night, incessantly.

It is as the books write by way of cycles. While one's soul is being completed in the degrees of *Nefesh*, he comes ever closer, and so his yearning and sorrow grow. It is so because the unsatisfied desire leaves behind a great affliction, according to the measure of the desire.

This is the meaning of "sound." The poet teaches us and says, "Awaken," meaning that you induce stimuli in the holy Divinity. "Sound," for you cause a great affliction, like no other, which is the meaning of "he groaned and moaned" because "What does Divinity say when one is afflicted, etc.?" And why do you do so? It is in order to "sever any shout."

This means, "The righteousness of the righteous will not deliver him on the day of his transgression." To Him who knows all mysteries, the desire in one's heart for His nearness is known, and that it might still be interrupted. Hence, He, the Blessed One, increases His stimuli, meaning the beginnings of the coituses, for if one listens to His voice, by way of "The Lord of thy shade," one does not fall by reason of the increasing affliction of the stimuli. It is so because one sees and hears that the holy Divinity also suffers as he does by the increased longing. Thus, one's longing grows stronger and intensifies each time until one's point in the heart is completed with complete will in a tight knot that will not crumble.

Rabbi Shimon Bar-Yochai has said about it in the Idra: "I am for my beloved and upon me His desire. All the days I was connected to this world with a knot connected to Him, to the Creator, and because of that, now upon me His desire, etc." It means, "Until He who knows all mysteries shall testify that he shall not turn back to folly." Hence, he is granted the return of the *Hey* to the *Vav* for eternity, meaning the complete coitus and the restoration of past glory, which is the meaning of "the great sticking."

All this is by the power and the virtue of the blowing, for they have severed any shout, and he shall not turn back to folly. Then one merits the complete consciousness in a never-ending coupling, called "knowing." In addition, one sees that all the many times of hardships that came to him were but "to know." This is the meaning of "at the same time," meaning "known to Him who knows mysteries," that times have created that power in him, to remain in his righteousness forever.

"In the same place," is the restoration of past glory, as it was before its diminution, as you have heard from me several times, that the Creator does nothing new at the end of correction, as the fools think. Rather, "And you shall eat old store long kept," meaning until he says, "I want."

"In the same woman ..." "...Grace is deceitful and beauty is vain; but a woman that fears the Lord, she shall be praised." This means that, during the preparation, the beauty and grace appear and the essence of perfection that one yearns and longs for. However, at the time of correction, when the earth is "full of the knowledge of the Lord," "I shall see an opposite world," as only fear and longing are the essence of the desired perfection. Then one feels that during the time of preparation, one was lying to oneself. This is the meaning of "a righteous who is happy," meaning the complete coitus for the one who is granted the great sticking. This is a complete righteous.

Show these words before the eyes of all the friends, and with that I shall bless you with writing and signing in the books of the righteous.

Yehuda Leib

My troubles are many, and I cannot let you know the greatness of my longing after you, but I am certain of the near redemption. Do not deprive me of your letters, at least one letter every week. Believe me, that while you write me, your answer will come right away.

I have not heard a thing from our friend ... and perhaps there is no need to those who fear Him? That, too, he should let me know. I miss hearing of him and his household.

All the best, and God willing, we shall speak at length of goodly matters.

Yehuda

Letter No. 20

1927, London

To my soul mate and student ... may his candle burn:

... Why have you not informed me of the *Dvekut* [adhesion (closeness)] of the friends, if it is going from strength to strength? This is the very foundation of our good future and of your success in teaching.

I am not ashamed to admit that my troubles are so numerous that I have no energy to play with you according to each and every one's wish, but you are carved within my heart all day and all night. I burn with thirst for your well-being and wholeness, and Lord knows how much I have labored and exerted on your behalf, and we are certain that they will not be in vain, and the word of the Lord will stand forever.

But why have you forgotten the teaching that I said in the holiday of *Shavuot* about the verse, "My beloved is like a gazelle," concerning the matter of "turning the face back," that the face is built during the escape and hiding, but in the form of *Achoraim* [posterior], which is the measure of sorrow for the distance and concealment? But in fact, those *Achoraim* are actually *Panim* [face/front], as our sages said, "turning the face back," so the face is in the back. This is the meaning of "I, the Lord, do not change; and you, O sons of Jacob, are not consumed," meaning as it is written, "They who seek Me shall find Me."

I wrote you the intention of the blowing [of the *Shofar*], to know why they blow and trumpet standing up ... "For the day is holy to our Lord." Although I know that my words will not reach you while you are hearing the sound of the *Shofar*, but it is written, "Before they hear, I will answer," which is why I wrote in its time.

You, too, show my letter to all the friends, and perhaps they will lend an ear to my words.

... From this day forward let us grow strong in Torah and *Mitzvot* "as an ox to the burden and as a donkey to the load," to raise Divinity from the dust, "arising contempt and wrath," and the sins will become merits because His glory will fill the whole of the earth.

God willing, I am certain that our salvation is near and we will be rewarded with serving the Creator together abundantly, and the Lord's wish will succeed by us.

Yehuda Leib

Letter No. 21

1927, London

To my soul mate ... may his candle burn forever:

I received your letter from the thirteenth of *Tishrey* [the first Hebrew month]. What you write me about, "I recognize how much I need external mortifications to correct my externality," thus far your words, I say that you neither need mortifications nor to correct the externality. Who has taught you this new law? It must be that you are not attached to me as before, and are therefore learning other ways.

Know that you have no other trusted friend in your whole life, and I advise you not to correct your externality at all, but only your internality, for only your internality is poised to be corrected. And the main reason why the internality is corrupted due to the proliferation of sins is the filth, whose sign is pride and self-importance. That filth fears no mortification in the world. On the contrary, it relishes them because the self-importance and pride increase and strengthen by the mortification.

But if you do wish to cleanse the sins off you, you should engage in annulment of the self-importance instead of the mortifications, meaning to feel that you are the lowest and the worst of all the people in the world. It requires much learning and education to understand it, and each time you should test yourself to see if you are not fooling and deceiving yourself. It also helps to lower yourself before your friend in actual fact.

However, you should be mindful that you lower yourself only before the right people. So if you wish to engage in it in actuality, you can annul yourself before our group, and not before strangers, God forbid. However, you must know for sure that you are the worst and the lowest of all the people in the world, for this is the truth.

Indeed, my advice is straightforward and easy, and even a weak person can keep it to the fullest, for it does not wear out the strength of the body, and it is the complete purity. Although I have not spoken to you about it, it was because you did not need it so, since while you were with me in the same place, you would gradually recognize your lowliness anyway, without any learning and deeds. But now that you are not with me in my place, you must engage in annulment of the self-importance in the manner just mentioned.

And the most important is to pray extensively and strengthen the confidence that the Creator will succeed in awarding you complete repentance, and to know how to cling to Him in one connection for eternity. This is the most important, and this is the difference between one who serves the Creator and one who does not. "Do not rest, and give Him no rest" until He forgives all your sins and transgressions, and brings you close to Him forever and for all eternity.

You should also cling to me in a way that the location does not separate us. Our sages said, "Cling to one who has been anointed and you yourself will be anointed." This is an important principle from the studies of the Baal Shem Tov, to mate with the righteous, may you be wise enough to understand it.

Believe me that on my part there are no preventions or heaviness. If I knew that there was more that I could do in your favor while being with you in the Land of Israel, I certainly would not leave you. But in truth, my journeying from you was also precisely for your benefit.

In fact, my departure from you was just for your own good.

Yehuda Leib, son of my teacher and Rabbi, Simcha Ashlag

Letter No. 22

1927, London

To my soul mate ... may his candle burn:

I received your letter from the fourteenth of *Tishrey* [first month in the Hebrew calendar]. But my friend, why aren't you pleased with the first order that I have set up for you, and ask for novelties? I have already told you that as long as you are not accustomed to the first order, you are not permitted to make for yourself other orders, neither easy nor strict. But here you are, pretending to forget, and you are knocking on my door seeking new orders. It must be the inciting of the inclination.

I must remind you the first order that I gave you, and may the Creator help you have no breaks with His work going forward, and only ascents ever upward until you are awarded with *Dvekut* [adhesion] with Him, as it should be:

1. Be prepared for His work, approximately two hours after midnight, and no later (meaning from the eighth hour after *Arvit* [evening service]).

2. On the first two hours, engage in "midnight *Tikkun*," afflict yourself about the exile of Israel and the affliction of the holy Divinity due to their iniquities, then pray and plead until the tenth hour.

3. From the tenth hour until the prayer is the time of delving in the holy books, *Beresheet Hochma*, and the like, and in the writings of the ARI. See that you thoroughly understand and internalize everything you study. If you do not fully understand, give the Creator no rest until He opens your heart and you understand Him, for this is the most important—that the Creator gives wisdom.

4. Set times for Torah, without any cessation for idle conversations, God forbid. See that you dedicate no less than five consecutive hours. You can set them for whatever time you wish during the day, as long as you do not stop for any conversation in between, they are consecutive, and specifically in the study of the revealed. Be careful not to forget anything from the study, so repeat it as you should. Also, it would be good for you to learn to be a teacher; it will be very helpful for you.

You can learn in a group with whomever you want during those five hours, but do not speak of things that do not concern the study, not even of manners of worship. If the partner wishes to study only two or three hours, you can finish afterward until you complete the five hours. During the rest of the day, succeed in negotiations.

Thus, you have what is yours, now hurry yourself and take the Creator with you, so you will succeed in behaving as I have written for you, and the words of Rashbi in *Idra Zuta* will come true in you: "'I am for my beloved,' etc., all the days when I was tied to this world, I was tied to it in one connection, in the Creator. For this reason, now upon me is 'His passion.'"

After a few months, when you have grown thoroughly accustomed to this order, let me know and I will add to you in the ways of the Creator.

In truth, I am not far from you at all, for it is all up to you, since time or place do not pose any hindrance in spirituality. Why don't you remember what I said on the festival of *Shavuot* about the verse, "My beloved is like a gazelle"? Our sages said, "As the gazelle looks back when he runs, when the Creator leaves Israel, He turns back His face." I interpreted for you that then the face returns to being in the *Achoraim* [back/posterior], meaning craving and longing to cling to Israel once more. This begets in Israel longing and a craving to cling to the Creator, too, and the measure of the longing and craving is actually the face itself, as it is written in "Bless My Soul," by Rabbi Yehuda HaLevi, "My face is to your prayer when you run to meet the Lord God."

Therefore, the most powerful at this time is only to persist and increase the longing and the craving, for thus appears the face, Amen, may it be so.

Send me many letters, and this will be encouraging to you, as well.

Yehuda Leib, son of my teacher and Rabbi, Simcha Ashlag

Letter No. 23

1927, London

To my soul mate ... may his candle burn forever:

... Concerning the comparison of your matter to the cascading of the worlds, of which your friends do not approve, it is because they learned from me that first you need to understand the upper worlds, for so is the order—from above downward first, then from below upward. It is so because a corporeal fountain can give birth only to corporeality, and wherever it looks, it only materializes. Conversely, a spiritual fountain emits only spiritual images, and any place on which it looks is blessed.

Even the corporeal images, when they sense their source, return to being truly spiritual, not compared to, or like, but truly become complete spirituality, as it is written, "It is changed as clay under the seal, and all things stand as a garment."

What you are asking of me, to repeat to you the matter of unifications because you were not rewarded with receiving them from authors, I wonder, how would you receive them from books?

I saw your allegories and poetic phrases that begin, "I shall carry my adages and say, 'words that are gauged by the *Omer* [count].'" Indeed, you gauge your words with the *Omer*, but exert further to bless the blessing of the *Omer*, for "an omer is the

tenth part of an ephah [measuring unit, as well as "where"]."
Ephah means great bewilderment, as you write, "*Ephah* is the
right [just] side, and *Asirit* [one tenth] comes from the word
Asurot [forbidden]," for there is a mother to the tradition, and
there is a mother to the Pentateuch, as in, "The king is held
captive by your tresses."

That measure indicates that through faith and confidence,
the heart's bewilderment is arrested, too, meaning not even a
trace of bewilderment remains. This is the measure of the *Omer*.
And yet, we should bless, and this I did not find in your letter.

It is said, "The greedy man curses and spurns the Lord."
That is, a prayer does half, and anyone who prays for himself
is incomplete, but halved, for the whole one has nothing to
pray for. This is why our sages warned us not to work in order
to receive reward, but for wholeness. This is a sublime secret,
and only those who have no awakening for themselves will
understand it.

This is why our sages said, "The host cuts and the guest
blesses," meaning that one must not lie to himself that the
landlord is giving him wholeness. Rather, he must feel the truth
as it is, in utter precision. This is why it was said, "The host
cuts," yet the guest must bless.

"Guest" comes from the words, "and smelled in the fear of
the Lord." And because he receives what the host gives him at
the cutting, as though it was complete, he is blessing anyway.
And the measure of his blessing is as the measure of his joy with
the gift, which is possible for him only through "His delight shall
be in the fear of the Lord."

This is what our sages said, "If he stole a measure of wheat,
ground it, kneaded it, baked it, and separated it, how will he
bless? He does not bless, but curses." This is very deep, for one
who steals does not thank the robbed one because the robbed

one did not give him a thing. Rather, he took from him by force, against his will.

The cutting and the reward that a person deserves all stem from the first iniquity, since "a transgression leads to transgression." "In the beginning it is as cobweb, and in the end it is as cart-ropes." Everything follows the beginning.

And yet, although he believes that all the deficiencies and cuts were done by the Creator, he still cannot think so about the first iniquity, as it is certain that harm will not come from the Upper One. It follows that he truly is a thief, as though he snatched from the Creator against His will.

"The tree of knowledge was wheat," as it is written, "One who robs a measure of wheat." *Se'ah* [measure] is as "In *Se'ahse'ah* [full measure], when You send her away, You will contend with her." Wheat is the first iniquity. Therefore, although "she ground and baked"—meaning they became cart-ropes, and then he separated the *Challah* from it, from the word *Hulin* [secular], "It is entirely for the Creator," implying the exaltedness and separation above reason—he is still not blessing, but curing, as it is a *Mitzva* that comes through transgression. For were it not for the first iniquity, this great *Mitzva* would not have happened.

All this is because he is a thief, and he does not see that a righteous pardons and gives, hence he does not bless wholeheartedly and does not make repentance from love, for then sins would become as merits to him. He would recognize that the measure of wheat is the Creator's gift, and not his own power and the might of his hand.

This is why our sages said, "The host cuts," and not "the guest," meaning the measure of wheat is also the Creator's gift, to "keep His covenant and to remember His commandments to do them." When the guest grows strong enough to believe that everything that the host has troubled Himself was only for him,

143

he blesses Him wholeheartedly. It turns out that that cutting in itself is truly a whole thing, after the blessing of the Creator from above downward.

But first, he must gain strength in his fountain of blessings from below upward. That is, he is called "a guest" for he can gain strength and exert by the scent, as it is written, "and smelled in the fear of the Lord," and as it is written, "One who steals from his father and mother and says, 'it is not a crime,' is a friend to a destroyer." In other words, the first iniquity is rooted in his body because of his father and mother, hence the person became a thief by saying that he is as abovementioned, and it is not the gift of the Creator. This is why he is regarded as stealing from his father and mother, and then adding sin to crime because he says, "It is not a crime." That is, he grows fond of the *Mitzva* of destroying, God forbid.

This is the meaning of the blessing of the *Omer*, that one needs to feel the Creator's gift even in the measure of wheat, meaning by the scent. At that time his joy will be whole in all his work, and by that the reward becomes whole again, and "The Lord knows the way of the righteous."

Yehuda Leib, son of my teacher and Rabbi Simcha,
may his candle burn

Letter No. 24

1927, London

To my soul mate ... may his candle burn:

I received your letter from the fourteenth of *Tishrey* [first Hebrew month] and I thoroughly enjoyed it. I commend you on your efforts in adhesion of friends, and may the Creator also give you the complete intention.

Please, my friend, do strengthen in the study of Torah, both revealed and concealed, for all you lack is strengthening in the burden of Torah, for the evil inclination resides only in a heart vacant from wisdom.

Also, be very careful of idleness because "through indolence the rafters sag," and it is the hardest *Klipa* [shell/peel] in the world. It is all according to the amount of actions: The sign of the idle is sadness, and the sign of the nimble is joy.

If it is not too difficult, I would suggest that you study to become a teacher, as it is good for the soul. But most importantly, pray and trust the Creator with everything you want to do, and it will help you accomplish successfully.

You already know that prayer and confidence go hand in hand. We must believe in complete faith that the Creator hears the prayer of every mouth, especially concerning the holy

Divinity. With this faith we acquire confidence, and then the prayer is complete, with confidence that we will be saved, and he is rewarded with confidence and joy all day, as though he has already been saved.

Remember what I told you—during the first hour after rising break your heart and engage in "midnight *Tikkun* [correction]" by thought. Afflict yourself in the affliction of Divinity, who is suffering because of your actions. However, do not prolong for more than one hour. Afterward, elevate your heart in the ways of the Creator, with faith and confidence in wholeness, and engage in Torah and work in gladness all day long. If you wish, you may engage in breaking the heart for half an hour before going to sleep, as well.

However, beware the tricks of the inclination, which wants specifically to sadden us while we engage in the work of the Creator. At such a time you tell the evil inclination, "Although you are right, wait, for I have a set time for it. I will think about it then, and not while standing before the king." This is why the priest had special garments for fertilizing the altar, and special garments for doing the work.

If you are mindful of these words of mine, you will be rewarded with bringing yourself close to *Dvekut* [adhesion] with Him, and you will succeed in doing the Creator's will.

Yehuda Leib, son of my teacher and Rabbi,
Simcha Ashlag

Letter No. 25

1927, London

To my soul mate, may his candle burn forever:

... What you wrote, that you do not understand the novelties in the Torah that I wrote to you, they should have been clear to you. When you straighten out the way you work you will understand them for certain. This is why I wrote them to you.

You explained regarding "sins becoming as merits to him," that when one repents before the Creator he evidently sees that the Creator forced him into all his iniquities, and yet he willingly gives his soul to correct them as though they were his own iniquities. By that the sins become as merits. But that still does not hit the center of the target because in the end you turn the coercions into merits, but not iniquities.

You also strayed further from the way by interpreting the sin of *Adam HaRishon*, condemning his soul to forced exile, and making the coercion a mistake. And what you explained, that it makes no difference whether the baby makes himself dirty or is made so by his father's deeds, for in the end he is dirty and must wash, I wonder, how did dirt come out of purity?

Your last words are sincere, that because you went into a place that is not your own, and due to your habit to cloak yourself with clothes that are not your own, you did not understand my words, which are aiming precisely and only for you. I wish these words were enough for you to stop wandering in others' fields, as it is written in *The Zohar*, "One must not look where he should not."

Regarding what you wrote—that I seem to speak in riddles—it is written, "The needs of Your people, Israel, are numerous." There is no time that is like another, much less those who go from door to door, to and fro, but the doors won't open. There is end to the changes in their situations. While I write words of Torah, or by heart, I say them so they will furnish for at least a few months, so they will be understood in the good times in time. But what can I do if the good times are few, or the broken is more than the corrected, and my words are forgotten?

Of course, the human intellectual mind will not examine my words at all, for they are said and are constructed from the letters of the heart.

And concerning your imagination that you entered and did not know how to come out because you grew tired of examining the matter, I will tell you that in general, one who repents from love is rewarded with complete *Dvekut* [adhesion], meaning the highest degree, and one who is ready for sins is in the netherworld. These are the farthest two points in this entire reality.

It would seem that we should be meticulous with the word "repentance," which should have been called "wholeness," except it is to show that everything is preordained, and each and every soul is already established in all its light, goodness, and eternity. But for the bread of shame, the soul went out in restrictions until it clothed in the murky body, and only through it does it return to its root prior to the *Tzimtzum* [restriction], with its reward in its hand from all the terrible move that it had made. The reward, in general, is the real *Dvekut*, meaning that she [the soul] got rid of the bread of shame because her vessel of reception has become a vessel of bestowal, and her form is equal to her Maker, and I have often spoken to you about that.

By that you will see that if the descent is for the purpose of ascending, it is regarded as ascension and not as a descent. Indeed, the descent itself is the ascent as the letters of the prayer themselves are filled with abundance, and with a short prayer, the abundance is small for lack of letters. Our sages have said, "If Israel had not sinned, only the Five Books of Moses and the book of Joshua would have been given to them."

What is this like? It is like a rich man who had a young son. One day, the rich man had to travel far away for many years. The rich man feared that his son would waste his wealth by poor judgment, so he exchanged his properties for gemstones, jewels, and gold, and built a cellar deep in the ground where he hid all the gold, the gemstones, and the jewels. But he also put his son in there.

He summoned his loyal servants and ordered them to keep his son from leaving the cellar until his twentieth birthday. Each day they were to bring down to him every food and drink, but absolutely no fire or candles. They were also to check the walls and seal every crevice so that no sunlight would penetrate. For his health, they were to take him out of the cellar each day for one hour and walk him through the city, but carefully watching that he does not run away. On his twentieth birthday, they were to give him candles, open a window for him, and let him out.

Naturally, the son's affliction was intolerable, especially when he would walk outside and see all the boys eating and drinking merrily on the street, without any guards or fixed hours, while he was imprisoned with few moments of light. And if he tried to run, he would be beaten mercilessly.

But he was most upset when he heard that his own father had caused him this affliction, for they were his father's servants, executing his father's orders. Naturally, he deemed his father the cruelest of all the cruel that ever lived, for who has heard of such a thing?

On his twentieth birthday, the servants lowered down to him a candle, as his father had commanded. The boy took the candle and began to look around. And lo and behold, what did he see? Sacks filled with gold and every royal delight.

Only then did he understand that his father is truly merciful, and that all his trouble was only for his own good. He immediately understood that the servants would certainly let him out of the cellar, and so he did. He came out of the cellar, and there was no guarding, no cruel servants. Instead, he is a noble man, wealthier than the wealthiest people in the land.

But in truth, there is nothing new here, for it becomes revealed that he was so very wealthy to begin with, but in his perception he was poor and destitute, oppressed in the pit all his days. Now, in a single moment, he has gained tremendous riches and rose from the deep pit to the top of the roof.

Who can understand this allegory? One who understands that the "sins" are the deep cellar with the careful watch to not let one out. I wonder if you understand it.

It is simple: The cellar and the careful watch are all "privileges" and the father's mercy over the son. Without it, it would have been impossible for him to be as wealthy as his father. But the "sins" are actual sins and not mistakes. They are also not forced by Divine decree. Rather, before he regained his wealth, that feeling dominated in the full sense of the word. But once he has regained his wealth, he saw that all these were the father's mercies and not at all his cruelty.

We need to understand that the entire connection of love between the father and his only son depends on the recognition of the father's compassion for the son regarding the cellar and the darkness and the careful watch, because the son sees in these mercies of the father a great exertion and profound wisdom.

The holy *Zohar* also spoke about it, saying that one who is rewarded with repentance, the holy Divinity appears to him like a softhearted mother who hasn't seen her son for many days, while they made great efforts and experienced ordeals in order to see each other, because of which they both were in great dangers. But in the end they came into that longed-for freedom and were rewarded with seeing one another. Then the mother fell on him, kissed him, and comforted him and spoke softly to him all day and all night. She told him about the longing and the dangers on the roads that she experienced until today, how she had always been with him, and that Divinity never moved, but suffered with him in all the places, but he could not see it.

These are the words of *The Zohar*: "She says to him, 'Here we slept; here we were attacked by robbers and were saved from them; here we hid in a deep pit,' and so forth. What fool would not understand the great love and pleasantness and delight that burst out of these comforting stories?"

In truth, before we met face to face it felt as suffering that is harder than death. But as the word *Nega* [affliction] is because the *Ayin* [the letter] comes at the end of the word, but during the telling of comfort-stories, the *Ayin* is in the beginning of the word, making it *Oneg* [delight/pleasure]. However, they are two points that illuminate only once they are in the same world. Now imagine a father and son who have been anxiously waiting for each other for days and years. When they finally see each other, the son is deaf and mute, and they cannot enjoy one another at all. It follows that the essence of the love is in royal delights.

Yehuda Leib

151

Letter No. 26

1927, London

To my soul mate, may his candle burn forever:

I received your last letter, from the fifth of *Kislev* [Hebrew month, roughly December], and regarding your surprise at the scarcity of my letters, I will tell you that I have many troubles, and I pray to the Creator to see me through.

I am surprised that you did not interpret the letters I sent to our friend regarding "The host cuts and the guest blesses," as he wrote me that he did not understand it. It seems as though you have grown tired of longing to merit the burden of Torah and *Mitzvot* due to the ravages of time.

And what can I tell you from afar, when you cannot hear my voice or my words, but only stare at dry and lifeless letters until a living spirit is blown into them? This requires effort, and in your opinion, effort requires time.

It is written, "A golden bell and a pomegranate, a golden bell and a pomegranate, all around on the edges of the robe. ... and its sound is heard when he enters the holy place."

The *Ephod* [vestment] comes from the words *Ei Po Delet* [where is the door], since the *Delet* [door] is in the place of the opening when it is closed. In corporeality, you can see the door just as you can see the opening. But in spirituality, you see only the opening. But you cannot see the opening unless with complete and pure faith. Then you see the door, and at that moment it turns into an opening because He is one and His name is "One."

That power, to heed the word of the sages in this reality in *Dalet*, is called "faith," as it is not established at once, but through education, adaptation, and through work. It is similar to the tutoring of a child, who would be like an unturned stone were it not for the tutor who rears him. This is why this work is generally called "a robe," as it is an overcoat, "beyond" human conception, and in which there is a combination, as in the edges of the *Kli*, which is the place where the yeast and the filth are collected.

During the training period, he is in a state of "to and fro," as are all those who seek the opening. And in the last moment of the march, when he is close to the opening, then, of all times, he grows weary and turns back. That march is called *Zahav* [gold], from the words *Ze Hav* [give me this], as it is written in the holy *Zohar*, that the walking is done through the craving and the longing for *Dvekut* [adhesion] with Him, and he longs and sings, *Ze Hav, Ze Hav*.

He is also called "a bell" because he does not have the strength to open and he turns back, thus spending his time going to and fro time and time again, looking for the opening. Also, he is called *Rimon* [pomegranate] because the *Romemut* [sublimity/exaltedness] of the above-the-intellect surrounds him from all sides. Hence, *again* he is called *Rimon*, for otherwise he would fall entirely.

In time, great filth and great anxiety assemble "all around on the edges of the robe," both in the form of the bell and in the form of a *Rimon* (which gathers) around the *Ei Po Delet* [where is the door], which has no edge...

But why did the Creator do so to His creations? It is because He must make the voice for the words, for the "mouth of God" [spelt the same as *Po Delet*] to appear when he comes to the holy place, as it is written, "when he enters the holy place."

Go out and learn from the letters of this world, that there is a sound only in anxiety, as is sensed in the strings of a violin. Due to the tension of the strings, there is anxiety [tension] in the air, which is the sound, and nothing else. And likewise, each human ear contains a kind of twist in the ear that physicians call "a drum." When another's mouth strikes the air, the drum shivers differently from each strike, and this is the entire merit of the chosen creature, the speaking species. Because of it, "all things [are] under his feet."

This is the meaning of "rejoice with trembling." Our sages said, "Where there is joy, there shall be trembling there." It is abstruse phrasing, for they should have said succinctly, "Joy and trembling will be together."

However, this tells us that the joy has no place without trembling. It is as they said—that where there should be joy and gladness, there is trembling, which is the place of joy.

You can also try it with a clapper [metal striker inside a bell] that is tingling on the iron of a bowl, thus making a sound. If you place your hand on the bowl, the sound will stop at once because the sound coming out of the bowl is the trembling of the bowl, and by striking with the clapper and placing your hand, you strengthen the bowl and reduce the trembling, hence the sound stops.

Thus you see the sounds—that the sound and the trembling are the same. And yet, not all sounds are fit for pleasantness, which is in the quality of the prior form, meaning the trembling. For example, the sound of a thunder frightens and is unpleasant to the human ear because the trembling occupies a large amount of the striking force, and also lasts too long. Even if the striking force were less, it would still be unpleasant to the ear because it is too long.

Conversely, the sound of a violin is pleasant to the listener's ear because it is proportional to the force that strikes, and is precisely proportional to the length of time. One who prolongs the time even a fraction of a minute will spoil the pleasantness.

It is all the more so with understanding the sounds for the word of God. It is precious, and clearly requires great precision in the force of the strike, divided into seven degrees. It is even more so with the time, not to spoil even a fraction of a minute, for there is pride there, as it is written, "You put my feet in stocks." Then you will know that all the angels rise in song, and in a place of joy there was trembling first.

Hence, not all anxieties are good, but one who is anxious for the word of God collects all the anxieties to a place and rushes the joy. This is the meaning of "Let the waters gather ... unto one place," and not otherwise, God forbid.

Our sages said, "A violin was hanging above David's bed. When the midnight hour came, a northern wind arrived and blew it, and it would play by itself." One who is anxious for the word of God, the anxiety comes instead of the northern wind, meaning as the *Rimon*. By that, "the host cuts."

The night divides, as in, "A prayer makes half." This is why he is lying in bed, which is the meaning of "He will never allow the righteous to fall." It is as it is written about, "And he lay down in that place." They explained, "There are *Chaf-Bet* [twenty-two] letters, which is a *Chaf* [also a spoon] that holds *Bet* [two] letters—the farthest points in the reality before us, as I have detailed in my letter.

Above his bed is the *Rimon*, as said above. And when the point below appears, the Creator goes out to stroll with the righteous in the Garden of Eden because the door is open and the holy Divinity says all her songs and praises. This is why David's violin is playing by itself, without any composition except for the trembling of the northern wind.

And if matters are still not clear, go and study the alphabet—that the *Bet*, with which the world was created, lacked nothing but the *Aleph* of *Anochi* [I]. This is its crack in the northern wind of the *Bet*. This is why "Out of the north the evil will break forth," which is a big breach.

Therefore, "Out of the north comes golden splendor." It begins with bells, and when the two letters unite appears the mouth of the Creator. This is why the anxieties must be collected in one place, to be anxious only for the word of God, and then one prepares "a golden bell and a pomegranate, all around on the edges of the robe."

Similarly, the upright will slowly be more than the broken, and will smell in the fear of God, and feel that "All that the landlord has troubled Himself with, He has troubled Himself only for me." He will know and see seven parts of the wind trembling, meaning that in addition to the wind of the fear of God, there are six more winds hovering over the Creator's Messiah, as it is written, "And the spirit shall rest ... the spirit of wisdom and understanding ..."

Our sages said about the such: "The host cuts." That is, although the host cuts, the guest blesses on the slice as though on a whole one. It is said about one who does not do so, "Robbers shall enter it and profane it," as it is written, "Will he even take the queen with me in the house," to come there with crassness, with more broken than is standing, arousing contempt and wrath.

This is the meaning of the chopped *Vav* [*Vav-Yod-Vav*] of Pinehas' *Shalom* [peace, farewell], as it stands with much that is broken before him, and the plague stopped. In his great sanctity that stands over the broken, the people reunited with Moses. His reward was that the Creator said to Moses, "And ... the covenant of everlasting priesthood," for eternity, as it is written in *The Zohar*.

This clarifies to Abraham the "this memorial" of his, which is there, so that one will not regard the details of the matters in which he is caught up, as this is the counsel of the inclination and the *Sitra Achra*, but only in general, as I have sufficiently explained here. This is the meaning of "All of man's works should be only with the aim to raise Divinity from the dust, from which the primordial serpent feeds."

And what can I do to those who vow and lean toward the view of the masses, and suffice for the halved comfort they receive through them, as people say, "Trouble shared, trouble halved"? This is why they work and settle, to receive reward. But if their ways have risen once and for all above ten feet, they would see the door because it is a wide open opening. Then there would no longer be two opposites in the same place and at the same time, as it is above the *Yod* [ten].

... It is written, "Though He scoffs at the scoffers, and He gives grace to the poor" (Proverbs 3:34). I shall start with an allegory, and perhaps you will understand:

A great, benevolent king wished only to delight his countryfolk, because he did not need any work to be done for him. Rather, his only wish was to benefit his countryfolk.

However, he knew that there are levels in the recipients of his benefit—to the extent of their love for him and the measure of recognition of the value of his exaltedness. He wished to delight abundantly, especially the worthy ones among his countryfolk, so the rest of the people would see that the king does not deny reward from those who love him dearly. Rather, in his goodness, he showers them with abundant delights that he has prepared for them. And in addition to the pleasures that he showers abundantly upon them, they have a special treat—they feel that they are the chosen ones from among the people. This, too, he desired to give to those who love him.

To keep from the people's complaint, lest they will lie or mislead themselves, as well, saying that they, too, are among the king's lovers, and still their reward is denied. And because of the king's perfection, he kept himself from that, as well, and therefore devised tactics to execute his plans in full.

Finally, he found a wonderful idea: He sent out a decree to all the people in the country, none excluded, to come to work a whole year for the king. He dedicated a place in his palace for that purpose and conditioned explicitly that it is forbidden to work outside the designated area, for it is abomination, and the king will not be pleased with it.

Their reward is in the place where they work. He prepared for them great feasts and every delicacy in the world whenever they wished. At the end of the year's work, he will take all of them to the king's own table, and they will be among those who see his face, the most eminent in the kingdom.

The proclamation went out, and every single one came to the king's palace, which is surrounded by guards and a wall. They closed themselves in there for the year, and the work began.

They thought the king had prepared watchmen to oversee their work, to know who was serving him and who was not. But the king hid, and there was no supervision. Everyone did as he saw fit, or so it seemed to them. However, they did not know about the wonderful tactic—that he placed a kind of bad powder in the delicacies and the sweets, and opposite that, he placed a healing powder in the house of work.

That clarified the supervision by itself: His lovers and those truly faithful to him—although they saw that there was no supervision in this place—kept the king's commandments carefully because of their love for him. They did their work as they were told and were careful to work precisely in the designated area. Thus, they inhaled the healing powder into their bodies, and when mealtime came, they tasted the sweets and delicacies, and found in them a thousand flavors such as they have never tasted, nor ever sensed such sweetness.

Hence, they praised the king extensively, for they were dining at the king's exalted table!

But the lowly did not understand at all the merit of the king—for which he should be loved with devoted and faithful love—or keep the king's commandment properly because they saw that there was no supervision. They slighted the area that was designated for work, and each worked where he saw fit in the king's domain. When mealtime came, once they had tasted the sweets, they felt a bitter taste because of the abovementioned dust. They cursed and despised the king and his despicable table, which he has prepared for them as reward for their work. They regarded the king as the greatest liar, who—instead of delicacies and finest delights—gave them these bitter and sour things.

Because of it, they began to devise for themselves foods from what was found in the city, to ease their hunger. Then their suffering was twofold, for their work had doubled, and they did not know the delight in the king's palace that was before them.

The lesson is that the Torah is divided into two parts: a part for worshipping the Creator, such as *Tefillin*, *Shofar*, and studying Torah, and a part for working with people, such as robbery, theft, fraud, and slander.

Indeed, the part between man and man is the real work, and the part between man and the Creator is the reward and the delights spread out across the king's table.

However, "All that the Lord has worked was for His sake," so the part of working with people should be in the king's place, too, meaning "to raise Divinity from the dust." In that there is a healing dust to the potion of death that is cast between man and the Creator.

This is the meaning of "He gives grace to the poor," in the Torah and *Mitzvot* between man and man, and between man and the Creator, "...to those who love Me and keep My commandments"—to make them do all the work in the designated area. They are the ones with the grace of holiness, and "they will inherit twofold in their land," for not only are they not working so hard for people, they are delighted all their lives by the grace of the Creator.

However, "He scoffs at the scoffers." They say that the king's palace is despicable, God forbid, because they experience holiness as a kind of mockery. Therefore, the wicked do not gain by their wickedness, so who would lose anything if he departs from them even when he hopes to be favored?

Yehuda Leib

Letter No. 27

1926, London

To the honorable student ... may his candle burn:

... I do indeed want to unite with you in body and soul, in this and in the next. However, I can only work in the spirit and the soul because I know your souls and can unite with them, but you can only work in the body, since you do not know my spirituality, so as to unite with it. If you understand it, you will also understand that I do not feel any distance from me to you, but certainly need the physical closeness. And yet, this is for you and for your own work, not for me or for my work, and with this I answer in advance many questions with regard to me.

But I do pray to the Creator to lead you on the path of truth, that you will be saved from all the obstacles along the way, and that the Creator will succeed for you all that you do.

As for you, you should meticulously follow the ways that I have set out for you regarding mind and heart, longing and prayers, and then the Creator will certainly make us succeed and we will soon unite in body and soul, in this and in the next.

To reply to your letter from the 26 of *Kislev*, the second day of *Hanukah* [December 2, 1926], you wrote that the world was created for work, and that He has created the darkness for the purpose of work—to have substance on which to work in it—since in the light, there is pleasure and not work. Accordingly, you asked, "What is the *Klipa* [shell/peel] of the right [side] for, for it feels the darkness as light, and the creature feels the darkness as separated from him, as though it is not his, so how can it continue throughout his seventy years? Such a person, why was he born?" You demand a complete answer for it, and it is not the great lights that you need, but only to remove the disgrace of hypocrisy from yourself, which reaches as deep as the soul. And you conclude that you can say about it ... "truth will show its way," and "it is already the fifth year" and so forth.

In truth, your words are confused, and therefore I do not know that truth. You said news: The world was created for work. If so, then should work remain forever? But it is known that eternity is rest! Also, your question about the creature replacing darkness with light without knowing the darkness in it, we need to know how to discern right from left, and you still have not been rewarded with seeing the darkness, since darkness and light are as the wick and the light. Therefore, we must see the candle and enjoy its light, and then you will know right from left.

However, why are you asking about the Creator, who gave great powers to the *Klipot* [pl. of *Klipa*]? I have already given you elaborate explanations about it, and primarily that the Creator protects Himself that one who clings to Him will not doubt Him, and this will never happen because He is Almighty, and I have no wish to elaborate here.

But I consider your words as "a prayer for the poor," which is a prayer in complaint. It is closer to being answered than all other prayers. See in *The Zohar* about the verse, "A prayer for the poor," etc., "And David was poor, but a poor one's prayer is in complaint," etc.

Also, your concern about a good sign, it seems that you need wholeness, as in merely a sign. This is a good sign because five years ago you were not complaining about that. I have already told you that from "And they journeyed from Rephidim" to the reception of Torah is only one journey. But know that my words must not calm your worry and comfort you, because at the end of the first year you were higher than you are now. And yet, do not give up on mercy.

You bring evidence from the writing to the purpose of creation, that it is for work: "What does the Lord your God ask of you but to fear the Lord your God ... and to serve the Lord your God." Indeed, there are two purposes: One should be before man's eyes, and one is for the Creator Himself. But the writing speaks of what should be before the eyes of the creature.

The matter is as is written in *Pirkey Avot* [*Chapters of the Fathers*]: "It is not for you to finish the work, nor are you free to idle away from it." That is, since wholeness is the purpose of the work and its conclusion, there is an open side to the *Sitra Achra* to come near and make one understand that he is incapable of it, and bring one to despair, since we should know that the end of the work is not at all our work, but the Creator's work. Therefore, how can you know the Creator and gauge if He can or, God forbid, cannot finish His work? This is insolence and heresy!

"And you are not free to idle away from it," even in that manner, if the Creator wishes you to work without finishing the job. This is the meaning of what is written, "What does the Lord your God ask of you?" That is, the creature must know only this: The Creator ... work, and will therefore do His will wholeheartedly, as in, "Open for Me one opening of repentance, as thick as a tip of a needle." By that he will be saved from the *Sitra Achra* ever approaching him. If a person is completed in that, he can be certain that the Creator will finish His work on His end, "And I open for you gates through which carts and carriages enter."

But if he is not ready to serve Him, even in a manner that he is not rewarded with the completion of the work and the opening of the hall, no fawning or lies will help him. I have already explained what is written in *The Zohar*, "On the evidence of two witnesses ... he who is to die shall be put to death," that it is *SAM* and he is dead to begin with, and it is not hard to kill the dead, though the dead has the *Klipa* of the right, since the harder *Klipa* is cancelled by proliferation of thanksgiving before the Creator, and proliferation of work.

I do not know if my words satisfy you, so do let me know and I will reply accordingly, because the question, "What is the proof?" is a wise man's question, if he is one who works.

Yehuda

Letter No. 28

1927, London

To my student ... may his candle burn:

... The above mentioned letter, which was not sent at the time of its writing, I will now reply to you about it. I will also reply to your latest letter from the beginning of the month, *Adar Bet*.

... Regarding your question about NHYM, that I did not explain the right, left, and middle about them, it is also because it belongs to the quality of the *Ohr Hozer* [reflected light], and I have already written to you that the qualities of the *Ohr Hozer* need all the clarifications in my book.

How many times have I commented to you that the spiritual qualities can never be better than the corporeal qualities, yet you insist that you do not feel the taste of servitude in cleanness.

In my view, any place where there is a desire for servitude is already lost there ... from the work, since delaying the contentment and the drawn-out abundance is called servitude, as our sages said, "A servant let loose feels comfortable." Therefore, while being tied under the burden of his master's enslavement, he is called "a servant" and "serving."

See in the "Preface to the Wisdom of Kabbalah," that work and labor extend from the *Masach* that delays the upper light, which it covets very much, while the reward extends from the *Ohr Hozer*. Thus *Malchut* returns to being *Keter* and comes out from servitude to complete redemption with simple *Rachamim* [mercies], which is *Keter*.

This is why our sages said, "A servant who is not worth his belly's bread [the bread that he eats]," since the *Ohr Hozer* is defined as NHYM NHY *de* ZA, and the *Malchut* that mate in *Hakaa*, as it is known.

If the servant were worth his belly's bread up to *Galgalta* [his head], he would be redeemed. But he is worth only up to his belly itself, meaning that his intention to delay does not have the hardness of the *Masach* in *Behina Dalet*, but in order to receive. It follows that his delaying *Masach* will be a vessel of reception, too, and not a *Kli* that delays, for which the *Keter* will, God forbid, become *Malchut*. Thus, only the belly is added from the *Keter*, and the bread that he eats [his belly's bread], hence he remains a slave.

All these discernments between the *Masach de Keter* and the *Masach* of the belly come to him by utter and complete loathing the vessels of reception into his own stomach, even the pleasure that extends to his belly by itself. It seems to him like the pleasure of one who itches and rubs boils (disease), which is a detestable pleasure to any person because the harm is obvious.

Through the detestable force in Nature, a second nature is imprinted in him, to truly loathe the pleasures of his guts. By that, his *Masach* is assisted by the delaying force as *Behina Dalet* that returns to being *Keter*.

But what shall we do to those who aren't so meticulous about cleanness and detestable things, even in their first, corporeal nature? We should feel very sorry for them because from their perspective, they are already cleansed, having come to loathe what should be loathed. However, they cannot discern very well due to the nature of their corporeality that they are not fleeing as carefully as they should, even with corporeal detestable things.

This answers your question about hypocrisy, for which you came up with the mistake that the world was created for work, and what is to me a reward, you inadvertently mistake for work. You should correct yourself before I come to Jerusalem, and even more so before Passover.

Yehuda Leib

Letter No. 29

1927, London

To my soul mate, may his candle burn:

I received your letter from the 22nd of *Adar Aleph* [Hebrew month around March]. Although you are displeased with the fact that your novelties are not receiving their due time to ponder and consider them, I regret it, too, and in my opinion, more than you. And yet, hope for the Lord and brace your heart.

And regarding what you wrote, you did well not going, although now is no time for humbleness because the majority of the book has already been printed, and all that is about to be revealed is deemed revealed. Therefore, you can publish the book as you wish.

As for me, I wish to know about those who forbid any novelties in Torah, and take out the new before the old. They treat my book in one of two ways: Either they say that there are no novelties or additions here at all, since everything has already been written in the writings of the ARI, and so it really is. The other option is to say that all my words are my own notions, for why did our sages not mention a word of all that is said in my words? Thus, who knows if you can trust such a person who wishes to create a new method in Kabbalah, which our fathers did not conceive, and then hang on this peg of theirs their entire unclean past?

In truth, I did not add a thing to what is written in the writings of the ARI, with the intention to remove the obstacle from the blind and the lame, perhaps they will see the goodness of the Creator in the land of the living. Therefore, it would be good if you rushed to become proficient in my entire book before it is exposed to the eyes of the external ones, so you may show them every single thing written and interpreted in the words of the ARI.

The core and the gist of all the explanations in my composition is the revealing of the *Ohr Hozer* [reflected light]. The ARI was succinct about it, as was sufficiently revealed to all the Kabbalists since the First [earlier Kabbalists], prior to his arrival in Safed. This is why he did not detail or elaborate on this matter.

However, in Branch Four, he introduces explicitly, and it is presented in *Tree of Life*, p 104b, Gate 47, "The Order of ABYA," Chapter 1. In that place, everything that I have innovated regarding the five *Behinot* of *Ohr Yashar* [direct light] is presented there, as well as the matter of the *Ohr Hozer*.

Indeed, know that the five *Behinot* of *Ohr Yashar* presented here are the heart of the innovations of the ARI's Kabbalah over that of the First. It was his only dispute with his contemporaries, supported by the verse in *The Book of Creation*, "Ten and not nine, ten and not eleven."

And yet, I should tell you that this is what caused great confusion in understanding his words, as in most places, he brings the ten *Sefirot* instead of the five *Behinot*. I also suspect that Rav Chaim Vital did so on purpose, to remove from him obstinacy and slander. In my explanation, I have already noted this quality, thoroughly proving that both are words of the living God, as explained in "General Preface."

See the essay, "The Knowledge," in "Gate to Introductions," where Rav Chaim Vital himself takes great care to show as equal the ten *Sefirot* and the five *Behinot*. However, they are not enough for the diligent students, which is why he only signed his own name on those words.

Regarding the *Zivug de Hakaa*, on which I elaborate and on which the ARI writes very briefly, it is because of the excessive disclosure of the matter among the students of the RAMAK [Rav Moshe Kordovero, the prime Kabbalist in Safed before the arrival of the ARI]. The ARI said about it that all the words of RAMAK were said only about the world of *Tohu*, not about the World of *Tikkun* [correction], since *Zivug de Hakaa* applies only to the worlds preceding *Atzilut*, as well as the externality of ABYA. But in the insides of ABYA there is no *Hakaa* but a *Zivug de Piusa* [coupling of conciliation], called "embrace of kissing," and *Yesodot* [foundations], as I will explain in the beginning of the World of *Tikkun*. But in the *Yesodot* themselves, this matter is applied everywhere, but in the form of reconciliation.

See in the "Gate to the Essays of Rashbi," beginning of the portion *Shemot* [Exodus], in the explanation about *The Zohar*: "And the wise will shine as the brightness of the firmament, ... illuminating and sparkling in the upper *Zivug*," concerning the two righteous—the righteous who entered it, called Joseph, and the righteous who came out of it, called Benjamin. The first is called "illuminating," which is the expansion of the nine *Sefirot* of *Ohr Yashar* [direct light] to it. The second is called "sparkling," which is "The one who lives forever." Look there and you will see that in my words, I added nothing, only arranged the issues for beginners, and this concerns only Rav Nathan Neta Shapiro and Rav Shmuel Vital, and there is no meticulousness in the matter.

Sometimes I stop an essay midway because it belongs to the World of *Tikkun*, and I do not want to confuse the student, only lead him in a safe and faithful way. Once I interpret succinctly the *Partzufim*, the worlds, and the *Mochin* in general, I will return to the beginning, and then I will be able to explain the complete essays in a wonderful order, as Rav Chaim Vital intended.

... One who afflicts himself with the public is rewarded with seeing its comfort, as both are the words of the living God. To the extent of the affliction, so is the measure of the tranquility, as they are truly one. The only difference is in the *Dvekut* [adhesion] with Him, as during the *Dvekut*, the judgments turn into simple mercies. The sign of it is that even one who has been sentenced to death but is seen by the king is pardoned and rewarded with life. Therefore, not during the *Dvekut*, the difference between those to two *MaT* [fallen] are 98 [*Tzach*-pure] in *Gematria*, for then "a righteous man falls before the wicked," and "a righteous man falls seven times, and rises again."

It is very hard for me to be in London during Passover, especially since I am still in the middle of my work. Although I'm very hopeful, it is my custom to enjoy only the present, which is the way to draw in the good future. Hence, I have much room for longing.

I am contemplating returning to Jerusalem after Passover, and I want to see you ready and willing in the king's palace, for on the joy of the holiday of *Matzot* [unleavened bread (meaning Passover)], you will come out from all those who seek the opening to and fro.

... As it is said, to draw a *Vav* in the *Matza*, and then the *Matza* turns into a *Mitzva* [good deed/correction], and the slice into wholeness, and how long will you engage in rules of carving? Our sages have already said, "Be not as servants serving the teacher in order to receive reward," for it will not satiate them prior to the actual reception. There is a maxim people use: "One who breaks all his bones, one of them did not break," but is rather strengthened by the crushing in the hand of the giver.

Then each of the two halves becomes wholeness, which is the meaning of "And the righteous inherit twofold in their land," for there is none who is broken here, and both are full and whole. It turns out that one of them did not break, and he has twofold bread because *Malchut* returns to being *Keter*. This is what Elisha asked of Elijah the prophet: "May it be twofold in your spirit upon me," meaning the spirit of the giver.

... Our sages said, "A man must be intoxicated [drunk] on Purim until he does not know," etc. That is, a man is rewarded with expansion of knowledge by a handsome wife, a handsome house, and handsome tools, as it is said in *The Zohar* about the verse, "And the children of Israel kept the Sabbath..."

But there is one who is rewarded with broadening of the mind through intoxication and rye, as it is written, "Give rye to the lost, and wine to the bitter-hearted." Indeed, it is about falsehood, for what can broadening of the heart give you and add to you in case of intoxication, when one is lying merrily, as though the whole world is his? This is why it is written, "The wine-joker," as he jokes about people with the gladness of falsehood and groundlessness.

This was Noah's sin, and the ministering angels mocked him for being drunk.

But there is a lowly and despicable *Klipa* [shell] called "the *Klipa* of Amalek," which cuts the words and tosses them up. That is, it is so material that it cannot be reconciled even with thirteen covenants and thirteen rivers of pure persimmon, since it tosses them up, too, and says, "Take what You have given them."

This is the meaning of what is written regarding Elisha, that he was plowing with twelve pairs of oxen, and he with the twelfth. The lowly works are called "plowing," and he was already at the lowest degree, meaning at its end, which is the twelfth.

In the degrees of the year, the month of *Adar* is called "the twelfth month." Then Prophet Elijah threw his mantle and made

175

it an offering to the Creator, since by gripping to the mantle of the giver he was rewarded forever, until the end.

Adar comes from the word *Adir* [huge/great], and extraordinary strengthening is called *Adar*. That strengthening comes to *Adar* only through much Torah. And although there are no wisdom or understanding in this place, nor counsel, Amalek still weakens and is ruined and becomes absent, and an heir comes in his place.

The thing is that idol-worship is cancelled only in those who practice it, who have connection with it. It is impossible to strike the wind with an axe. Rather, the wind that strikes repels the wind, and iron to iron, etc. And since the essence of Amalek is a joker, destroying everything in materiality, without knowledge but only with mockery, it is impossible to uproot him from the world with the spirit of knowledge. On the contrary, it is with something that is above reason, meaning through the wine of Torah.

From the whole of the light of Torah, that huge force remains. Through it, you will understand that although the wine is not rife with rye, it is a good remedy for destroying and annihilating the seed of Amalek (as it is written, "to disturb them and destroy them," "an eye for an eye," "it was turned to the contrary"), in the feast of Queen Ester, who is standing in the bosom of, etc., and dipping and sitting in the bosom of, etc., meaning that our sages said that it is permitted to change on Purim, in welcoming of guests, and with costumes.

It is as they said, "A man must be intoxicated on Purim," meaning that they said, "It did not say, 'learned,' but rather 'poured water,' to teach you that servicing the Torah is greater than studying it." By servicing, he was rewarded twofold, and not at all due to the study, as they are two opposites in the same subject. This is why they are called "twofold," and the prohibition is the permission, for a key that is fit for closing is fit for opening.

This is the reason for sending [Purim] gifts to one another, since there is no distinction between one with *GAR* and one with *VAK*, because of the two gifts that they send to one another. It is as said in *The Zohar*, Song of Songs: "Your love is better than wine," meaning that the friendship extends from the wine of Torah, as he is attached in utter completeness to the Creator, even in a place devoid of *Hochma*. This is not from the wisdom of Torah itself, but from the wine of Torah, which springs out of the profusion of Torah.

This is the meaning of "And their memorial will not perish from their seed," meaning the maleness, as it gazes on the wicked and they are gone, and the matter that there are no *Achoraim* here at all becomes revealed, and these days of Purim are remembered and done. "And Mordechai went out from before the king in royal apparel." Everything depends on the male, even the displaying of Ester.

I have been brief because I have spoken about these matters at length several times. I hope that the Creator will expand your boundaries in all the additions related to the above matters, for the matter is very near to you, and how long will you keep testing the Creator, and if you believe in Him, you will certainly not turn back often.

And why did the Creator have faith in Rashbi that he would not turn back? When he said, "I am for my beloved," etc., "All the days when I was connected to this world, I was connected to it in one connection, in the Creator. Therefore, now 'His passion is for me.'"

However, man sees the eyes, and the Creator sees the heart, for your mouths and hearts are not the same to do them, and the spice for it is the Torah.

Indeed, I have learned much Torah from you. You instilled drops of idle words, but in response to them came forth drops of Torah.

I haven't the strength to fight with your materialism. Instead, the fine light of my teaching has illuminated on you even in previous generations, but you yourselves did not work at all opposite your materialism, and you are not inspired by the greatness of the Creator and the greatness of His servants, and His holy Torah. I have been standing and warning you about that for a while, and this is the wall that separates you from me for a long time now; woe unto this beauty that has withered in this dust.

Know that this work is highly capable, before I came to you, as it is external work, and one who cleans his clothes in front of the king will not gain honors. Therefore, fix yourselves in time so you may enter the hall, for I see no other fault but that, and "He who said to His world, 'Enough!'" Time is short, and the work is plentiful in the place of Torah, so hurry and journey from Rephidim to the light, by the light of the living, and together we will be blessed with the blessing of redemption that has redeemed us and redeemed our fathers, Amen, may it be so.

Yehuda Leib

Letter No. 30

1927, London

To my soul mate, may his candle burn:

I received all of your letters, and regarding your wish to receive an advance for the book, for it is finally to be revealed, happy are you, for the merit of humbleness is to conceal how capable one is. It is as our sages said, "Everyone knows why a bride enters the *Huppah*," etc., for all the great and important matters come in humbleness. It is as written in the holy *Zohar* abut Rabbi Aba, who knew how to reveal in intimation, and all according to the ability. And yet, beyond the ability, there is no merit in humbleness, but the initial humbleness is present and instills upon him the blessing forever.

Yehuda Leib

Letter No. 31

1927, London

President of the children of Manasseh, Gamaliel, son of Pedahzur

To the students, may the Lord be upon them:

... I shall reply to both of you together, as it all stems from the same desire. The holiday is approaching, and as you know, I tend to keep to myself at such times and not waste time.

Although I do not have many expenses on basic needs for the holiday because I've already obtained the *Matzot* and the wine, I am preoccupied with receiving the newborn child from all that has happened to me during the months of conception since *Tishrey* [approx. September]. The child is very dear to me, a child of entertainment, and so my heart goes out to him and to all his needs.

You must have noted to write in the previous letters that you will prepare yourselves to long for the Creator and for His goodness in these days, prior to my coming to you, for the time is suitable for it, if you wish, since time and place do not part between us whatsoever concerning the needs of the Creator and the lot of the Creator. And the box of corporeality? Put it behind you, and we are one.

Our sages have already wondered, "Ester from the Torah, where from?" They said, "I will surely hide." The thing is that from *Lo Lishma* [not for the Torah] one comes to *Lishma* [for the Torah], that the light in it would reform them. Therefore, they were right to ask, "How can there be concealment to any person?" Even if you say that he is wicked, that he engages in Torah and *Mitzvot Lo Lishma*, still, the light in it has to reform him.

They answered that there are two concealments, as in, "I will surely hide" [Heb: *Haster Astir*]. One concealment is due to the diminution of the moon, as it is written, "lights," with deficient writing, since the *Vav* is missing from the *Ohr* [light] in it, *Ohr* without the [letter] *Vav*. The second concealment is due to the sin of *Adam HaRishon*, considered that he threw filth at her, and he was diminished in the first one, too, creating *Mar* [bitter] instead of *Maor* [illumination]. In the work of creation, He brought the medicine before the blow, as it is said in the verse about light, "Let there be light," and "And there was light," to be sufficient for both concealments.

The second light was blemished by the inciting serpent, and *Vav-Reish* remained of it. The *Vav* was already missing in the first light, living a storm over the head of the serpent and his company, "*Arur* [cursed] are you than all the beast," etc. From the first, *Aleph-Reish* remained, and from the second, *Vav-Reish* remained.

This is why its legs were cut off and he walks on his belly, and I have no time to elaborate further. This is the meaning of using the seven days of creation, which were concealed for the righteous at the end of correction.

However, all the corrections are in the receivers of the light. Since they are unfit to receive the upper light, they are rebellious against the light because the light is bestowal, and when it is received, it is called "illumination," which is the internality that reforms him, that which clothes in the vessels of reception. The upper light dresses in the letters of all the prayers, and "He is one and His name, 'One,'" which is the meaning of our fathers being immersed in mire and bricks, from the idols of Egypt on the forty-nine gates of impurity. Then the King of all Kings, the Creator, appeared to them and redeemed them.

The reason is that they had to discover all the letters of the prayer, so the Creator waited for them. However, when the prayers ended, He rushed to them and redeemed them, "And His divorce and His hand come as one."

When Righteous Mordechai brought Hadassah, he was rewarded with her because she was the daughter of his uncle, Avichail. And although "The vision of the glory of the Lord's fire is as consuming fire at the mountain top," she had a good pasture and oil with him, as it is written, "On his right was a fiery law unto them." He understood by the light of his righteousness and extended on her a thread of grace. By that extension, he extended the quality of "line" into holiness for fourteen days (for the quality of "line" is *Hesed* [mercy]), due to the two abovementioned diminutions, as in, "And her father indeed spat in her face." Finally, he was rewarded with, "And Esther found favor in the eyes of all who saw her," even the actual nations of the world.

First, she corrected in *Achoraim*, meaning she stands from the bosom of Ahasuerus, dips, and sits in the bosom of Righteous Mordechai, which is purity, as in, "interpreted as pure myrrh" (This is why they explained that Mordechai is the translation of the Torah [into Aramaic]), meaning the "bitter" from the serpent. He cast filth in her (which is the meaning of "To most of his brothers," and not "To all his brothers"), and the *Aleph* from "He and I cannot dwell in the world" fled from the illumination in her, for a man cannot dwell in the same place with a serpent. He was rewarded and purified for her because he extended to her his champion, his acquaintant. And yet, the illumination is still written with a deficiency, meaning the *Vav*, due to the diminution of the moon.

However, in return for it he was later rewarded with "Royal apparel" and a great crown of gold, as it is written, "The two great lights." Then "Mordechai from the Torah," as it is written, "flowing myrrh," meaning freedom from the angel of death, in the actual holy language.

It is so because the whole purification is in the *Achoraim*—the translation—and complete freedom is in the holy language. The forty-nine pure faces and the forty-nine impure faces are from the diminution of the moon. This is why the first correction is the coming out of the vessels in purity, and the second correction is a new name, which the mouth of the Lord will determine, "Her name is *HaVaYaH* [the Lord]," and "In every place, offerings are presented unto My name."

I have elaborated thus far to give you a taste of the bitterness of *Mitzva*, should you wish, for the meaning of "And made their lives bitter," without the two *Alephs* of *Tohu*. Although the filth of the serpent was only in the first light, he attributed the corruption to the upper one—that the lack of the *Vav* due to the diminution of the moon proved that the *Aleph* was also missing there, God forbid. He dressed them as light [*Ohr*] and *Kli*, the oil for the illumination and the light, taking the *Aleph* of "illumination" from the "illumination" and from *Ohr* (for the *Vav* was already missing), and the *Aleph* of *Ohr*, assembling them in one another. Thus, he made *Maror* [bitter], meaning the angel of death, where the two *Reish* became *Tav*.

When rewarded with "flowing myrrh," then the Creator came and slaughtered the angel of death, who becomes a holy angel once again. There aren't forty-nine and forty-nine here, a scale of merit and a scale of fault, which are twenty-two letters. Rather, "He is one and His name, 'One,'" for "The enemy will not deceive him, and the son of wickedness will not afflict him," "The wicked are overthrown and are gone."

Therefore, first, the gods of Egypt must be imprisoned, on the tenth of the month, to be hung in the Torah, "that he cannot prefer ... but he shall acknowledge the firstborn, the son of the hated one, by giving him a double portion." This is the meaning of the preparation for the plague of the firstborn, the son of the hated one.

By chaining the gods of Egypt to the legs of the bed, they drew upon them great lights in the cut off place. *Yakir* [recognize] is like *Yakir* [cherish], and there is no "visiting," but there is "preferring," since there is no flaw, as it was said, "My darling son, Ephraim, a child of entertainment," for he "folded his hands," and put his right hand on the head of Ephraim.

This is the meaning of "a lamb for the fathers' house," from "the hands of the Mighty One of Jacob." And on the four days of the first-fruit, it was slaughtered on the fourteenth and the mouth that forbade (which is the meaning of twice, *Yaccir* [recognize] and *Yakir* [cherish]). It is the mouth that permitted, and in the light of "The Lord is to me, and the night will be as light."

Then, "a lamb for the house," and "In that very day, all the hosts of the Lord come forth," etc., "I and not a messenger," etc., "And you will dip in the blood that is on the doorstep," at the bottom of the legs of the bed. "And you will touch the post, and the two *Mezuzot*," meaning the *Tikkun* [correction] that fills the abovementioned two diminutions, which is two *Mezuzot*, from the words, "from this" and "this," as in, "the faith of the craftsman," and "the faith of a faithful one." The daughter that was trained is really his mother in the faithful one, as I have already interpreted for you. Then, "You will touch the post," etc., for it is literally bloods, and I have no time to elaborate, and the bright ones will understand.

How I long to hear from you the enunciation of redemption and the blessing of redemption, "Who redeemed us," etc., for "On *Nissan* [Hebrew month, spring] they were redeemed, and on *Nissan* they will be redeemed." That is, the past and the present join as one because he sees his back as he does his face.

This should not be surprising to you. After all, a box of pests [bad reputation] is hanging behind each one, and how can you equalize with the one ahead of you?

However, this is only in the present, for eternity is present, making the future equal to the present and the past, meaning to the ones rewarded with the light of truth, clothed in only one and unified desire. Anything more than one desire, it was said about it, "Any excess is deemed gone." It is in the unification of the true *Dvekut*, from the recognition of his heart that is full of the light of *HaVaYaH* to the brim.

Even when he directs his heart to heaven, one should be very careful with the unity of the desire, to be unified in true unity, internal recognition in the extent of the *Dvekut* on the height of the Lord's palace ... for His hand will not be short, as it is written, "Indeed, I live, and the glory of the Lord shall fill the whole earth."

This is the meaning of Israel's redemption, as in, "I am the Lord, I and not a messenger, nor an angel or a seraph."

One who has many desires, the Creator has many messengers and many degrees. The Kabbalists write that there are 125 degrees even in *Nefesh de Assiya*. But one who has only one heart and one desire does not have all the calculations, all the degrees that are made by seraphim [angels] and animals, and holy ofanim [another type of angels]. Rather, "And I was trusted by him," a child of entertainment, for a servant of the Creator has contentment with his servitude. This is a clear sign that the

Creator has contentment with his loyal servant, and conversely, it is, God forbid, to the contrary.

Thus, all we need is to aim the heart to entertain with Him, for the entertainment is for Him alone, and not to cause sadness whatsoever. Also, a wise son always looks at his father's face, whether he is happy with him, as he has one intention—to delight the father, and nothing else.

This is the meaning of "Now it shall be said to Jacob and to Israel, 'What has God worked?'" Our sages interpreted that angels and seraphim learn the knowledge of the Creator from Israel. This is the meaning of "'And it was very good,' this is SAM," as he blossoms in one, but when that power for holiness is taken from him, then "And in all your might" comes true in us. This is the meaning of being rewarded with revealing Elijah from the time of the revival of the dead. He flees in four, and then that force to work and to be encouraged is established in us in one, meaning very good, which we hope for soon in our days, Amen.

I have been brief in this letter due to lack of time. But God willing, it will suffice for you to prepare yourselves and be rewarded with all the abovementioned prior to my coming to you. Then, where there are vegetables on the table, there will be meat and fish, for after all the abovementioned meriting you will begin to be ready to receive His light through me, as is the Creator's will in advance.

Although it may be a wonder in your eyes, in your minds, you should still believe me that I do not mean to boast, God forbid, for the Creator's benefit is your benefit. If you are small in your own eyes, look at your Maker, the one who made you—a wonderful craftsman does not do low and lowly things. This folly is the flaw from the serpent, who casts filth in her, to consider himself low and lowly and not feel that the Creator is by his side, even, and only at the bottom of his lowliness. And what I see, I shall say, perhaps the Creator will be to your liking soon in our days.

Yehuda Leib

I did find one correction on the first page of the preface, second column, where instead of "except," which I wrote, it was written, "but" or "only." It must be from ... may his candle burn, who already argued with me about this word, and then I kept silent about his argument. But now I noticed and found it interpreted in Kings 12, "There was none that followed the house of David, except for the tribe of Judah," as well as in Kings 2, 24, "None remained, except for the poorest sort of the people of the land." And he interpreted the *Fortress of Zion* and replied to me.

And concerning remission of the many debts that some of you ask in letters, I ask, "Why should you not pay me my debt to write me a letter each week as I have asked you?" Indeed, all debts stem from the same *Mitzva*.

The same

Letter No. 32

1927, London

To the honorable students, may the Lord be upon them:

Yesterday I received the 200 copies of *Pticha* [Preface to the Wisdom of Kabbalah], and today your letter. You are all unanimous about my letters being short, while I myself wrote in detail, for it takes time because the nature of every great thing is that it takes much time to conceive.

What the rav wrote ... that he did not understand my letter because it is all initials, it seems that he still does not know that he does not know, because in truth, it is the end of the words and not their initials, for each day I wait for the Creator to finish for us, for we are not free to be rid of Him.

Concerning his comment about my writing, that it would be a wonder for them once they are rewarded with all that is written, and then they will need to receive His light through me, he wrote that he is not surprised about it whatsoever. It is because he did not understand my writings, as he himself admits. But how will he understand the wonder? However, I see that it is a wonder in my eyes, too, and may he be experienced and test my words.

And what he wrote concerning settling down in Israel, I agree. I, too, am in favor of enjoying ancestral merit because the covenant of the fathers has not ended and the case is important.

And what ... wrote as an interpretation to my letter, that *Dror* [freedom] in *Gematria* is *Kodesh* [sanctity], he should have said the opposite—that *Kodesh* is *Dror*. And concerning his writing that he wants to know when I will return to my home, I want to know if he is already ready to receive me and enjoy me, and God willing, I will let him know on my part in due time.

I also received the letter from rav ... and what he wrote except for *Yaccir* [will recognize] and *Yakir* [will cherish], that he cannot properly support, he should know that he is the center of all my letters, and if he does not understand that, he won't be able to truly understand the matters.

... It is said in RASHI, portion, *Chayei Sarah* [The Life of Sarah]: "Sarah was a hundred years old, as twenty for punishment (to sin)," (and in *Baba Batrah*, 58a), "Everything before Eve is as a monkey before a man." These are only intimations, but simply put, the *Chaf* is replaced with a *Kof* because they are from the same pronunciation, GICHAK, hence "Ephraim, my darling son," can be interpreted that the son cherishing the father or the son recognizing [knowing] the father, for they are truly one utterance: The one who cherishes recognizes, and the one who recognizes cherishes, without any difference.

There is a clear sign given in the name of the Baal Shem Tov by which to know how much the Creator is playing with a person—to see in one's own heart how much he is playing with the Creator. So are all the matters, as in, "The Lord is your shade." This is why one who still feels some difference between cherishing and knowing requires the unification of the heart, as from the perspective of the Creator they are both one.

This is a very deep matter, that the Creator is truly in the heart of everyone from Israel. But this is on His part, so what does man need? Only to know it—the knowing changes, and the knowing finishes. This is the meaning of "The Lord is your shade."

And what he asked—which one is first, the disclosure of Elijah or the resurrection of the dead, or do both come at once—it is not the same for all and there are several degrees in it. It requires much elaboration to explain and there is nothing more to add here.

Rav ... did well ... but it seems that you, too, did not read the pamphlet as attentively as you should have, for you cannot show them that all my words are present in *Tree of Life*, and I did not add a single word, other than writing explicitly that *Malchut* in every place is the will to receive, which is already accepted from the writings of the ARI in general, without any need to reference it accurately. It is presented explicitly in *The Zohar* and in the *Tikkunim*, and besides that there is no change of wording.

His comparing my book to *The King's Valley*, I saw it for the first time here, and last week I wrote from it. However, all the foundations of this book are renewed and arranged by the Kabbalah of the *Geonim* [genius], which begin with *Tzimtzum Aleph* [first restriction], followed by the world of *Malchut*, then *Avir Kadmon*, then *Tehiru*, and then *Atzilut*. However, he fills those matters with orders of the ARI ... which are truly not similar because the ARI spoke of nothing more than a line and *Tzimtzum*, and only then *AK* and *Akudim*, *Nekudim*, and *Atzilut*, as is presented in *Eight Gates* and in all the writings of the ARI.

The studies of the *Atzilut* that are attributed to the ARI are not at all from the ARI but from some abbreviation from the book, *The King's Valley*, itself. This is why Kabbalists who follow the ARI did not like this book.

I wrote you that first you should study the pamphlet until you can say to anyone and show their ignorance because you will be able to truly find everything in *Tree of Life* and in *Eight Gates*, especially if you look in Branch 3 and Branches 4 and 5 in *Panim Meirot*. Branch 3 explains the *Ohr Hozer* [reflected light], Branch 4—the four *Behinot* of *Ohr Yashar* [direct light], and Branches 5 and 6 explain the *Hizdakchut* [cleansing/purification] of the *Masach* by which the *Histaklut* [looking] of *Ohr Hozer* is done, and you can prove to anyone who must listen to what he is saying. If you do so, you will certainly prove that you are right.

The book, *My Desire Is in the Lord*, by Rav Chaim Vital was found among my books tied together to the Kabbalah book by Hacham Mas'ud, who gave it to me as a gift. I need it very much, so I ask that to have it sent to me as soon as possible.

Yehuda Leib

Letter No. 33

1927, London

To the honorable students ... may the Lord be upon them:

Two nights ago a wonderful thing happened to me: A man asked me to come over to his house to see his books, among which there were also Kabbalah books ...

I saw there a large book, about 180 pages, two printer sheets, titled, *The King's Valley*, by one of the wondrous ascended ones, Rav Naphtali Ashkenazi, printed in Amsterdam in 1648. The author established a complete order to the wisdom of truth, as in the book, *Tree of Life*, beginning with the *Tzimtzum* [restriction], and ending with the lower worlds *BYA*. It is based on the foundations of the ARI with his own explanations, and he is also assisted by the Kabbalah of the *Geonim* and the *Rishonim*, similar to Rav Yaakov Kafil.

When I opened the book I saw in it many issues and foundations that were not introduced in any of the books of the ARI or the *Rishonim*, except in the book, *Studies of Atzilut*, presented in his book, letter by letter.

This surprised me. I went over the book meticulously until I realized that the book, *Studies of Atzilut*, attributed to the ARI, is completely false and fabricated. Instead, a copier abbreviated this book, *The King's Valley*, and turned into a short composition, which is the book, *Studies of Atzilut*, that we have.

Moreover, that copier was completely ignorant and did not understand anything about Kabbalah, so he confused the pages of the book in a terrifying manner. Out of every ten pages, he took half or a third of a page and copied them verbatim, then put them together into a single issue.

In consequence, one issue in the book, *Studies of Atzilut*, consists of ten thirds of pages from ten separate issues in the book, *The King's Valley*. This is why it is so perplexing. I cannot put in writing my anger at this wicked fool, since it took me a long time to sort matters out for myself. But because of the sublime holiness of the issues presented there, I was fond of them, and so I spent a great deal of time—above and beyond—on this book.

I understand that the same thing happened to all the great ones, therefore I wish to make it known that 1) it is not from the writings of the ARI, 2) it is distorted and confused to the point that it is forbidden to look at it. It must be put away so as to remove obstacles from future generations. One who wishes to understand the holiness of the matters will look into the book, *The King's Valley*, where the matters are presented in their full sublime glory. I am contemplating interpreting the matter in the introduction that I will write.

That book is precious. It was probably printed only once, approximately 300 years ago, and this was my first time to see it. It must have been an act of Providence because I took with me the book, *Studies of Atzilut*, but when I wanted to read in it I could not find it. I looked for a place where I could borrow it but could not find it anywhere. In the end, I did find it, in my bag, to my surprise.

Regarding the personal questions, I pray that he will succeed wherever he turns, for I cannot settle private affairs these days, as my own troubles surround me. Hence, in His light we will see light.

Yehuda Leib

Letter No. 34

1927, London

To the honorable students, may the Creator be upon you:

I think that I do not need to write you words of Torah because you have plenty in writing and in print. But who knows if they are still news to you, for "He renews in His goodness the work of creation each day and always." Hence, one should be impressed and praise only with news.

Before Passover I wrote you novelties in the Torah, as it is said, "A good day of labor in the Torah" (the Torah of a festival). With this you will understand the words of our sages concerning fear of heaven, that "the whole world was created only to command this." We should make a precision: It should have said "that" ["this" is used as male form and "that" as female form], since the *Malchut*, which is *Halachah* [code of law] and fear of heaven, is called "that," and the Creator is called "this."

However, it is known to those who are meticulous that when we speak of male and female together, we pronounce it in male form, and the Creator is called "this." It is as written in the words of our sages, "In the future the Creator will make a dance for the righteous, and each will point with his finger and say, 'Behold, this is our God ... this is the Lord for whom we hoped.'"

But prior to the correction of making a dance for the righteous, and *Machol* [dance] comes from *Mechila* [pardon], it is said, "He shall not enter at any time into the holy place," due to the circle of twenty-eight times, fourteen for better and fourteen to the contrary. Rather, "By that shall Aaron come into the holy place," meaning by the fourteen for the better, which is called "that."

Our sages said, "The whole world was created only to command this," meaning the unification of the Creator and His Divinity, which are then called "this." That is, up to here we must rise in the fear of exaltedness, in turning his reception into bestowal, while the giver, who is above the circle, can certainly bestow upon every time, even to the fourteen that are to the contrary, for in bestowal there is absolutely no evil, as has been thoroughly explained.

This is the meaning of the words, "Keep that forever for the inclination of the heart of Your people." As long as we have not been awarded unity with the Creator as one thought, but rather as two thoughts, we therefore ask, "Keep that," give us strength and power to come to the holy place by keeping the word, "By that shall Aaron come into the holy place." "Remember and keep were said in one utterance," and by that it ascended to unite in the true unity, blessed and exalted be His name forever.

It is written, "Take no rest, and give Him no rest until He establishes, and He makes Jerusalem a praise in the earth." So we rush our pleas above, knock by knock, tirelessly, endlessly, and do not weaken at all when He does not answer us. We believe He hears our prayer but waits for us, for a time when we have the *Kelim* [vessels] to receive the faithful bounty, and then we will receive a reply for each and every prayer at once, since "the hand of the Lord will not be short," God forbid.

This is the meaning of the words, "Children in whom there was no blemish ... and who have the strength to stand in the king's palace." It teaches you that even those who have been rewarded with pardon for iniquities—which became as merits, by which the matter appears after the fact, and in whom there is no blemish—still need more strength to stand in the king's palace, meaning to stand and pray, and wait tirelessly, knock by knock, until they elicit the complete desire from the Creator.

This is why we should learn this trade before we enter the king's palace, meaning muster power and might to stand as a pillar of iron until we elicit the desire from the Creator, as it is written, "Take no rest." Although the Creator seems silent and irresponsive, let it not cross your mind to be silent, too, "Take no rest." This is not what the Creator aimed for with His silence, but rather to give you power to stand afterward in the king's palace when you have no blemish. This is why, "and give Him no rest." Naturally, all the works are taught while one is still outside the palace, for afterward there will be no time to dedicate to crafts.

Regards to all the students. Due to my worries, I cannot answer in greater detail, and I shall hope for the Lord and for His kindness.

Yehuda Leib

Letter No. 35

1927, London

To the honored disciples, may the Lord be upon them:

The surprise of ... at my zeal and devotion to *The King's Valley*, which I wish to publish, is because he did not understand me. It is not *The King's Valley* that I am zealous for, but its abbreviation, which is the study of *Atzilut*, which the copier maliciously attributed to the ARI.

In his abbreviation, he has done two harms: 1) He wasted the time of all who search their hearts for nothing and to cause fear, due to the far ones who are drawing nearer in his lines and cause bewilderment. 2) These are words of the wise rav, author of *The King's Valley*, in the writings of the ARI. By that he caused immense confusion. So I am zealous because of my time, which was lost.

Concerning the abovementioned book, the author is undoubtedly a very high and holy man. However, his words are built on the foundations of MAHARI Sruk, who, in my opinion, did not understand the words of his teacher, the ARI, as well.

However, the words of Rav Sruk spread to all the holy ones that were in the land because the Rav Sruk nevertheless arranged the words he had heard from the ARI, hence they are understood by anyone with a degree in attainment, for the greatness of mind and attainment of MAHARI Sruk are immeasurable.

For this reason, the author of *The King's Valley* relied entirely on his foundations, along with all the Kabbalists overseas to this day because of the questions in the words of Rav Chaim Vital, which are brief and disordered. This is also one of the reasons why I was moved to put my own words into a book in arranging the Kabbalah of the ARI, which came to us from Rav Chaim Vital, who understood, as the ARI himself testified, and as MAHARI Sruk admitted, too.

It is surprising that the HIDA did not resolve to save *The King's Valley* from the quandary of the *Makor Chaim* [*Source of Life*], who did not lie at all in the Kabbalah of the ARI, God forbid, except that he relied himself on MAHARI Sruk. This is more or less the case with all the Kabbalists and authors from overseas, not one excluded.

In my view, MAHARI Tzemach, MHARAM Papash, MAHARAN Shapira, and MHARAM Di Lozano also relied extensively on MAHARI Sruk, so why was he not mad at them?

As for me, I hope to, God willing, purify the words of the ARI without admixtures of names and attainments from others that have mingled into his words to this day, so that in time will be accepted by all the greats, and they will not need to water the foundations of the ARI with other fountains but his.

It is interesting that ... was surprised that I did not mention the RASHASH? Why did he not reply to him that the RASHASH begins his book from the world of *Nekudim*, while I stand in the middle of *Akudim*? And other than some fragmented words in *The Sun*, which also belong to the five *Partzufim* of *Atzilut*, he did not say a word about these matters.

What he contended regarding the *Keter* commentaries in the second edition of *Tree of Life*, you can tell him on my behalf that he does not understand the explanation there. There he speaks of the *Sefira Keter*, which includes the ten

Sefirot of *Ohr Yashar* [direct light] and ten *Sefirot* of *Ohr Hozer* [reflected light], which is the inner *AK*, the middle between *Ein Sof* and *AB-SAG-MA-BON*, but which was revealed outside of it. Similarly, each *Partzuf* contains *Keter*, such as the inner *AK*, which includes twenty *Sefirot*, for which *The Zohar* calls them "twenty." The book, *Tree of Life*, says about it that it can be called *Ein Sof*, it can be called "emanated," and both are words of the living God.

But I speak only of the *Keter* of the ten *Sefirot* of *Ohr Yashar*, which can only be called *Ein Sof* and Emanator, and cannot be called "middle," and much less by a formless name, and the root of the four *Yesodot* [foundations] of *HB TM*. It is so because prior to the disclosure of the *Sefira* of *Bina* of *Ohr Yashar*, there is not even a root to the *Kli*, as I have elaborated in Branch 1, that the *Kli*, the potential, and the execution are all from the emanated.

Concerning the inner light of *Igulim*, he confused my words once I divided them into two points—saying that the illumination of the surrounding light is from the surrounding *Ein Sof*, and the inner light is what the *Igulim* can receive by themselves, which are two discernments.

Near there, in the third *Behina*, I interpreted the inner light: The light that comes to them is called *Ohr Pnimi*, meaning that it comes to them by themselves. It is called "the light of the *Reshimo*." That is, the *Reshimo* still has the strength to draw and suckle from *Ein Sof*, except by a limited illumination, which is therefore called "a *Reshimo* that remains after the great light from prior to the *Tzimtzum*," and I have elaborated there.

Conversely, those who imagine that the matter of the *Reshimo* in every place indicates that it is as though a part of the holy light was carved and remained attached to a place after the departure of the light, this is a gross mistake because each light is attached to its root. It extends from its root incessantly, both a great light and a small light, which remains after the departure, called *Reshimo*.

In *Behina Dalet*, I interpreted the surrounding light in the following way: "Now *Ohr Ein Sof* illuminates bestowal from its place." What I mean is that that light does not come with the quality of the place of the *Tzimtzum*, which is limited and measured like the *Ohr Pnimi* [inner light]. Rather, it illuminates unboundedly and does not distinguish between great or small that the emanated has made for himself.

These matters are explained in many places in *Preface to the Gates* and in *Gate to Introductions*. There is no dispute at all between him and me, except in the meaning, but not in the phrasing whatsoever. I, too, say that the light of *Reshimo* is *Ohr Pnimi*, but I interpreted it so there will not be mistakes about it.

And what he wrote, that he was not set up toward the desired goal, which is the intention, tell him that this is my whole intention with the arrangement of the introductions, since many err in it, and each one builds a podium for himself because the ARI and Rav Chaim Vital did not arrange by themselves. For this reason, I had to clarify my foundations in the explanation of the ten *Sefirot*, in which many grossly err, and in the explanation and order of the *Partzufim* of AK, in which most were grossly mistaken.

Once I explain the order of the *Partzufim* of *Atzilut* and the ascents of the degrees properly, I will explain the book, *A River of Peace*, printed with great contradictions because it was printed without the awareness of the RASHASH, and things he said in his childhood ... which he regretted as an adult, were put together. But if he had composed them himself, he would certainly proofread what was needed.

However, it was known that it was not his friend, but others stole and printed it while he was not at home, and he regretted it, as is known. I saw other commentaries explaining his words, but these commentaries testify that they did not even begin to understand the RASHASH, except for one book, *The Teaching of a Sage*, which attains partially, but not thoroughly. God willing, it will all be explained properly.

However, the method of the RASHASH goes against all the authors until today, for which I could not negotiate with his real words before I demonstrated his real foundations in the studying of *Tree of Life*, which, God willing, I will disclose in the future.

I will also put together an index of all my words in *Panim Meirot uMasbirot* [*Bright and Illuminating Face*], for I did not add any interpretations to what is written and explained in *Eight Gates*, in *Tree of Life*, or in *Preface to the Gates*. I also accepted some things from the book, *My Desire Is in Her*, by Rav Chaim Vital, but I accepted nothing else into my foundations from the rest of the writings of the ARI, fearing for the purity of their compilers.

It is even more so with the Kabbalah of the First, the Genious, and all the others, which I hardly saw at all. My reference to Maimonides in his interpretation to *The Book of Creation* was not to be as a foundation for the wisdom, but as a foundation for purification from corporeality. Rav Chaim Vital also quotes him on this matter, and so I quoted Maimonides on that matter.

I found it necessary to elaborate so you could listen to the ones you should, attentively and open-mindedly, and the words of the wise are heard in peace. God willing, I will put together an index so you may see each and every phrase.

Currently, I am preoccupied with setting up the introduction of the book, after which I will set up the index, the glossary, and acronyms. My many troubles are delaying me, especially as these are works to which I am not accustomed, which are therefore delayed from day to day.

Concerning the new synagogue, I'm very happy, and I wanted to hear how things are going with the other synagogue, which they were hoping to make in the Old City.

Regards to you,
Yehuda Leib

Letter No. 36

1927, London

To my soul mate ... may his candle burn:

... What you wrote about the cleanness of the clothes, I agree with you. And what is written, "Ten *Sefirot* of Direct Light," with what is the light attained, and what is the concept of the *Kli* [vessel]? This is explained in the rest of the book for anyone who seeks—*Behina Dalet* [fourth discernment], which is the one with the *Masach* [screen], is the *Kli*, but she is not a vessel of reception, but a vessel of bestowal. By that she returns to being *Keter*.

The concept of the light is all this wisdom, for all that the wisdom discusses is only measures of Reflected Light, while in the Direct Light they are all equal, according to the abovementioned four *Behinot* [discernments], as is explained there. And the division of the nine bottom *Sefirot* of Reflected Light is already written there—that they connect in the *Kelim* [vessels] of Direct Light.

In the fourth pamphlet that I will send this week you will see in the introduction of the *AHP* in *Panim Masbirot* [Kind Face], item 11, the longitude, attributed to the Direct Light, and the latitude, to the Reflected Light. By that you will observe that the Reflected Light is discerned primarily by the amount of extensions of light of *Atzmut* [essence] in the *Partzuf*, which is not extended to the emanated without the Reflected Light. This is why it is called "illumination of the line," "thin line," and examine there carefully.

Yehuda Leib

Letter No. 37

1927, London

To my soul mate ... may his candle burn:

I received all your letters. Be strong and we will grow strong; do not fear and do not dread them. Let it be a sign for you that when success approaches, the fear and dread of them grow.

Concerning your questions whether to go to America, I do not know how to measure your spirit in the work of the Creator. Perhaps the enemies will find in it a soft spot to weaken you from His work.

And although "emissaries of good deeds are not harmed," meaning when he engages in it—when he does not spend on it more time than necessary for the *Mitzva* [good deed/ commandment/correction]—if he is slacking and loses time more than keeping the *Mitzva* requires, the *Klipot* have a place to grip.

Therefore, test yourself: Begin with preparations and supplies, and see and measure your strength. If your thoughts do not trouble you when not in the act, but rather, promptly after the necessary act you take yourself to the work of the Creator and can reject the worldly matters that drip from these matters, you will know that you are a strong man and go, for the Creator has sent you, and the Creator will bless your way and your works.

But if you cannot take away the excessive thoughts, even when they are not necessary and during the engagement, and they trouble you when you do not engage in it, as well, then it is not you that the Creator has chosen for this great thing. Rather, you still need to cleanse and hurry in any thing that helps, as it should be with the emissaries of the merciful one.

Yehuda Leib

Letter No. 38

1927, London

To ... may his candle burn:

I received your letter and I congratulate you for the *Semicha* [Rabbinical certificate] you have received. This is the first wall that barred you from going forward. I hope that from this day forward you will begin to succeed and go from strength to strength until you come into the king's palace.

I would like you to get another *Semicha*, but from now on hurry up and spend the majority of your time preparing your body to muster strength and courage "as an ox to the burden and as a donkey to the load." Do not lose a minute, "for the way is long and supplies are scarce."

And should you say, "Where is this preparation?" I will tell you, as I heard from the ADMOR of Kalshin, that previously, one had to first obtain all seven external teachings, called "the seven maidens that serve the king's daughter," as well as terrible mortification. And yet, not many gained favor in the eyes of the Creator. But since we have been rewarded with the studies of the ARI and the work-ways of the Baal Shem Tov, it is truly possible for anyone, and the above preparations are no longer necessary.

If you step in those two, which by the Creator's grace I have been favored by Him and have received them firmly, and my

209

view is as close to you as the closeness of the father to his son, I will certainly pass them on to you when you are ready to receive from mouth to mouth.

But the most important is the labor, meaning to crave how to labor in His work, since the ordinary work does not count at all, only the bits that are more than the ordinary, which is called "labor." It is like a person who needs to eat a pound of bread a day to be full. All his eating does not merit the title, "satisfying meal," but only the last bit from the pound. That bit, for all its smallness, is what defines the meal as satisfying.

Similarly, out of every service, the Creator draws out only the bits beyond the ordinary, and they will be the letters and the *Kelim* [vessels] in which to receive the light of His face.

Yehuda Leib

Letter No. 39

1927, London

To the famous *Hassid*, may his candle burn:

Regards to you.

I must inform you that I just received a very distressing letter about my sacred pamphlet being handed over to the external ones, to abuse it as they please. Now you will understand my stern warning to keep a secret, and why I have not sent the pamphlet until now. This is what I feared, so I wanted to first send the pamphlets to the MARAN, and to the rav.

Indeed, that which I dreaded came to me, and the hands of illiterate have betrayed me, doing what I did not order, after my stern warning to not disclose my secret to any person, whoever he may be. And now they have defamed me in the eyes of the generation and have failed me on the path of my exalted work to bring contentment to my Maker. Who can forgive this to them? Heaven will testify to my labor in all my strength to extend His holiness to that generation.

And yet, the *Sitra Achra* always finds her people, doers of her missions, setting obstacles before me wherever I turn to benefit others. Thus far are my words, and "those who are with us are more than those who are with them," and the Creator does not deprive me of my reward. Bit by bit, I pave the way, at times less, at times more, but always with profit (reward), until I am rewarded with taking down all the enemies of the Creator with the help of His great and terrible name.

As for you, do not fear the fear of fools. Those who slander, my little finger is bigger than their waist. So the Creator desired, and so He made me, and who will tell Him what to do and what to act? The merit of my law is greater than the merit of their fathers. Similarly, the contemporaries of Prophet Amos defamed him and said that the Creator had no one on whom to instill His Divinity but that stutterer, as it is written in the *Psikta* [a Midrash].

However, it is written, "A truthful lip shall be established forever, and a lying tongue is only momentary," for in the end, the truthful people are the winners. Amos remains alive and existing forever, and who has heard or knows what had happened to his adversaries?

So it is here. The sayers can harm only their own kind, so it follows that the storm swirls on the head of the wicked, the truth lives on and does not weaken by all the lies. Instead, it grows even stronger by them, like a sown field that is strengthened by the manure and dung that are thrown in. With the Creator's will, the blessing of the field increases and multiplies by them.

I still do not feel the harm that will reach me from them concerning the dissemination of my teaching, so I do not know how to calculate my way to instill light and save it from their evil. And yet, it is certain that if I feel any harm, I will take my revenge against them, as is the law of Torah, and I will contend forcefully with them. I will do all that is within my power to do, as it is the Creator I fear, and there is no other force but Him.

As a rule, you should know that it is not for my own need or my own glory that I have composed the book. Rather, it is only for His sake, for I noticed great confusions in the writings of the ARI because the ARI did not write or arrange them by himself in the full depth of this sublime wisdom. When Rav Chaim Vital heard and wrote the words, he was still not in the degrees of wholeness necessary for attaining those words at their root. He was young then, thirty years old, when studying with the ARI, as it is written in *Gate to Reincarnations* (Gate 8, p 49). It writes, "Now, in the year, 1571, and I am twenty-nine ..." Then, on Passover he was already serving the ARI, and the Rav [ARI] fell ill on July 21, 1572. The next Tuesday, on the Fifth of *Av* [July 25, 1572], he passed away.

You therefore find that at the time of his demise he [Chaim Vital] was only thirty, and the ARI lived thirty-eight years, as it is known, and he wrote some more there (Gate 8, p 71).

At the time of his passing, Rav Chaim Vital was not at his [the ARI's] side. These are his words verbatim: "Rav Itzhak HaCohen told me that at the time of my teacher's passing, when I came out of his room, he (Rav Itzhak HaCohen) entered and cried before him saying, 'Is this the hope that we all hoped in your life—to see great good, Torah, and wisdom in the world?' He replied to him: 'If I found even one complete righteous among you, I would not be taken away prematurely.' While saying it, he asked about me (about Chaim Vital). He said, 'Where did Chaim go? Has he left me at such a time?' He was very saddened. He understood from his words that he had some secret to pass on to me, so he (Rav Itzhak HaCohen) said to him: 'What shall we do from now on?' He (the ARI) replied: 'Tell the friends on my behalf that from this day on they will not engage at all in this wisdom that I taught, for they did not understand it properly. Only Rav Chaim Vital shall engage in it, *alone*, in a whisper, and in hiding.' He (Rav Itzhak HaCohen) said, 'But is there no hope at all?' He said, 'If you merit, I will come to you and teach you.' He replied to him: 'How will you come and teach us if you are now departing from this world?' He replied, 'You have no knowledge of the concealed, of how my coming to you will be,' and he promptly passed away."

I have elaborated in copying the words of Rav Chaim Vital's book, *Gate to Reincarnation*, so you may see that the ARI forbade Rav Vital to teach what he had learned to others because at the time, he did not sufficiently understand what he had heard from the ARI. This is why he would not even arrange the writings he had heard from his teacher, and his successors arranged them, the third generation—Rav Yaakov Tzemach and Rav Shmuel Vital.

Each of those compilers did not have the complete writings of the ARI because six hundred pages from the writings were stolen while Rav Chaim Vital was alive. Out of those, Rav Yaakov Tzemach compiled the majority of *Tree of Life*, as well as some other compositions. Rav Chaim Vital ordered another part to be buried along with him in the grave, and so they did. He left a third part as inheritance to his son, Rav Shmuel Vital, from which the famous *Eight Gates* were compiled.

After a long time, Rav Yaakov Tzemach assembled a large group of students, who dug the third portion out of the grave. From them the first and next editions of *Tree of Life* were composed, as well as *Perpetual Burnt-Offering*, and other compositions.

You therefore see that each time, the compiler had only a third of all the writings, which together make up one entity and one structure. I wish it were enough, but since they had only a small portion of the writings, they did not understand the depth of the wisdom at that time, and they terribly confused the matters by not understanding how to arrange them.

Know for certain that since the time of the ARI to this day, there has never been anyone who understood the method of the ARI to the fullest, as it was easier to attain a mind twice as great and twice as holy than the ARI's than to understand his method, in which many hands fiddled—from the one who heard them through the first writer, to the last compilers, while they still did not attain the matters as they are in their upper root. Thus, each one inverted and confused the matters.

And now, by the Creator's will, I have been rewarded with conceiving [impregnation of] the soul of the ARI, not because of my good deeds, but by a higher will. It is beyond me, too, why I have been chosen for this wonderful soul, which no one has been granted from his passing until today. I cannot elaborate on this matter because it is not my way to discuss wondrous things, but I did find it my duty to ease your mind because ... before a flow of great waters from servants that burst out at their master and expel from their waters cast up mire and dirt, to fall under the work that their animate soul has worked, since they still did not completely understand how to separate it from the spiritual soul. You should know that one must not fear such forces, which spring forth only to wash away all holiness, and the Creator saves us from them.

I think you will believe me, as it has never been my way to fabricate or exaggerate, or pursue respect and gain a name among the fools, which, until today, I have tolerated and had no desire to even fight with them.

To reinforce your not being confused by their armies of the *Sitra Achra*, I will give you a clear sign that we received from the ARI, by which to know who is a true righteous and who is not a true righteous, but is worthy of being righteous, for which he should be treated respectfully, too. Do you believe that we should cast lots [flip a coin] about it, to know who is serving the Creator and who is not? After all, the signs and the tokens do not determine in this matter, as is known among the *Hassidim*, so it is a lot that we need, God forbid.

Rather, know that Rav Chaim Vital asked the ARI that question, and it is explained in the book, *Gate of the Holy Spirit*, the seventh of the *Eight Gates* by the ARI, page 1. Here are his words, word for word: "The sign that my teacher gave me was to see if all his words come true, or if all his words are for the Creator, and he will not be wrong in even one of his words (relating to a letter that he learns from his friend who needs, etc., as it is known to those who know the wisdom of the hidden). He should also know the secrets of Torah and how to explain them, and then we can definitely believe in him." Rav Chaim Vital ends with this sign, and these are his words, verbatim: "According to his words we can know and recognize his greatness and merit to the extent of his knowledge."

The explanation is as previously written, that when a person is righteous and *Hassid*, and engages in Torah and prays intently, angels and holy spirits are created out of him. This is the meaning of "One who performs one *Mitzva* has acquired for himself one advocate." The follies that come out from his mouth become a chariot to the souls of the first righteous, to go down to teach Torah to that man.

He also says there that if the *Mitzvot* [commandments] are incomplete, incomplete angels and spirits are made of it, which are called "tellers." It is about that that he gave the abovementioned sign that if the Torah and *Mitzvot* are complete, he is rewarded with complete attainment and knows how to explain all the secrets of Torah. If he is lacking in it, meaning knows how to explain only some of them, his works are certainly incomplete.

Indeed, all those who can be my adversaries, it is because they do not even understand my words, so how can they be deemed complete righteous? Thus, I have given you a clear sign.

I've already written to you that my book needs no endorsements because I did not add even a single word to the words of the ARI, and I have also made an index for every single concept, showing their place in the writings of the ARI, and the ARI does not need the endorsement of our generation. I did that deliberately, seeing the ways of the *Sitra Achra* toward me in advance. My own work and additions in all those two commentaries are hardly recognizable. Thus, how will they hold out the campaign against this notebook? If they do have complaints about my studying and being more proficient in the writings of the ARI than they are, this is not an argument. They shouldn't have spent their time on vanities; they had time to study the words of the ARI, and since they were idle, now they will eat their own flesh.

My regards to you and to ... and ... Tell him that all his ways are as this deed, whose intention is good but the deeds are not, and everything follows the act. But what can I do to him? He is my flesh and blood. Therefore, let him inform me in great detail the whole story and how it unfolded from beginning to end, and I will reply to him.

I also ask that you will let me know your thoughts about this letter, and more of what is happening between you, in great detail and elaborately, for I need to know all the details in order to maintain the shield, for the work of the Creator is no small matter.

Yehuda

Letter No. 40

1927, London

To the honorable students:

This week I received a double portion of letters from the portions *Shlach* [Send] and Korah. Last week I did not receive any letters and I thought that you did not write today because on the third day of the portion, Korah, it has been a full year since I have left you.

Regarding the impression of ... with the question ... regarding, "You did not see any image," to the point that he wrote me that even Solomon's wisdom would not be enough to answer such a question, I call on him the words of our sages: "Do not judge your friend until you are in his shoes." If I had even Moses' wisdom, of whom it was said, "And he beholds the image of the Lord," he would be able to blunt his teeth, too, for there is a form in spirituality.

What I wrote is according to the view of fools who interpreted the word "form" and the word "image" as one. But I am surprised at you—in a place where I ground wheat into flour for human consumption, you turned the flour into wheat again to chew on like a beast of the wild.

I elaborated extensively on the matter of form and disparity of form, which is only the difference between the Emanator and the emanated. It is necessary that we find some discernment for which it will be called "emanated" and not "Emanator," and I placed "the name" on that discernment, to be able to engage in it and speak of it.

This is why I called it "disparity of form" and "equivalence of form." Sometimes I call it, "great *Dvekut* [adhesion]" and "little *Dvekut*." It can also be named by any name we want in order to explain this matter.

Once we have ground [analyzed] the matters from several pages in the book, he made them wheat again, and materialized the box of the form, clothing it in a corporeal image until his hands and legs were hopelessly tied up in this image. It is written explicitly in the Torah, "For you did not see any image," while here it writes that there is form, disparity of form, and equivalence of form ... I elaborated in your words to evaluate your inclination toward externality, that one needs to look into one's actions.

The precision that Rav ... makes regarding the name *Ein Sof* [infinity] and "the light of *Ein Sof*," the wording in the book, *My Desire Is in The Lord*: "And all those worlds and *Malchut* were included in the upper world, each of them. Also, they are included in *Keter*, and the whole of *Ein Sof*, inside of which all the worlds, etc., and everything was one unity, and all was *Ein Sof*," thus far his words, word for word.

And what he wrote in the title of the book, *The Holy Tongue*, p 20, I did not know the initials of that title, nor suffixes.

And what he imagines to be my words in the beginning, that "The light and all the abundance are already included in His essence Himself," has no connection to my words regarding the *Hitkalelut* [mingling/inclusion] of the bottom worlds in *Ein Sof*. There, I explain specifically the matter of *Ohr Pashut* [simple light], which does not change wherever it is, and the difference

between the Emanator and the emanated is actually in the
darkness. This is why I wrote very precisely, "In His essence,"
which has neither a name nor a word. I do not even refer there
to the light of *Ein Sof*, God forbid.

I do not understand you whatsoever, how you scrutinize
but do not taste what you are saying, and compare one issue
to another like food to a barrel. It must be due to multiple
engagements or a desire for multiple engagements.

And what roams as a "thought"—to know where she belongs,
he caught my tongue in *Bina*, and in the order, ABYA—is said
in *Atzilut*, as well as in *Tikkuney Zohar* [*Corrections of The Zohar*],
"Upper *Hochma* is called 'a thought.'"

Indeed, it is from the wondrous and concealed secrets. But
see in *Gate to the Essays of Rashbi*, these are his words in "The
Hidden Midrash of Ruth": Moses means *Daat*, as in *Tifferet*, and
Rabbi Akiva is *Bina*, called "Being." Had the Torah been given
from the part of *Bina*, the *Klipot* would have no clothing in the
Torah. But the Creator wished to give them a part and a grip,
similar to how the first sparks in *Hochma* raised 320 sparks. This
is the meaning of "So it came about in the Thought."

You find here that Rabbi Akiva as *Bina* is called "being,"
but this is difficult because it is known that "being" is the name
of *Hochma*. And yet, see in Branch 2 in *Panim Masbirot* (as well
as in the introduction on the *AHP*) in the "Preface" regarding
the ascent of *Malchut* to *Bina*. It explains that *Behina Dalet* rose
to *Hochma* and became *Nukva* to *Hochma* of *Behina Dalet* that
was established as Upper *Ima*. This is why *Bina*, which is *Behina
Bet*, went out, meaning below *Behina Dalet*, whose *Sium* is called
Parsa, since out of that *Bina* that went out, the two *Partzufim*
YESHSUT were established below the *Parsa*.

By that you will understand that that *Malchut* that went up,
really did go up to *Hochma* and acquired Upper *Ima* there, and

she is called "being." She is also called "a thought," and there is the mitigation of the *Dinim* with *Rachamim*. This is why it is where the 320 sparks rose, as they are from *Behina Dalet*.

However, they did not rise to the actual *Hochma*, but rather to Upper *Ima*, who is *Hochma*. This is the meaning of "All is clarified in the thought," since there is their root.

Sometimes *Bina* is called *Nukva* of *Hochma*, which is why I said that *Malchut* rose to *Bina*, meaning received the form of Upper *Bina*, which is called "a thought" and "existence from absence." This is the deepest of the deep, which is why the authors were succinct here.

And what I wrote in *Panim Masbirot*, p 6, it writes, "nine *Sefirot, Toch* and *Rosh*," it is no longer in the pamphlets, but was written "*Toch* and *Sof*."

And what Rav ... that I should ask on his behalf, it is similar to a working steam engine. Any machine that you attach to the steam engine with a strap will be just as strong. Thus, it is only *Dvekut* that we need.

Yehuda Leib

Letter No. 41

1927, London

To the honorable students, may the Lord be upon them:

I received your letter, and I am now sending the introduction. Although I have not proofread it, not even in writing, I trust you to understand how to proofread it perfectly. I cannot send you paper from here, simply for lack of funds.

The introduction will probably consume a printer-sheet and a half, six pages, and with the index and references, it will be two complete pamphlets, eight pages.

But the introduction is one complete thing, and there is no division in it whatsoever, for they are matters of the highest importance, as you will see once you understand. You should hurry with it as much as possible so that I can be during the festival.

... And we hope that everything will be for the sake of the Creator and for our sake. We need only exert in His law and in His work, to fill the lack and to correct what is broken...

I do not understand your lack of longing for my replies. As for me, I find myself truly near you, not in any way less than when I was with you. I share your sorrows and your joys, just as though I were with you in the same house and we were speaking to each other. But you know two, and I know one, hence my words are few.

Please follow everything I wrote above concerning the wholeness of the introduction.

Yehuda

Letter No. 42

1927, London

To the honorable ... may his candle burn:

With the words below, I will open my heart to you: I am very surprised that the friends aren't missing my approaching return home as they should be. But I think of you that you are nonetheless the best among them because you cannot write me and explain your words, so you are more in need of a face-to-face encounter than the rest. Because of it, I think that you are longing more than they, so I will speak and feel better.

... But on the other hand, let us count the gains you have acquired in all your days with me. Although it is not yet clear who is to blame, but be that as it may, the hope is dwindling and requires strengthening.

On my part, I cannot help you in that, except to guarantee that the fault is not at all mine, but yours alone, due to your lack of knowledge or weakness of faith and so forth. This is why all my prayers for you did not help you because you still did not understand how to execute it.

Therefore, let me give you a complete introduction, which you will keep and feel better: When the Creator is fond of a person and calls him to cling to Him, of course he is ready and willing for it with all his heart and might; otherwise He

225

would not invite him to His meal. If the faith in his heart is as a stake that will not fall, he understands this faithful calling and recognizes his place forever. Then, he does so and eats, and sees the king's face. And it does not cause him diminution because his mind and faith are complete.

Our sages said, "Fear the Lord your God, including wise disciples." It is to include those who unite in true unity, and happy are those who live up to it.

You can see the validity of the words in you, yourself. When the time was ripe and you were fit for bonding, I did not waste time to wait until you came to my house. Rather, I was promptly at your place. And although you did not see me physically, you felt my love and the sublimity of holiness at the bottom of your heart.

Then, all that was left for you to do was hurry and greet me with love. One who craves does and completes his part. So you did, sending feelings of love, sublimity, and joy to my ears all the way from your home to the hill, with faithful passion.

But once you have climbed up the hill and greeted me, the joy and love began to wane. It happened for your lack of faith in me and in my sincere love for you, as you to me, as the water-face to the face. This was the first flaw between me and you, for with that thought you immediately departed and drew far from me, to that extent.

Indeed, so is the nature of anything spiritual—the matters are woven in lightning speed, and conception and birth are near. Therefore, once your belly conceived fear, "You promptly gave birth to straw." That is, you doubted yourself, and your pleasant, sublime, and exalted thoughts about me, that they were exaggerated, that maybe it is not so, and then, "of course it is not so." Thus, I was necessarily separated from you, and kept all my work and labor in deposit for a better time.

At the right moment, I returned with you as before, and you, too, repeated your previous acts, more or less. At times you wished to hear from me explicit words about it, as one speaks to one's friend, and not in any way less. But I am not good at that, as it is written, "For I am slow of speech and slow of tongue." You, too, should not hope for it in the future unless you merit sanctifying your corporeal body, with the tongue and ears, to such an extent that it will equal the merit of the spiritual.

But you cannot understand it because you have no perception of the hidden. But I, all that I am permitted, I do not withhold at all, and "more than the calf wants to eat …"

Let me picture for you your abovementioned issues with me in an allegory: A man walks along the way and sees a lovely garden. He hears a voice calling him, coming from the king, who is walking in the garden. Excited, he jumps the fence in one leap and is inside the garden. For all his excitement and rush, he does not feel that he is walking before the king, and the king is near him, strolling right behind him.

So he walks and thanks, and praises the king with all his might, aiming to prepare himself to meet the king. He does not notice whatsoever that the king is next to him.

But all of a sudden he turns his face and sees the king right next to him. Naturally, he is overjoyed. He begins to follow the king, praising and glorifying as much as he can, the king before him and he, behind the king.

So they walk and stroll up to the gate. The man walks out the gate and returns to his initial place, while the king remains in the garden and locks the gate. When the man sees that he has been separated and the king is not with him, he begins to look for the gate through which he came out when the king was before him. But there is no such gate at all, but only as he came in the first time, when he was walking before the king and the king was behind him without his noticing.

So it should be now, but it requires great craftsmanship. Understand it and study this allegory, for it is the same between us. While you were with me and I felt the chill that was born in you compared to the past, you should have nonetheless concealed your face from looking at me, as if I know nothing of all that had happened to you and went through your heart along the way to me.

This is the meaning of "And they believed in the Lord and in His servant, Moses," because in return for, "And Moses hid his face," he was rewarded with, "and the image of the Lord does he behold." That is, if you had believed in my prayer for you, and while I was with you, hearing all the praises and glorifications that you thought of me, there is no doubt you'd be ashamed of the coldness instead of the warmth. And if you were properly ashamed and regretful, you'd be rewarded with the Creator's mercy over you, and then, more or less, the excitement would return to you, and you would be rewarded with uniting with me properly, as a stake that will not fall forever.

Yehuda Leib

Letter No. 43

1927, London

To the honorable ... may his candle burn:

... Our sages have already said, "The fear of your teacher is as the fear of heaven." This, therefore, will be the measure of exaltedness that such a man obtains by his sanctity, for his exaltedness will by no means exceed the exaltedness of his rav.

What the Rijnaar boasted about—that he was awarded a higher degree than all the sages in his generation because he acquired more faith in the wise than all of his contemporaries—we need to understand that faith does not come by lending. Such faith can be acquired by six year old children, too, but as a feeling of the exaltedness and the inspiration to his soul from the wisdom of the wise who have shared from His wisdom to those who fear Him.

I have already said and elaborated that the biggest *Masach* [screen] is in the work in the children of the land of Israel, since the domination of the Canaan *Klipa* is in this place, and each one is as low as the ground, his friend is even lower than the ground, and many others like him.

Allegorically, you can say the words of our sages about the verse, "Leave Me and keep My law"—"I wish they would leave Me" means that they were proud of the exaltedness.

And although "he and I cannot dwell in the same place," still, "Keep My law," be attached to a genuine righteous with proper faith in the wise. Then there is hope that the righteous will reform you and will sentence them to a scale of merit as is appropriate for the presence of the Creator. What could come out of their humility and lowness so the Creator will not move His abode from them, if they have no genuine righteous to guide them in His law and prayer, and lead them to a place of Torah and wisdom?

It is already known that it is forbidden to marry one's daughter to an uneducated man. By that they gradually dry out like dry bones, God forbid. And what can you do for them if not repeat such words from time to time until the live one will pay attention?

... It is written, "And Moses would take the tent," etc. Why did he pitch his tent outside the camp? The fools believe that he did it to stop the flow of *Hochma* due to the sin. This is unthinkable, since after the sin they need the fountains of Torah and *Hochma* thousands of times more than before, as our sages said, "Had Israel not sinned, they would have been given only the *Five Books of Moses* and the book of Joshua."

However, it is to the contrary. It is a true remedy for opening the fountains of wisdom to a faithful source, since once Moses had pitched his tent outside the camp, the craving for him inside the camp increased, as one who has bread in his basket is not like one who, etc., and along with it the adhesion with him. Thus, they were rewarded with expansion of Moses' soul between them, for which they were called "the generation of knowledge."

I have already said and mentioned the words of Torah that I said on the festival of *Shavuot* prior to my journey from you about the verse, "Run My beloved, and be like a gazelle": "As

230

the gazelle turns its face back when it runs," etc., for having no other way to make a *Panim* [face], they devise this tactic—bringing the *Panim* to the *Achoraim* [back]. It is as is written, "So is the Creator when," etc., "turns His face back," since the sensation of separation and *Achoraim*, and the inability to receive the *Panim* of *Kedusha* [holiness] increase the sparks of craving tremendously, until the *Achoraim* become *Panim*, since the tablets were written on both sides. You should be noticing these things by now.

Yehuda

Letter No. 44

1927, London

To the honorable students, may the Lord be upon them:

... I must praise Rav ... whom I feel closer to me than the rest of the students, and I am deliberately praising him in his presence, so he will give praise and thanksgiving to the Creator for it, that after my leaning away from him for a short while, he was rewarded with connecting to me to a great extent. It must be a present from the Creator.

And concerning my not answering his questions in private, it is because so is my way in important matters—to change addressees from one to the other so as to not give a foothold to the *Sitra Achra*. Hence, each one must exert himself to understand all the letters, without minding the addressee whatsoever.

Do not suspect me that his words are not properly engraved within my heart. Rather, I carry the load with him in all his labors, troubles, and pains.

It is true that for some months now he has been mentioning before me the great pain he has had in the side of his head. I wanted to quickly write him a proven remedy, which is to exert in Torah, but my way has always been that before I make my remedy known, I ask of the Creator that he would obtain by himself. After he obtains by himself, I, too, will come and fill up the words, "For Judah and more to call," and I will tell him the remedy.

This is why I so rejoiced when I received from him after some weeks, words of Torah about the verse, "And the man Moses was very humble," that he discovered it with a genuine mind—that the whole issue of salvation is in obtainment of *Hochma* and the secrets of Torah. I praise and thanked the Creator for it.

But afterward I received a letter from him, from which I understood that he had broken, "Let he not break his word," and he once again perceives ways and salvations prior to attaining the secrets of Torah, since he wrote me that the pain has once again gripped his entire head.

Therefore, I hereby remind him that he had already resolved that there will not be complete, eternal salvation before he attains the flavors of Torah, and the flavors of *Mitzva*, and therefore he must not be sorry, except for the attainments of the Torah.

It is known that the Creator does not marry His daughter to an uneducated man, as our sages said, "Anyone who marries his daughter to an uneducated man, it is as though he ties her and places her in front of a lion."

... It is known that the woman is always called after the man: He is a *Melech* [king], she is a *Malkah* [queen]; he is *Hacham* [wise], she is *Hochma* [wisdom]; he is *Navon* [intelligent/ understanding], she is *Bina* [intelligence/understanding], as it is as is written in *Tikkuney Zohar*. It therefore follows that the wife of an uneducated person is named "folly," since he is a fool, who does not know how to be watchful with kings' honor.

The permanent residence of the evil inclination is a heart that is empty of Torah. But the Torah and *Hochma* reject the evil inclination from the heart, bit by bit. And because he is a fool, a woman of folly is prepared for him—*Klipat* Noga [Noga Shell], who seduced Eve.

This is what the writing says, "Anger rests in the hearts of fools." You find a perfect reason why the king should not give his daughter to an uneducated man. Unless your soul truly desires the daughter of Jacob, you need not give many gifts, as is believed by the external ones, of Hamor—father of Shechem the Hivite. Rather, exert for attainment of flavors of Torah and flavors of *Mitzva*, not one of them missing, for then his desire and her desire will meet and unite with one another, and the love will complete its thing by itself, without any assistance from the side, meaning by humans.

Yehuda

Letter No. 45

1927, London

To the honorable students, may the Creator be upon them.

As I prepare myself to return to my home, I so long to find you ready and willing to hear the word of the Creator properly.

Currently, I feel shame for ... and for ... who were among the best and the highest of the friends, and now, who knows? Perhaps ... may his candle burn is drawing nearer to me more than they, and if he is rewarded with complete confidence, he will rise and live, as it is written, "You desire truth in the inward parts, and in the blocked, You let me know." That is, by obtaining confidence, all the wisdom of the worlds, upper and lower, is bundled and revealed, and all that is required for this attainment is a pure heart, which has already loathed self-love and is entirely dedicated to His name.

Therefore, he did well not being impressed at all by ... and ... slighting him because his lack of sophistication. Rather, let his heart be haughty in the ways of the Creator, and small and great are there.

What else can I do for ... who wishes to learn everything from me, except for the matter of lowliness, for he is thoroughly displeased with this engagement, and he is confident that he is better and more comely than the blind and dry people, and all the more so than his brother, who has an ugly face? He is even certain that I, too, thank him because he was not shy of writing me. It seemed to me that for his sake, he should dedicate considerable time to this engagement.

And yet, my intention is not as the lowest of the low, meaning as the lowly, who seek lowliness, for that one is even worse than pride itself because who will swear on a stone that it is a stone? Certainly, there is he who thinks that it is gold. However, he should know and believe that all creations are as "clay in the hands of a potter—when He wishes, He makes longer, and when He wishes, He makes shorter."

Also, he should not be angry at the wicked, but rather have mercy on them no less than he has mercy on himself. As long as he has not been rewarded with the higher mercy, how will he know what to detect and anger over? On the contrary, the mercy on them increases even more because they are robbed without consolation.

Like a father whose two sons are sick, where one has the funds to purchase medicines, one hasn't the funds. Clearly, the father's heart has more mercy on the son without the funds for medicines, for the one with the funds for medicines will be cured if he seeks out cures, and if he does not, it is as though he has committed suicide. But the other son, the mercies of the father and of all who see him cut through heart.

Therefore, why do you so slight your brother, who has an ugly face, and you are angry with the world for respecting him more than you? In my view, he is more worthy of respect than you are, and he is simple. So is the nature of the world, and although he did not see, his fortune saw, and this is easy to understand.

Last week, I learned from ... that he has resolved to resign from my engagement, that I had burdened him with too much, and to come to me, to London, without asking my permission, for how will he ask me? Does this relate to me? Also, even a small child running from school knows that to sit next to his rav's table, with great contentment, and to entertain himself with the secrets of Torah and high secrets, is far more agreeable than to engage in the *ways* of his rav, in lowly and contemptible matters. From those, one can only come to great troubles, for lack of ability to pray even as a simpleton.

I reply without questions, for one who deals with me in this way at this time, when he is thirsty and longing, I greatly benefit him. Moreover, let his deeds be with me when I am rewarded with bringing him under the wings of Divinity, for then he can think, has the Creator spoke only with Moses? The Creator will speak with me, as well. I, too, have a set table, to furnish all the upper worlds, and how can I annul myself now before the bodily engagements of my rav and the questions he had taken?

The honor and fear of equalizing with the Creator relate primarily to that time when he has already been rewarded with the holy Divinity being clothed within his heart forever, for you should believe that your rav's bodily matters are truly engagements of the soul. This is why our sages said, "It did not say, 'studied,' but 'poured,' indicating that serving is greater than learning."

A student should be in true annulment toward the rav, in the full sense of the word, for then he unites with him and performs salvations in his favor. A student cannot cling to his rav's soul, as it is above his attainment, and as it is written, "My God."

As ... may his candle burn, wrote me, he believes that the body of a righteous is as great as the soul of another. While he did not hear what he himself said, for he finished with ... he still agreed with my trip to America. Had he heard what he had said, he would not have agreed so easily. However, it is true that the body of a true righteous is as great as the soul with which the righteous, the saints of the Upper One, are rewarded. So may you be rewarded with clinging to my body, and then you will certainly see your world in your life. This is why our sages praised the service, as it is closer to *Dvekut* [adhesion] of the student with the rav.

It is hard for me to understand ... for how can it be after all the troubles I went through for his sake—composing the handsome and comely composition, namely my book, *The Light of the Face*, with various adornments for him, on fine paper and with a clear type font, a complete introduction, and a general preface, index, and a list of acronyms? These have become the two great lights, properly illuminating and explaining.

Also, almost each week I write him a long and elaborate letter, sometimes even two in the same week, as best as my fingers can produce. I cannot suspect that he is not a good guest, that he will not say, "All that the landlord has troubled himself with, he has troubled himself only for me." And yet, I find him sitting surrounded by the holy wall, for had he not sat outside the wall, he would certainly not equalize himself with his inclination, conducting this sapless custom.

I also fear that alongside that custom of his, he says to himself that he is adhered and connected to me more than all the friends, for the heart's aim follows the words, and the Creator seeks the heart. And since the point in his heart is clung to me, he needs nothing more than to repeat the actions. These are needed and appropriate, but for those of little knowledge who have no other way. For a decorated (handsome) Jew such as him, a good heart bests them all, so he no longer needs to display any actions with qualification or advantage.

It is true that I have not yet heard from all the friends any impressions of my book, *The Light of the Face*, except for ..., who for every section that I sent wrote me praises and accolades galore from the bottom of his heart. I am therefore certain that this will help him ... and he can more or less feel the value of the man and his work. This is why his heart is a human heart, which is at least behooved to be impressed, as I have already written in the interpretation of the verse, "My dear son, Ephraim." *Yakir* [dear] is like *Yaccir* [know/recognize], and *Yaccir* [know/ recognize] is like *Yakir* [dear], meaning they are interdependent and are as one.

Remember what ... wrote me, admitting without shame that he understood that whole letter well, except for the issue of *Yakir* and *Yaccir*, that he must insert an elephant through the eye of the needle [study hard]. He attributed it to the possibility that he needs more forewords and knowledge of the righteous. This is why he was able to write to me in the last letter that there is a hidden lock on my books, which he does not know or understand.

What could I reply to him? I therefore determined that what the mind does not do, time will do, and it will become clear to him that recognition is according to the appreciation. That is, the inspiration by and annulment toward the real good. This is what raises and sustains the exaltedness and preciousness, and then the recognition is accumulated in him, followed by the raising of the preciousness. Thus they rise in the rungs of sanctity until they are rewarded with satisfying the deficiency and correcting the wrong, up to the real and complete unification.

In that letter, I wrote that *Yaccir* is like *Yakir* on the 310, but they are one and the same, as it is written, "And they believed in the Lord and in Moses His servant." It is also written, "One who doubts his rav, it is as though he doubts Divinity," since the upper will [desire] is equal in matters that are measured and come in truly the same amount.

And what can I say to you, natives of the land, who believe that I am abroad and you are in the land of Israel!

The holy Torah will testify on my behalf, in what Moses commands us in the portion, *Masa'ey* [Journeys]: "Command the children of Israel ... for you are coming unto the land." In these verses he points out and clearly marks the borders of the land, in a way that anyone who comes to the land of Israel will no longer have any doubt.

He decrees and says, "It shall be to you the side of the Negev ..." "Negev" comes from the word *Negiva* [wiping], for "The salvation of the Lord is as a wet garden." Therefore, the departure from His light is called "Negev." "It shall be" implies joy, indicating the salvation of the Creator, which includes the letter, "It shall be to you the side of the Negev," meaning that they knew that the side of the Negev was considered a recognized side and boundary.

It is written, "And you will soon perish," meaning from Zin desert, by Edom. "Zin" comes from the words *Tzinim* and *Pachim*, which our sages said are not in heaven, but rather by Edom, for as soon as Edom is involved, the Creator says, "I and he cannot dwell in the world."

This is why he says, "And it shall be to you the boundary of Negev." "Boundary" is the end, where the abovementioned wiping ends, "From the end of the Dead Sea eastward" means as soon as you begin to touch the edge of the kingdom of heaven. "Eastward" is like "as before" [the same letters are used in Hebrew for both words], the wiping will promptly end, and the abundance of the goals of His might will begin to appear before you.

It adds further, "And your border shall turn from Negev." That is, because the beginning of sunrise was after the "wiping," and "in its boundary," the narrow turns outward and twists to the north of the world diagonally, as RASHI interpreted, to The Ascent of Akrabim [scorpions]. In other words, this is why scorpions are coming up before you.

"And pass along to Tzina [Tzin]." Terrible *Tzina* [chill] spreads through most of the bones, bursting forth from Zin desert on the east, for he is *Tzin*, and she is *Tzina*. It is translated (into Aramaic), "from the south to the ascent" of Akrabim.

"And pass along to Tzin," as our sages said, "Even if a serpent is wrapped around his leg he will not stop." But according to everyone, a scorpion does stop. Therefore, "And his outcomes shall be from the south to Rekam Ge'ah [Kadesh-Barnea]," because envy consumes like fire in front of the scorpions, until he must come to Kadesh-Barnea, which is Rekam Ge'ah.

In other words, his thoughts take on a clothing of pride, extraordinarily, until "And it shall go forth to Hatzar-Addar," for although he boasted with a mantle of hair and will not cause to sin, like those who are first to the kingship, he still feels he is standing in the court, standing outside. This is why that place is called *Hatzar* [court] *Addar*, meaning that they contradict one another.

"And pass along to Atzmonah," Atzm-on-ah. He is *Etzem*, and he is *Atzmon*, and she is *Atzmonah*, for the place causes, and it becomes like a hard, unbreakable *Etzem* [bone/object]. Likewise, the elephant does not have joints in its bones and cannot turn back its head. When it wants to look back, it must turn itself entirely, from head to tail, as is known to those who know the nature of animals.

He concludes and says, "And the border shall turn (for you) from Azmon to the brook of Egypt," meaning that Atzmonah returned to being Atzmon. This is why he returned to the brook of Egypt, of which the Creator said, "You shall not return that way henceforth." However, it is still not the actual exile in Egypt, but rather the edge of that exile.

"And its exit shall be at the sea." That is, once it was taken and allotted in the brook of Egypt, it is rewarded from there with the coming forth of wisdom, to roam in the sea of wisdom. RASHI interpreted it: "That strip that protruded to the north was from Kadesh-Barnea to Atzmon, and from there on the narrow grew shorter ... to the brook of Egypt."

Interpreting his words: It is written in the name of the ARI in *The Brightness of the Firmament*, and I believe in *Gate to Introductions*, as well, that the world was initially created with a *Bet* [בּ]. It is known that there is a point in the middle of the *Bet*, which is *Hochma* [wisdom], and the north side is open (see RASHI, *Beresheet*). Afterward, that point of *Hochma* in the *Bet* expanded like the *Vav* and returned to the north of the *Bet*, like that, ם, and became a blocked [final] *Mem*.

This is the meaning of the words of our sages, "But it could be created in one utterance"; that *Mem* is one utterance.

However, *Hochma* would have been unable to expand because that ם is a blocked letter in all four directions, so the *Hochma* was restricted once again as a point in the middle of the *Bet* [בּ], like the *Vav*.

At that time the *Hochma* expanded to be given as a reward for the righteous, which is why "the world was created with ten utterances, to avenge the wicked who are destroying the world, which was created in ten utterances."

Because the border turned from Atzmon to the brook of Egypt, it is written, "I saw the wicked buried, and they came." It is also written, "I was at ease and He shattered me. And He has grasped me by the neck and broken me to pieces. And He set me up as His target."

It is all because of the abovementioned strip, where the *Yod* expanded into a *Vav* to the north of the *Bet*, and the border was necessarily made shorter for the brook of Egypt. This is why all the enemies of Israel are lost there, and the children of Israel come to the sea to draw the fountains of wisdom [*Hochma*] to renew the world as before, meaning to "give good reward to the righteous, who establish the world, which was created in ten utterances."

The writing ends, "As for the western border, you shall have the Great Sea." This is the primary source for being granted with the great *Hochma*, called "the Great Sea." From there begins the drawing of the air of the land of Israel, which the Creator has sworn to give to us.

To rush us toward that thing, the text repeats and says, "This border shall be your west border." That is, all the exits from the sea of wisdom are only that border, meaning the Great Sea, the sea of the land of Israel, *Mochin* de *Gadlut*! It is impossible to be rewarded with them unless they have traversed all ten borders. This is the meaning of "and changed my wages ten times," after which one is rewarded with settling in the land of Israel, a land flowing with milk and honey, and good, broad, and pleasant land.

Behold, I have given you horses. If you can place riders on them, you will come to settle in a good, broad, and pleasant land for all eternity. Until then, do not say that I have journeyed from the land of Israel. Rather, you are negligent at that, and do not properly long to sit in it together with me.

Because I read the portion to you, I will conclude with the prophet: "Hear the word of the Lord, O house of Jacob and all the families of the house of Israel. ... Who say to a tree, 'You are my father,' and to a stone, 'You gave birth to me.' For they have turned their back to Me, ... and where are your gods, which you have made for yourself? Let them arise if they can save you in the time of your trouble ..."

Is it even conceivable that our holy fathers at the time of the Temple and the prophecy were fools, calling the tree and the stone, "Mother and Father"? Only fools who make others fools could think so about our fathers.

Rather, the tree is the tree of life, and the stone is the tree of knowledge. That is, what is revealed to a person, it is tested and tried that it is the counsel of the Creator, since through those tree and counsel he extends the light of the upper life, called "the tree of life." What is hidden from human concepts and tactics—and which is still doubtful whether it is a good tree or a bad one in the eyes of his Master, to be favored by Him—is called "the tree of knowledge of good and evil," or *Even* [stone], from the word *Avin* [I will understand], meaning I will observe and see if it is a good counsel or a bad one.

One who sits and regrets for a long time is also called *Meducha* [mortar/issue], as our sages implied, "Prophet Hagai sat on this *Meducha*." It is called *Meducha* because it is ready for the fools to grind and crush their bones there, as it is written, "If you pound a fool in a mortar with a pestle ... his foolishness will not depart from him."

We should ask, "How is the fool placed under the pestle in the mortar in fervent devotion, yet does not depart from his folly whatsoever?" Also, although he sees for himself that the fool is killed like moth, he will not depart from his filth? But the fool finds for himself a reason even while sitting inside the mortar, and seems to find contentment in it.

We need not be surprised at it, for it was said about such matters, "Do not judge your friend until you are in his shoes." This is why this god is called "gods of stone," or a "figured stone," for it does not reward its worshippers whatsoever, who worship it devotedly, and they have no one to save them in their time of trouble.

Opposite the gods of stone are those who worship the tree, who settle for the slight illumination they can salvage for themselves. As the hand of the Creator is too short to save them in their time of trouble, they do not move from the tree that they see because it seems to them that the landlord, too, cannot save his vessels from there because that tree is already tried and tested by them as the father of life. Thus, they forget, or pretend to forget that holiness is increasing, not decreasing.

This is a sign of sanctification and sanctity, as it is written, "Do not say, 'The first days were better than these,' for it is not from wisdom that you ask this," as those who serve another god are infertile and do not bear fruit, and wane and diminish like the fruit of the festival. They will die without wisdom, and are always feeling that "the first days were better than these."

This is what the prophet complained about them, for after all their days in the abovementioned foreign works, as the disgrace of a thief who has been found, "they say to a tree, 'You are my father.'" That is, as though saved from a fire, they delight in their lot, for that tree is to them like the father of life. "... and to a stone, 'You gave birth to me.'"

And once they have received their lot, the prophet compares them to people laid between the mortar and the pestle. The prophet asks further, "And where are your gods which you made for yourself? Let them arise, if they can save you in the time of your trouble." That is, "Think how much those gods have given you and how much they have saved you from your troubles."

He continues and asks about them saying, "According to the number of your cities are your gods, O Judah." That is, in each awakening, these invocators were stubborn and confident compared to the abovementioned sides—the tree or the stone. Finally, all the kings of the east and the west could not disrupt the works from you, and each city becomes Godly to you, like the word of God.

Do write me and clarify how much you understand of this long letter, and how much you do not. Specifically, detail at length all ten boundaries that I have depicted for you, and interpret for me more than I have written in it, for I have written succinctly.

And most of all, do not be ashamed to let me know all that you do not understand, and all your interpretations, for then I "will respond to the grain, to the wine and to the oil," and not one of your words shall be returned empty handed.

Yehuda

Letter No. 46

1927, London

To...

I received your letter and I was happy to see his handwriting, which was to me a sign of his good health. Concerning what was said, that he does not consider the rav a Kabbalist, as I think, I do not know who said and who suspected that that rav is a Kabbalist, so I think that the honorable rav thinks that I long for his approval to support my words of Torah. I have already written that I want it only in order to obtain the funds to print the books because I do not have the endorsement of a renowned person who is important in this place, as I have written there.

For this reason, I think that the honorable rav wishes to know more about me and to deliberate with me on that matter. In that, too, I am willing to comply, and I will reply to the best of my ability, especially since he retired from the trying that is mentioned there. For this reason, I am impartial on this matter and I am like a wise disciple who comes prior to the act, who is obeyed, and I will answer first things first.

1) What he wrote, that he does not see at this time anyone who is a Kabbalist, I wonder how one can sit in a certain place and see throughout the world, and especially, to see who is a Kabbalist. And yet it is true that I, too, have not seen a genuine

Kabbalist in my time, but I understand that Israel is not widowed and there is no generation without the likes of Abraham, Isaac, and Jacob. And besides, "We did not see" is no evidence.

2) What he informed me concerning a Kabbalist, as in, "Let a double portion of your spirit be upon me," who asked what he asked and what he replied. He explained that he asked to be a receiver and the received together, "And this is why he replied to him, 'If you see that I am receiving from you now that you are receiving from me.'" I admit that I do not understand the brevity of his words. It is similar to one who asks his friend for a gift, and he replies to him, "If you see that I am giving you a gift, then you will have the gift." This is not an answer whatsoever, much less that it does not require a twofold requisite, as written there.

3) "I saw in my teachers from ... and from ... that they had that degree," thus far his words. In my view, there is no doubt that one cannot see any degree in one's teachers, much less if he still has not been rewarded with it himself. Our sages said about the likes of that, "One does not understand his rav before he is forty," and even in one's friend it is impossible to see that which is not in his own domain. I wanted to hear the honorable rav's opinion about that.

Now I will toy a little with his words, concerning the receiver and the received as one. These words can be understood only literally, meaning that anyone who receives the abundance from the Creator boasts with the crowns of the Creator, and one who is rewarded with feeling during the act how the Creator, too, boasts about having found him ready to receive His giving is called "a Kabbalist." And this is certainly a high degree, as it is written, "I have found My servant, David; I have anointed him with My holy oil."

By the meaning of the words, "a double portion," I will explain, as in, "Let the wise," etc. It means as it is written,

"He cannot prefer the son of the loved one," etc., "He shall acknowledge him to give him a double portion." It is known from Rabbi Ber of Mezeritch that "a double portion" is the mouth in which that spirit that the fathers trusted was concealed, see in the *Idra*. I will interpret it below, and from that he will understand the above.

It is known that there are two righteous—a righteous who came into her, and a righteous who came out of her, as in, "As her soul went out," for which their *Zivug* [coupling] stopped. It is known in the *Zivugim* [pl. of *Zivug*] of ZON that in the future, their *Zivug* will be whole, and then she will be called "a double portion." This is why Elijah told him, "You ask a hard thing," implying to him how far it reaches. That is, "If you see me when I am taken from you," taken is in *Kubutz* [a punctuation mark], which means taken from you, meaning the opposite of what you thought thus far, that I was your master and that you were taken from me. Rather, I am taken from you, and then "It shall be so unto you" because then you will be rewarded with "a double portion." This is why Elisha did not have the strength to ask him about it anymore. (It is somewhat similar to what is written about the pious man [*Hassid*] who considered him his rav [teacher].)

But in the end he was rewarded with it, as it is written, "And Elisha sees and he cries, 'My father, my father, the *Merkava* [chariot/structure] of Israel and his horsemen.'" That is, he saw how all the lights that were included in his master, Elijah, where all are drawn and ignited from him, himself. This is why he found it very difficult, as it is written, "a hard thing." In other words, he could not tolerate it until he cried, "My father, my father," which is the double portion, where the bottom ZON are as the upper AVI.

This is why "he saw him no more," since he saw only himself. He was very stressed by that; hence, "he held his clothes and tore them into two tears." Explanation: The lights in general, "the *Merkava* [chariot/structure] of Israel and his horsemen," are implied in the words "his clothes," ... until he was rewarded, as it is written, "And he picked up Elijah's mantle that fell from him." This is the mantle ... which until now he regarded as lowly and externality, but now he understood, picked it up to its place, and then he was indeed rewarded with a double portion.

Henceforth he had the fall of Elijah's mantle as an example for raising *MAN*. This is the meaning of the words, "And he took ... which fell from him ... and said, 'Where is the Lord, God of Elijah, too?'" "Too" is the *Kli* [vessel] of *Nefesh* [soul, spirit, light of *Nefesh*], as it is written, "And He breathed into his nostrils the breath of life, and the man became a living soul." This is the fall of in between, as mentioned regarding the tearing of the clothes that was made to him, as in, "Too ... and Elisha went over." "And they said, 'The spirit of Elijah rests on Elisha,'" meaning all the degrees of Elijah, his master, were connected in Elisha.

By that we understand what is written in the ARI's *Assortments from the Torah*, that Elisha is an incarnation of Cain, of whom it is written, "and his offering He did not accept." Indeed, Elisha consists of the letters *Eli Sha'ah* [my God accepted], meaning as we said, "a double portion."

(the rest is missing)

Yehuda Leib

Letter No. 47

1927

To my dearest ... forever and ever:

I received your words today and there is one thing that I see in them: your great fear of my moving away from you even as a hairsbreadth.

It is inherent in people, and also gives permission ... to draw true abundance to the other side. And where the abundance of fear should affect you, to look into your own heart, always and forever—so as to not distance your heart from me as a hairsbreadth— you turn this fear on me, that my heart will not draw far from you. Thus, you are laboring to correct what is fixed, what was never broken, while the broken place remains broken and without attention. I know that these words, too, will be unclear to you and you will not understand where they are coming from, and at a time of joy you might think more, God forbid.

I do feel for you, my dear, to toss into your mouth a drop of truth, which is not obliged by any of the 613 organs of the human body. How many times have you learned it from me? And still, whenever I offer you a word of truth you fight me fiercely.

Indeed, so is the nature of spirituality: One who is adhered to the Creator feels himself as un-adhered. He worries and is insecure about it, and does all that he can do by his strength to be rewarded with *Dvekut* [adhesion]. A wise one feels opposite from one who is not attached to the Creator, who feels content and satisfied, and does not properly worry, except to keep the *Mitzvot* [commandments] of worry and longing, for "a fool does not feel." And just as one cannot teach one who is blind from birth the essence of absence of vision, except by giving him eyesight, so is this matter.

I have already written that you are wrong to say that I have journeyed from you. You should instead understand that you have journeyed from *me*. Believe me that my eyes and heart are always with you, without feeling a distance of place or time at all. Were it not required for the listener to know, you would be witnessing it.

But on the contrary, physical remoteness can act within you faster. And in truth, this is what I hoped, and do hope, if you understand further.

It is also true that I judge you favorably, assuming the air of Jerusalem while I am still before you, and especially during concealment from you. This is why I have established for you conducts by which you can still hang on and not turn back.

And the single most special one about them is the adhesion of friends. I sincerely promise that this love is able. And I shall remind you of every good thing that you need. And if you nonetheless braced yourselves in that, you would certainly go from strength to strength on the rungs of holiness, as I have promised earlier.

How can I forgive this to you: The ladder that is placed on the ground is empty; no one is climbing it, and instead of today you say, "tomorrow." You tell me, what will you gain from my forgiveness? Let me know and I will answer you.

I am not an issuer of decrees or a maker of laws, and this you, too, should know. Unless I feared sliding back, I would not go out of my way, for it was extremely difficult for me. But I am as one who regrets the loss of time ... but my soul suffers from it more than was anticipated, even in a standstill, much less when you, God forbid, fall back. This I saw ahead of time and wished to fix in advance.

Therefore, let me remind you the validity of love of friends in spite of everything at this time, for it is upon that that our right to exist depends, and upon that our near-to-come success is measured.

Hence, turn away from all the imaginary engagements and set your hearts on thinking thoughts and devising proper tactics to truly connect your hearts as one, so the words, "Love your friends as yourself," will literally come true in you, for a verse does not reach beyond the literal, and you will be cleaned by the thought of love that will be covering all transgressions. Test me in that, and begin to truly connect in love, and then you will see, "the palate will taste," and all the people will not separate between me and you.

And concerning your negligence in coming to the prayer, I know and feel your fate and sorrow. And unless I saw that the measure of loss does not decrease by the justness of the cause, I would not say a word.

Yehuda Leib

Letter No. 48

1927, London

To the students, may the Lord be upon you:

I received all your letters, and what ... wrote me about the humiliations and the papers about him, he should believe me that I share and fully sympathize with his pain and misery. He should know that I feel his pain more than he himself.

But the Creator will grant him doubly, and if he could brace himself and act the conduct of a servant of the Creator to say with honesty, "The Creator permitted all who afflict me," I would advise him to greatly strengthen himself in that, and it will help him in all his ways.

Concerning his questions whether he can show the letter and the words of Torah of the sage's fruit, "And you will be only joyful," he can certainly show it to all the friends.

In the letter of ... may his candle burn, I am glad to see that he has already begun to do what I want him to in this matter.

And what ... wrote, that he sees no other way but come to my house himself, I agree with him on that, and my thoughts are already occupied with preparing supplies for the way and to rush my arrival at my home as much as possible. I have much work to do regarding that, to stand up to all the preventions that rise against me to detain me here for longer.

He should ask my son ... why he has not informed me of the complete reconciliation that I learned about.

And thank ... for the information concerning the friends' party on the fifth of *Sukkot*, and concerning the whole issue between the friends, I have already written that we need not do much about it because with the Creator's help, He will finish for us, who have already begun for the glory of His name.

Yehuda Leib

Letter No. 49

1927, London

To the students, may the Lord be upon them:

While I trust you to keep your commitment to devotedly observe every utterance I utter in Torah and *Mitzvot*, I order you to begin to love one another as yourselves with all your might, to ache with the friends' pains, and rejoice in the friends' joys as much as possible. I hope that you will keep these words of mine and execute this matter to the fullest.

I received the letters and everything in them, but at the moment I cannot answer in person. And besides what I have already replied to each and every one in the previous letters, I promise to speak more elaborately.

Concerning the abovementioned order, I mean specifically among the friends, because it is written, "your friend." About people from the outside, it requires much scrutiny because there is more to lose than to gain due to their clinging to corporeality and self-importance, and among the friends this must never be accepted; be very careful.

Awaiting salvation for it is close...

Yehuda

Letter No. 50

1927, London

To the honorable students, may the Creator be upon you:

I received your letter from the portion, *Shoftim* [Judges], along with the novelties in the Torah of all except for ... and I do hope to receive his letter today.

It would be very good if you wrote your novelties in the work of the Creator, as well as your questions on the matter. And it makes no difference whether I answer you and comment, or I do not write and do not comment, because your very question is half the answer, while I bring before the Creator to answer you in due time. I am surprised that you still do not sufficiently understand it.

I do have one comment for you: When you write me novelties in the Torah, you do not understand at all if the ways of which you speak are already in your possession, or at least at your degree, meaning whether you can do them or they are still above your degree. Rather, wait for the Creator to grant the understanding how to do them. Likewise, you should be mindful to always interpret as a prayer to the Creator, so you are rewarded with the novelty you have attained or an intimation, as an apology for not being rewarded with it yet, and so forth.

The beginning of our longed for, pleasant future is approaching us, and so I crave and long for you to be next to me in body and in soul (meaning that you would draw near me, and not me to you, which is impossible, as well as pointless).

I must also apologize that last *Tishrey* [first Hebrew month] was a very favorable time but you were not near me then. I looked for ... all through that month but he was nowhere in my area, and I only saw one or two of you. Naturally, I was sorry about that all through last year.

The reason for it is the pride and self-importance that have snuck into you, and to that extent the hatred between you (due to it) in clinging to materialistic friends who are not from our society. ... Clearly, if you hate one of the members of the group, it is a clear sign that you are not in complete love with me, as well.

And although the evil inclination shows you that friend's bed, meaning that his actions are bad and sinful toward the Creator, you should have prayed and trusted the Creator for his sake, that He will certainly help him because he is my student.

And if you already understand about that friend that the Creator cannot help him, and that my prayers also cannot help him in a time of need, then the judgment reflects back on the hater. From now on, come and see, and pay attention that you do not fall into that trap any more.

... You also need not notice at all if I actually, verbally expel a friend ... judge him favorably, in truth.

Let me tell you the truth: In my departure there is greater unity than in my nearing. Like any craftsman who is toiling in his craft to complete his work in the best way, a stranger must not look at him in the middle of his work because he will not understand his conduct in his work, except for a craftsman as great as he.

I have elaborated on that so you may know that your soul depends on it.

Although I do not tend to offer private guidance, I must still comment on what I have already warned you several times: No one should share the "novelties in the Torah" that he attained, nor should he "admonish" whatsoever. Even the desire for it is a terrible flaw.

The exception is what I have permitted while I am away—to share novelties in the Torah with one another from what I have *already said*, as accurately as can be explained, but very precisely, without any additions of one's own.

Also, you must not speak of the words of Torah that I said, and which that friend has not heard from my mouth. He should be educated attentively and wisely.

I find it necessary to warn about the above because I feel that you have already stretched the line that you have given to yourselves. Know for certain that by this keeping you will be granted with saying novelties in the Torah before the Creator, and to admonish yourselves. But one who scatters his qualities in those will not be established in the eyes of the Creator. In that matter, an ounce is as much as a pound, and the Creator will help you and guide you to the doors of truth.

Yehuda Leib

Letter No. 51

1927, London

To the faithful soul mates:

Because the time of our celebration is approaching, I hereby point to it.

It is written, "And you will be completely joyful." The grammar feels as though it should have said, "And you will be glad." But this is what I have explained several times, that the whole difficulty in worshipping Him is that in the worshipper, there are always two opposites in the same subject, that His uniqueness is simple, but must clothe in man's body, which consists of a body and a soul, which are two opposites.

Therefore, in any spiritual concept that one attains, two opposite forms are immediately created in him—one form on the part of the body, and one form on the part of the soul. By nature, a person cannot scrutinize the body and the soul as two subjects. Rather, he is composed by the Creator as one, meaning as one subject.

It is similar to the tying of Isaac, when the Creator said to Abraham, "For in Isaac shall a seed be called to you," and the Creator said to him, "And offer him there for a burnt-offering." From the perspective of the Creator, it is as was written, "I the

Lord do not change." But in the perception of the receiver, they are opposites.

This is why it is written, "And you will be completely joyful," for "'but' and 'only' are diminutions," and the joy of the festival certainly requires wholeness. However, both must be perceived by the receiver as they are for the joy of the festival.

It is also written, "Who is blind but My servant, or deaf as My messenger whom I send?" And it is also written, "The deaf heard, and the blind looked, so as to see." There are many others likewise, meaning as our sages said, "You, too, prick up your ears," as though he was never at the court of hearing, the sentence of choice, to find out who is indebted and who is acquitted, for both are the words of the living God. That is, it is written, "I the Lord do not change," as from His perspective there is but one form here.

This is the meaning of the *Mitzva* [commandment], "Sit," as in "dwell," meaning as King David asked, "that I may dwell in the house of the Lord all the days of my life, to behold the pleasantness of the Lord." The "House of the Lord" is the holy Divinity, as in, "The righteous sit with their crowns on their heads." When they are granted the most, then You are to him like a home, constant and eternal.

The Creator wished to say to His servants, "Go out of the permanent housing and sit in temporary housing," meaning only under His shade. This is the meaning of a "light *Mitzva*," the *Mitzva* of the *Sukkah* [hut], where a person sits under the shade of the waste of barn and winery, which is the actual shade of the Creator. And although they contradict one another—for in corporeal eyes and in corporeal hands we see and feel that the shade comes from the waste, in truth it is the Creator Himself. However, from the perspective of the receiver, it is necessary that those two opposite forms will be depicted in him.

The thing is that before the complex man was created, there was no waste here. But once man was created and the waste and the judgment were felt, the quarrel began in his organs. It is as our sages said, "The hay, the straw, and the chaff are discussing with one another. One says, 'The field was sown for me,' and one says, 'The field was sown for me,' etc. When it is time for the harvest, everyone knows for whom the field was sown." All these quarrels and deliberations continued through the terrible days because three books were opened because of them: righteous, wicked, and intermediate.

Once those who were acquitted in the judgment were sorted out and whitened as wheat through the Day of Atonement, and the wicked went promptly to death, as "chaff that is blown away by the wind," for everyone knows for whom the field was sown, we arrive at the commandment, "Go out of the permanent housing and sit in temporary housing." That is, know that it is only temporary housing, and "the banished one will not be cast out from him." It is as was said, "Even if the whole world tells you that you are righteous, be wicked in your own eyes." This is also the meaning of the words, "And you will be completely joyful."

This is why the festival of harvest [*Sukkot*] is called "the time of our joy," to tell you that one should sit in the shade of a *Sukkah* in great joy, just as in the king's house, the kingdom's most eminent. "Sit" is as "dwell," without any difference whatsoever.

And yet, he should know that he is sitting in the shade of a *Sukkah*, meaning the waste of barn and winery. However, "Under His shade I delighted to sit," since he hears His word, "Go out of the permanent housing and sit in temporary housing," and both are words of the living God. Then his exit delights him as much as his entrance, as it is precisely the abovementioned, "The deaf heard, and the blind looked, so as to see."

Otherwise, there would not even be a shadow of a *Sukkah*, for it is not toward us, those who scrape the walls as blind, sitting under the shade of a shade, meaning twofold darkness. It was said about them, "shall inherit locust," two words [locust is a translation of *Tzaltzal=Tzel Tzel* (shade, shade)], since their thatch is still fit for reception of impurity like one who puts thatch in pegs, which have no *Rosh* [head], or in broken vessels, where there is still waste, since they are still in a state of *Tohu* and the breaking of the vessels.

By that you will see that one cannot keep the *Mitzva* of *Sukkah* before he has been rewarded the degree of unification, *HaVaYaH ADNI*, which is the meaning of "The sun in her sheath."

It was also said explicitly regarding the nations of the world: "In the future, when the Creator brings out the sun from its sheath, and each one kicks his *Sukkah* and leaves, and it crumbles, Israel too?" They explained, "Kick, they do not kick." It is explained that if a person is not rewarded with a sun in its sheath, he cannot keep the *Mitzva* of *Sukkah* altogether. This is the meaning of *HaVaYaH ADNI* being 91 in *Gematria*, implying "Go out of the permanent housing."

This is the meaning of "Stay with me one more day," as in the small meal of the *Atzeret* [assembly on the eighth day], meaning that thanks to the complete joy of the festival, as in, "completely joyful"—accepting the two opposites in the same subject and not revoking one before the other—one is rewarded with the eighth day. This is the meaning of "Stay with me one more day," the day of which it is written, "a day which shall be known as the Lord's, neither day nor night, and it shall come to pass that in the evening there will be light."

Explanation: A day is the works of the righteous, and a night is the works of the wicked, as it is written in *Midrash Rabah* regarding "And God said, 'Let there be light'": "I still do not know which has the Lord chosen—the works of the righteous or the works of the wicked, when it says, 'And God called the light 'day," to teach you that He chose the works of the righteous."

Therefore, at the end of correction, as in, "The banished one will not be cast out from him," it is written, "a day which shall be known as the Lord's, neither day nor night," meaning the abovementioned choice. But in the evening, which pertains to the waste of barn and winery, "there will be light," and all thanks to the delay on the eighth day.

This is why it is called "the festival of the *Atzeret*," as though *Otzrin* [gathering] the oil from the olive, meaning "oil squashing," which is the essence ... of all the servitude of "only" a day, and it is crushed in a crusher. "Truth shall spring out from the earth," "And the Lord shall be king over all the earth," for it will be entirely for the Creator because "only" is part—half permitted and half forbidden, "half of it for you, and half of it for the Lord." But in the eighth day, the *Atzeret*, it becomes entirely for the Creator.

Yehuda Leib

Letter No. 52

1928, London

To ... may his candle burn:

I received your letter and the note. ...interpreted for me the verse, "Seek the Lord while He is found; call upon Him while He is near." This is perplexing. If the Creator is already with him, and He is already close, why is there still a need to seek and call upon Him? He explained that the writing speaks to those who have already been rewarded with constant closeness to the Creator. The prophet warns them that although it seems to them that there is nothing more to seek or to obtain, we should never think like that, for it is like cutting down the plantings. Rather, one should seek further and call upon the Creator for greater attainments.

Let me interpret this according to our way. Clearly, anyone who is been rewarded with his Maker's fondness, the Creator grants all his wishes, as do lovers and friends who complement each other's wants, each according to the ability. And because that person has been rewarded with befriending the Creator, he necessarily consists of body and soul. Therefore, he is not ... for them room to display them before the Creator.

Still, "Love covers all transgressions," and especially before Him there are no obscenities or transgressions, as it is written, "No filth will defile You; a fire that consumes fire will not burn

271

You" (see, "Poem of Unification"). Therefore, through the genuine love between him and the Creator, it is inevitable that man will also reveal bodily desires before Him.

Clearly, the Creator will not fail in fulfilling His loved one's every wish, both proper and improper, since the Creator's capability is tied to His will. But once the Creator has satisfied his desire, that person himself seemingly regrets the excessive wishes he presented before the Creator, and we learned that from above there is giving and not taking, since the Creator has already sanctified him.

It therefore follows that the person must mend the abovementioned wrong, in two: 1) that he insulted the Creator's honor by presenting bodily wishes before the king, 2) that he was not cautious in appreciating the gift of the King of all Kings, whether great or small.

This is so because there are two values to each gift. The first value is the gift—whether it is great or small. The second value is the giver—whether he is important or unimportant.

Naturally, when an important person gives even a small thing, the gift has great value, according to the importance of the giver. It is as our sages said ... to be in the king's palace, and must come out to be corrected. And once he goes outside, he loses all the attainments he has already been rewarded with attaining because the Creator's gifts are united in "world, year, soul." That is, there must be a chosen "soul," a chosen "time," and a chosen "place." And since he has changed his location, his year and soul change, too, and then a person is in great bewilderment.

The prophet warns about that: "Seek the Lord while He is found," meaning return and continue to attain all the matters of spirituality that he attained, for in matters that concern the soul, the Creator is found for all. It is written about that: when

He is found, "Call upon Him when He is near," being the bodily matters, which he has already attained because He is near.

The prophet warns that here it is forbidden to ask because it is an insult to the king to come to Him with bodily wishes. Rather, one must "call" Him only "by that name." That is, when he presents his prayer before the Creator, one must mention all His benefits, which He has done for him before with benevolence, satisfying bodily wishes for him, so it is a given that He will satisfy the matters of the soul for him now.

This is the meaning of the words of our sages: "The heaven between me and you will make a way for a plea." The words are profound. In these words, the rest of the *Haftarah* [final part of each Torah portion] is explained—that the foreigner concerns bodily matters, and the eunuch concerns matters of the soul, and the bright ones will understand.

The above interpretation is immensely profound; who will understand it? Therefore, I will explain by way of "seventy faces to the Torah": When a person introspects and feels his poor state, he awakens to return to the Creator and pours out his prayer in great longing to cling to the Creator. He thinks that all those prayers and all that awakening are his own powers, and sits and expects the Creator's salvation, whether small or great. When time passes and he sees no sign of welcome from the Creator, he falls into despair because the Creator does not want him, since after all this longing, He did not turn to him at all.

It is written about that: "Seek the Lord while He is found," when the Creator presents Himself to you for asking. Then you will necessarily seek Him, too, for it is man's way to move first. In other words, the Creator first gives you the heart to seek Him. When you know this, you will certainly grow stronger, as strong as you can ask, for the king is calling you.

So it says, "Call upon Him when He is near." That is, when you call on the Creator to bring you closer to Him, know that He is already near you, for otherwise there is no doubt you would not be calling Him. This is also the meaning of the verse, "Before they call, I will answer," meaning that if you are calling Him, then He has already turned to you to give you the awakening to call upon Him.

"While they speak, I listen," meaning the measure of the Creator's listening depends precisely on the measure of the longing that appears during the saying of the prayer. When one feels excessive longing, he should know at that time that the Creator is listening to him attentively.

Clearly, when he knows that, he pours his heart out even stronger, for there is no greater privilege than the King of the world being attentive to him. This is quite similar to what our sages said: "The Creator longs for the prayer of righteous" because the Creator's desire for a person to draw near Him awakens great power and longing in the person to crave for the Creator, for "As in water of the face to the face, so the heart of man to man."

It follows that the saying of the prayer and the hearing of the prayer go hand in hand until they accumulate to the full measure and he acquires everything. This is the meaning of "spirit draws spirit, and brings spirit." Note these words, for they are the first foundations in the ways of the Creator.

You wrote and asked that I would accept you as a student. You also suspected that I am displeased with you because I already have enough students. But to tell you the truth, it is harder for me with you than with others, as you are of a more eminent lineage. You must have heard that Rabbi Elimelech refused any students with eminent lineages, and the rav of Rufshitz pleaded with him and cried bitterly, but to no avail, until all scent of eminence has faded from him. This is what he said to him: "Why is it my fault that my father is so eminent?" Once he recognized the sincerity of his words, he accepted him.

Do not be surprised that in the eyes of landlords, it seems that the eminent one is closer to the Creator than an ordinary person, as he sees and observes the good deeds of his father from his youth, and the childhood rearing is set more firmly in the heart.

The thing is that in each and every movement in His work there are two opposites in the same subject, as I have elaborated in previous letters, as the receiver consists of body and soul, which are opposites. Therefore, in each attainment, great or small, He makes two opposite forms.

There are two concepts in the work of the Creator: 1) "prayer and plea," 2) "praise and thanksgiving." Naturally, both must be at their highest. To complete the prayer, a person must feel the Creator's closeness to him as mandatory, like an organ that is hanging loosely, for then he can complain and pour out his heart before Him.

But opposite that, regarding the complete praise and thanksgiving, a person must feel the Creator's closeness to him as an addition, a supplement, as something that does not belong to him at all, for "What is man that You should know him, the son of man that You should think of him?" Then he can certainly give praise and thanksgiving to His great name in wholeness for choosing him from among all those who are standing ready to serve the Creator.

It is great work for the complex man to be completed in both those opposites, so they are set in his heart forever at once. The second discernment, to feel himself lowly and far, and the kindness of the Creator as a supplement, is a far harder concept than the first. For the most part, all those who are rejected fail only in the second concept.

By that you know that the one of eminent lineage is farther from the second concept than an ordinary person because he feels the Creator's kindness toward him as mandatory.

Nonetheless, I have no such suspicion because I have already enslaved myself to the Creator, to serve Him in any way I can. No work is too heavy for me to do for His great name. On the contrary, I always love and relish at great exertions that bring Him contentment, and the evidence is that I chose the land of Israel as my workplace, where the ruling of the *SAM* is the greatest. And not only that, but in *Jerusalem*, where even the holy ARI was afraid to open his seminary. ... I also collected into my seminary all the eminent ones from Jerusalem ... by which you can know that I am not avoiding work. Thus, everything depends only on you; always remember that.

Time is short, and the good day is approaching, so I cannot elaborate for you on that. But if you believe me, you will also be rewarded with understanding me.

Yehuda Leib

Letter No. 53

To my soul mate ... may his candle burn:

... Indeed, you have caused me much work concerning the separation and hatred that has been sown and grown among you to an extent that I did not foresee. Each of the students, may they live forever, is like an organ in my own body, and behold, there is no peace among my bones due to my sin. Therefore, I must begin to cleanse myself like a newborn baby until I merit making peace between the students, may they live forever.

In truth, prior to my departure from my home, I hoped that I would be rewarded with seeing all the kids [young goats] as grownup goats in my return, for which I have taken upon myself these man's jolts and huge troubles, which I had never experienced previously, nor even something near it. Because of it, I truly have been rewarded with great and wonderful salvation for all of you, and the doors of heaven have been opened over us.

However, the separation and the hatred, whose only root is in the *Klipot* [shells/peels] and the yeast of the *Klipot*, have been against us, obstructing our ways because through there, the *Klipot* have found a way to sneak into the bodies and twist the holy channels.

I need not interpret for you the measure of longing and sorrow that you have caused me by that. I openly admit that until now I did not understand the ARI, who so regretted the dispute that occurred within his group until the manuscript came through. Now I see that there is none so wise as the experienced. And yet, I hope to mend everything upon my return home.

The prophet asks and answers, "What does the Lord require of you? Only to do justice, to love mercy, and to walk humbly with your God." These words are very profound, and who will find them?

It is brought in *The Zohar*: "The Creator has three worlds, and this is the meaning of 'Holy! Holy! Holy!' concerning the abovementioned three worlds. And in each one, the whole earth is full of His glory." Interpretation is according to the words, "Justice and law are the foundation of Your throne." It is also written, "Open for me the gates of justice," and it is known that justice becomes Godliness to you, such as a word of Godliness, etc.

Yehuda Leib

Letter No. 54

To my soul mate, may his candle burn:

Today I received your letter with all the adventures that happened to you, and what you wrote from the night of fourth of [the Torah portion] *VaYechi* [Jacob Lived]: "If the light had surrounded your entire body you would have been saved from all your troubles."

It seems that you have not fully grasped what I said to you before your journey: "There is no other salvation but the attainment of the Torah." The whole *Merkava* [chariot/structure] of the *Sitra Achra* is only to fool people in other business, to deny this truth from them. This is the meaning of the exile in Egypt in mortar and bricks, and the boasting of their king, "My Nile is mine and I have made it."

See what is written in that portion: "This shall be the sign to you that I have sent you: When you have brought the people out of Egypt, you shall worship God on this mountain." That is, when the Creator wished to verify for him the sacred situation with which he has been rewarded then (as explained in the writings), He verified it with that sign, that he doubtlessly be once again rewarded with the reception of the Torah in that place.

Understand that thoroughly: Even though the face of the Creator appeared to Moses in complete clarity, so much so that he was afraid to look at God, he still needed the guarantee of the Torah, for otherwise the Creator would certainly not make him look.

It is written, "Seek the Lord while He is found, call upon Him while He is near." "Seek the Lord while He is found" means where He is present, and you will not fail with the *Sitra Achra*, who always deflects a person to seek Him where He is not present. Thus, one scatters one's labor in vain. Hence the prophet warns, "Seek the Lord where He is found," meaning in a place of Torah, and not in a place where there is no Torah, for He is not present there at all.

He also says, "Call upon Him while He is near." When the Creator shows you a bright face, it is the time to call Him—to contemplate and reflect on the secrets and the reasons [also flavors] of Torah, which is the reading—perhaps the Creator will open man's heart to be rewarded with the blessing of the Torah.

This is the meaning of "The Creator, the Torah, and Israel are one." By that you can also observe the need that the Creator had at the event of the first prophecy to Moses to pledge to him with this sign of acceptance of the Torah.

This is the meaning of the words, "Who will ascend into the mountain of the Lord, and who will stand in His holy place? He who has clean hands and a pure heart, who has not lifted up his soul to falsehood and has not sworn deceitfully."

It is said that prior to a person's exit from the mother's womb, he is sworn: "Even if the whole world tells you that you are righteous, be as wicked in your eyes." This matter requires explanation: Our sages have already said, "Do not be wicked in your own eyes," much less when the whole world testifies that he is righteous, should he regard himself as wicked? I wonder. We should also understand the words, "Be as wicked in your eyes," which implies that in his own heart he can know the truth—that he is righteous.

The thing is that there are two works: one is in the heart, and one is in the mind. That is, to turn the vessels of reception in both of them to being in order to bestow. At the time and moment when a person purifies the vessels of reception of the heart, he immediately becomes worthy of His light, which pours out incessantly. That light is called *Nefesh* [soul], after the disclosure of the *Nefisha* [rest] in all the organs.

This is the meaning of the words, "Who will ascend into the mountain of the Lord, and who will stand ...?" meaning gain an eternal level and will not fall again. It is precisely "He ... who has not lifted up his soul." In other words, once the Creator has turned to him and brought him a little closer, he needs to strengthen himself immensely and take that light for the scrutiny of Torah, to find its secrets and increase his knowledge of the Creator. This is the meaning of raising the eyes of the holy Divinity, as it is written, "A bride whose eyes are beautiful, the rest of her body does not require examination."

And if a person does not mind raising the eyes then he carries the light of *Nefesh* futilely. Even worse, he swears deceitfully because at the time of birth, he was sworn, "Even if the whole world tells you that you are righteous." That is, even if he is rewarded with the light of *Nefesh*, where all the organs and tendons of his small world feel that he is a complete righteous, placed in the Garden of Eden, he still must not believe it whatsoever until he raises up the eyes of *Kedusha* [holiness].

This is the meaning of "Who will ascend" and "Who will stand"—precisely "He who has clean hands," who has been rewarded with cleaning both his forms of reception—of mind and of heart. "And a pure heart" means that he has already been rewarded with attaining the flavors [also "reasons"] of Torah and all its secrets, as it is written, "And you will know this day and reply to your heart that the Lord, He is the God … there is none else."

"Who has not lifted up his soul to falsehood" means that he understood how to work and use the light of *Nefesh* that the Creator illuminated for him, "And has not sworn deceitfully," but raised the eyes, as said above. Delve deeply into all that is said here for it is a true and sincere counsel to avoid being trapped by the counsel of the *Sitra Achra*, who always fools into seeking the Creator where He is not found. Hence, each day one should remind oneself of that.

But what can I do for you if you do not appreciate my words properly, and therefore scatter your energy futilely? I wish you would hear me from now on because my words are always in "neither add nor subtract," and are therefore still standing and waiting for a listening heart.

My words are being said in due time because the abovementioned precise work is very capable in these days, which are called in the books, "*Tikkun Shovavim TaT* [correction of the naughty, *Tav-Tav* (acronym)]."

Let me disclose to you that the books offer only intimations that are completely abstruse to the masses. Indeed, they marked *Shovavim TaT* as an acronym for *Talmud Torah* [Torah study], and there is no other correction but *TaT*, and "One who does not know the commandment of the Upper One, how will he serve Him?"

The thing is that the upper light that approaches a person to direct him toward revival is called *Nefesh*, due to the reception of *Nefisha* [rest] in the organs, each according to its measure in its time. However, it cannot exist without *Ruach* [spirit], meaning attainment of the Torah.

This is why that person is called "naughty," like a little boy who places both hands in a bag full of money, jumping and dancing about, not knowing what to do with the money because he does not know the shape of the money or how to negotiate. It turns out that one who gives a gift of a bag of money to a little boy does not do him any good. On the contrary, he makes him naughty and drives him crazy.

This is the meaning of the words, "He will make my soul naughty." In other words, if the Creator does not give the *Ruach*, but only the *Nefesh*, He makes a person naughty and crazy. However, from *Lo Lishma* [not for the Torah] one comes to *Lishma* [for the Torah], meaning as he ends, "for His name," meaning that through that he will be rewarded with *Lishma*.

This is why he said, "Return, oh naughty boys," meaning those who have not yet been granted with *Ruach*. This is the meaning of attainment of the Torah. Also, as I spoke to you prior to your journey, this is the meaning of the *Klipa* [shell] of Pharaoh, king of Egypt, which was such a hard *Klipa* that no slave could escape Egypt because of the lights that they had to give to all those who fell into their hands, until they could not retire from them.

It is as is written, "My Nile is mine and I have made it," as I interpreted for you while you were still here ... This is why the enslavement in the [Torah] portion, *Shemot* [Exodus] begins with the exile in Egypt, and does not end before the portion *Yitro* [Jethro], at the time of the reception of the Torah, as in, "This shall be the sign to you that I have sent you: when you have brought the people out of Egypt, you shall worship God on this mountain," as I have explained above.

Therefore, it is very possible for any person who wishes to complete what is desired of him, for in these sequences— *Shovavim, Teruma* [donation/contribution], *Tetzaveh* [command (verb, imperative form)]—he will examine his works and correct his ways for the reception of Torah. ... He will gather all the sparks of light of his soul that were captured by the *Klipa* of Egypt into a place of Torah with great longing and yearning. Through studying with the external mind, as in, "Whatever you find that you are able to do by your hand, that do," we will be rewarded with our hearts' opening in His law and the depths of His secrets, and we will be granted the reception of Torah as explained in the portion, *Yitro*. The rest of the sequences, *Mishpatim* [ordinances], *Teruma* [donation/contribution], *Tetzaveh* [command] are the teaching from the making of the calf and the breaking of the tablets.

The *Tikkun Shovavim* is implied in the books in relation to ejaculation in vain, called "night ejaculation." However, they are the same issue, as I have explained that one who did not purify the vessels of reception of the heart, the vessels of reception of the mind are necessarily filthy, too, and his faith is flawed because he cannot believe what his eyes do not see.

Just so, one whose vessels of reception of the heart are flawed necessarily contemplates once a day or so, and will come to night ejaculation.

At the same time, it is necessary that he will come by a thought of heresy, called "a bag of ejaculation," since the vessels of reception of the heart and the vessels of reception of the mind go hand in hand, and then "The righteousness of the righteous will not save him on the day of his transgression."

It follows that all the lights that he received fall into the hands of the *Sitra Achra*, and delve in it, for I have been brief. All this continues until one is rewarded with extending *Ruach* along with the *Nefesh*, meaning reception of the Torah.

I cannot continue with this any longer, and it is time that you will take my words to heart. Perhaps the Creator will resolve to pour upon us spirit from on high until the will of the Creator succeeds by you ...

Yehuda Leib

Letter No. 55

1932, Jerusalem

To my dearest ...

Today I received your letter with the news about the sons, may the Creator give the blessing.

By and large, I had some contentment with that letter. Although you did not altogether refrain from giving bodily matters the lead here, too, there is still much of the point in the writing, as you yourself wrote.

As for your saying that I am angry or concerned about you for not writing me anything for two years now, it is how you feel. My reply is that although this feeling is not generally disappointing, it is disappointing in its form, as the Creator knows that nothing bad can come to me from those who perceive the body. As then, so now, I am the same: "Woe to this beauty that withered in this dust," and from here are all my joys and sorrows.

Following this introduction, I will grant your wish. You wrote, "I ask very much that you will write me some novelties in the Torah."

We should carefully consider the words of our sages, whose every word is like embers. They said, "An hour of repentance and good deeds in this world is better than all the life of the next world, and an hour of contentment in the next world is better than all the life of this world." It seems as though the beginning and the end contradict one another, for once they determined that an hour of the next world is better than all the life of this world, they must be meaning the *spiritual* life in this world, meaning repentance and good deeds. After all, we cannot suspect that the Mishnah speaks of a life of perceived pleasure, as it is for the wicked, the fools, and the insensitive.

Our sages have already instructed us: "The wicked, in their lives, are called 'dead.'" That is, the form of life that the wicked can resemble, that form is death itself, the opposite of life and happiness. Thus, the death that the wicked perceives, being the absence of the perceived pleasure, is a false perception, since absence of bodily pleasure is not the opposite of life, to merit being defined as death.

Rather, the presence of bodily pleasures, which the wicked received and with which they rejoice, are woven for them into an iron partition that separates them from the life of lives, and they sink in the world of death, as it is written, "He is Satan; he is the evil inclination; he is the angel of death."

Accordingly, it is evident that the words of the Mishnah, "the life of this world," indicate the *spiritual* life in this world, for the words of the wise heal and they will not speak falsehood.

It was of this that they said, "An hour of contentment in this world is better." Thus, why did they add, "An hour of repentance and good deeds in this world is better than all the life of the next world"? We mustn't forcefully divide that repentance and good deeds require labor and patience, for which they are separate from the life of this world. This is why they first said, "An hour of contentment of this world" is better than it.

However, labor and exertion that are devoid of pleasure are better than the spiritual pleasure in this world, for it is even higher than all the life of the next world. However, such words are acceptable only among those with little knowledge. They will never be accepted by the wise. Our sages have already determined for us in the holy *Zohar*: "Where there is labor, there is the *Sitra Achra*, for the *Sitra Achra* is in deficiency," as are all who follow her. But regarding sanctity, there is wholeness there, and all who work in holiness are in wholeness, without any effort, and only in delights and happiness.

Before we delve into the heart of their words, I will thoroughly define for you the meaning of these words—"this world," "the next [world]"—in the words of our sages. It is as is presented in *The Zohar* in the title, *Sefer HaBahir* [*The Book of the Bright One*]: "Rabbi Rechimai was asked, 'What is the next world, and what is to come?' He replied to them, 'In the next world and came.'" In other words, the abundance is still to come.

You can evidently see the difference between this world and the next world. This one is what we attain in the present, or attained in the past. The next world, however, is what we have not attained, but which should come to us in the future, after some time. However, both speak of what *one attains and receives in this world*, since the meaning of the anticipated reward of the soul is presented in the abovementioned *Zohar*, defined only in the words, "in the future."

In other words, prior to the correction, people in this world are utterly unfit to receive it, but only the souls, which are devoid of bodies, or after the end of correction, when this world rises in the great merit of the world of *Atzilut*. Yet, we needn't elaborate on it for now.

It is said, "Initially, our fathers were idol-worshippers. Now the Creator has brought us closer to His work, Terach, Abraham's father." We must understand the intention of the sayer with this reference to Terach, Abraham's father. Is it to remind us of the best of times, the time of our freedom?

But we find such as this in the holy Torah, as well, as it is written, "And Terach died in Haran. And the Lord said unto Abram, 'Go forth from your country,' etc." This proximity is perplexing and bewildering, for the first appearance of the Creator to the first father, who is the root and the kernel of Israel as a whole, and the entire correction, containing all the hoped for abundance and happiness to be revealed to us, and the abundance in the worlds to all the righteous and the prophets from beginning to end.

It is so because the law in sanctity and spirituality is that the root contains within it all the offspring that come and appear because of it, as it was said about *Adam HaRishon* that he included all the souls that would appear in the world. Likewise, the firstborn includes all the children born afterward, as is known in the books.

Thus, there should have been secession in several writings between Terah's name and the first appearance of Abraham, for he is the root of everything, as said above.

Here I must explain the basis of idolatry. It is as the books write about the verse, "There shall be no foreign god within you." It means that the Creator should not be to you like a stranger, since working for a stranger is a burden. This is why it is idol-worship. [The literal translation of idol-worship is "foreign (strange) work."] Rather, worshipping the Creator should be with love and joy, and then its place is in holiness, and not otherwise.

It is also said in the name of the Baal Shem Tov, "You shall have no other gods over Me," for one who believes that there are other forces (over Me) besides the force of the Creator, who is called *Elokim* [God], is idol-worshipping, and this is profound.

It is so because a worshipper of the Creator does not need any change in the corporeal set up. It is beautifully and wondrously arranged, as written in the "Poem of Unification," "You forgot none of Your wishes, nor missed a thing. You did not subtract, and You did not add, and You did not work in them in vain."

The corporeal setup is arranged in such a way that all the people of the world will unite and be qualified for His work, as it is written, "All of the Lord's works are for His sake." This is the meaning of "There has never been joy before Him as the day when heaven and earth were created." It is also written, "And God saw all that He had done, and it was very good."

However, it is arranged in a manner suitable for such work, suitable for the wonderful reward, which "Neither has the eye seen a God besides You." This is the meaning of the work and the reward that are set up before us in this world, in corporeality.

We see here that any reward is according to the pain that the worker feels during the work. But the concept of labor and suffering that appear during the work is valued and measured according to the postponement of the payment from the time of the labor, for it is natural that the payment puts out and uproots the suffering from the labor. That is, it is not perceived as sorrow, not even a bit.

Think for yourself: If you swap a cow for an ass, then you've received the contentment you feel with the ass, completely equal to the cow. At the very least, it is not less than that, or you would not swap it with the ass.

Likewise, if the owner paid the worshipper such payments and rewards that were not satisfactory for him, at least as much as before he worked, it is certain that he would not swap his work with the reward. After all, the worker's intention is to gain and receive contentment through the swap, and not increase his sadness even more; this is clear and simple.

Indeed, there are exceptions, but this refers to the majority of people, for the real price of labor is true only in the majority of people, not in specific individuals.

But for all the above-said, common sense denies that at the end of the day, it seems that the body will not make rational calculations, and that it feels the work more or less as debt, and the payment does not put out the present fiery pain of labor.

But in truth, the calculation is correct, for the body does not enjoy or suffer from the future, but from *the present*. Therefore, if the owner paid the worker his due in the present, meaning moment by moment, where for every feeling he would pay him a penny, there is no doubt that he would not feel his effort whatsoever, as the payments would put out and uproot the pain.

But the owner will not do so. Rather, he pays his payments and the reward at the end of the work, after a day, a week, or a month. This is why the animal body, which does not enjoy or suffer from the future, will pain and worry, as it truly loses all its labor for the animal sensation.

It follows that the body that receives the payments did not work at all, and the body that worked did not receive a thing for it. This is why it is separated, for it enjoys only the present moment, and the sensation of the future feels for it like a foreign body.

Come and see: The merchant, owner of the shop, who really does receive his pay in the present, meaning for each minute that he troubles himself and suffers while serving the customers, really does not feel his effort whatsoever. On the contrary, he is delighted during the pay. The labor, which is tied to the pay, is uprooted for him. He is not like the worker who receives his pay in the evening, and feels unhappiness and sorrow during this work.

This is what I said, that any sense of pain and suffering in reality is only for the removal of the payment from the time of the work. Also, if you scrutinize further you will find that according to the time-gap between them, so the pain increases during the work, as accurately equal as two drops of water.

With the above said, we understand the two names, "righteous" and "wicked," for one does not go idle in this world; we necessarily have some sense of the reason for our being in the world—for blessing or, God forbid, for cursing. That is, the blessing we are commanded to bless the Creator is done by itself.

Likewise, a rich person who gives a gift to a poor one knows for certain that the poor person blesses him for it. He does not need to lend his ear to what he utters from his mouth. But if a person strikes and curses another, he knows for certain that the other one is cursing him; he does not need to think about it.

Just so, one who enjoys being in the Creator's world, at that time he is blessing his Maker, who has created him in order to delight him. He hardly needs to utter anything.

Conversely, when a person feels some pain while in the Creator's world, at that time he does the opposite. And although he does not utter any condemnable words from his mouth, still, *the feeling rules.* This is the title, "wicked," for when he feels some pain, he necessarily condemns, as the grievance is expressed in the feeling itself, and need not be shown publicly.

Even if he utters a blessing, it is akin to blarney, like a landlord who is beating his servant while the servant is saying, "I so enjoy the beating; I am simply overjoyed." It was said about the such, "He who speaks falsehood shall not be established."

By these words you will also understand the definition of the title, "righteous." It refers to a person who is in the world of the Creator, yet always receives good and pleasant sensations, and is in constant pleasure. For this reason, he always blesses the Creator, who created him in order to furnish him with such a good and delightful world. He, too, certainly does not need to explicitly utter the words, for the feelings themselves are the blessings that he blesses the Creator, as explained in the above allegory. This is why he is called "righteous" [also "just"], for he justifies Creation and feels it as it truly is, as it is written, "And God saw all that He had done, and behold, it was very good."

This is the meaning of "A righteous lives by his faith." It comes to teach us the power of the righteous, for it seems to be incomprehensible for a common person because how can a person be in this world yet be spared pain and suffering? Even more perplexing, he is in constant pleasure. It seems to contradict reason.

And yet, with the above said you will understand that the very concept of labor and pain that existsin life is present only in the form of removal of payment from the work. Therefore, although the payment can put out the suffering and uproot it, they do not affect him during the work, and he has time to experience them, as above-detailed.

It is as the store-owner, whose pain from the labor is completely uprooted. When he searches for it, it is gone during the payment and the servicing of the customers because the reward and the labor come together, without any time difference for the pain of labor to appear.

Now you will clearly understand the words of *The Zohar*, "Where there is labor, there is the *Sitra Achra*, for the *Sitra Achra* is in deficiency, and all her works are in deficiency." It is so because one who has been rewarded with complete faith, the future is to him exactly as the present, for otherwise it would not be considered complete.

For example, if a trusted person promises me something, it is as though I have actually received it. If my sensation is somewhat deficient, meaning that I feel it would be more pleasant if I actually received that thing, then that very extent is missing in my faith in him.

It is therefore obvious that a righteous person, who has been rewarded with complete faith—to the extent that our sages said, "Your landlord is trusted to pay you the reward for your work"—necessarily feels every ounce of the pain of his labor in the payments he receives from the Creator, *although he hasn't actually received them yet.* But for this, his faith illuminates for him completely, in a manner that the giving itself has no room for adding even the smallest bit of contentment.

Had the giving been slightly less valuable than the promise, even in the slightest bit, then he has yet to reach complete faith, and he would therefore *not be considered righteous.* However, he has necessarily reached the completion of faith, where the promise serves for him as giving, and he feels no division between future and present. Thus, he is like the storeowner, for whom the pain from the labor cannot appear while he is serving the customers because the labor and the payment come together. This is the meaning of "A righteous lives by his faith."

By that we can understand the words of *The Zohar:* "Where there is labor, there is the *Sitra Achra,* etc., and there is holiness only in wholeness." It is a clear sign; if he has been rewarded with clinging to holiness, he has necessarily been rewarded with complete faith.

Therefore, from where did he get the sensation of labor? It must be that the *Sitra Achra* is on him because his faith is incomplete. Thus, he necessarily feels pain, and then he is called "wicked," as detailed above at length.

This is the meaning of "The wicked, in their lives, are called 'dead,'" The wicked is "short lived and full of anger," and "A righteous lives by his faith."

Now you will understand the philosophers' question about our holy Torah in the commandment to love the Creator. By Nature's law, there cannot be commandments or coercion in love. Rather, it is a thing that comes by itself, etc., as they elaborated in their foolishness.

According to the above you will understand the question here about the Torah being given only to the children of Israel, who were rewarded first with complete faith, as it is written, "And they believed in the Lord and in His servant, Moses," and also first to "We shall do and we shall hear."

In this manner we have attained all 613 *Mitzvot* [commandments] to do them with complete faith first, as it is known that this is the house's door. Therefore, the extent of the words, "And you shall love the Lord your God," depends completely on the individual, on trying as hard as one can to come to that perpetual level of always receiving abundance of sanctity, strength, and every delight in endless pleasure.

In that state, the love is guaranteed for him by itself, as it is set up in the laws of Nature, in a way that the measure of the love and its commandment are tantamount to our qualification to receive from Him endless pleasure, pleasantness upon pleasantness, as is the way with holiness—it increases.

This is certainly in our hands, meaning the correction of the faith. With that, the light of His love will certainly come by itself because the sensation of receiving the pleasure is in itself the expression of love and blessing for the giver, like a candle and its light, and this is simple.

Yehuda Leib

Letter No. 56

1932

To ... may his candle burn:

I received your letter today and I understood it. And yet, I believe that you should also know my view regarding your words, although in my estimate, you still do not perceive them. For this reason, the words will not delight you, nor will they be pleasant in your view, and for that, the truth will show its way.

Many say, "Who will show me good?" And yet, very few find it. We should therefore understand where is that great and relentless obstacle that mercilessly fails so many.

I have already pointed out to you several times the famous law in the holy books, that nothing is given unless by merit, meaning through labor, which everyone calls "awakening from below." Without it, no bestowal from above, called "awakening from above," will ever happen.

These words and laws are known to all, but their extent is not known, or they do not *want* to know it. For this reason, there is a big edifice of the *Sitra Achra*, which stands and makes allowances in the matter—that it is not necessary to exert beyond human capability. In dire times, one has an entire lore from authors and books showing the kindness and mercy of His guidance with a person who is not so meticulous. He has a thousand pre-prepared proofs for it, instantaneously, as it is written, "The Creator does not criticize His creations."

They said about the such, that the Torah is called SAM, for if he is not rewarded, the Torah itself becomes to him a potion [Sam] of death, for they are learning Torah from SAM, the wicked, and from him they understand. His words of Torah are immediately accepted by the heart, and are always kept in the memory, for they are contemplated day and night, God save us from him and from his followers.

What shall we do for those, and how can we reach out to them, or slightly move them from their places when they are not at all ready for an awakening from below? I wish to say that even if we succeed, with the Creator's help, to draw upon them the greatest awakening of the body, to crave and covet Him, they will still not want, or won't be able to—with that power of theirs—to give the measure of awakening from below that is needed for an awakening from above. This is something about which the Creator has never made allowances, since days of old until this day and always, for "He has given an unbreakable law."

It is said about it, "In full measure, when You send her away, You contend with her." The Creator measures a person one portion at a time. It is also written, "For the iniquity of the Amorite is not yet full," referring also to our topic. The iniquity of the Amorite is the *Klipa* [shell/peel] that keeps and surrounds the fruit, called "awakening from above," or "the land of Israel." That *Klipa* will not move from its place even as a hairsbreadth before Israel complement entirely the necessary measure of awakening from below, called "merit," meaning the labor and exertion beyond human capability.

Anything that one can do is merely called "work"; it is still not considered "labor." When Israel reach that point, they complement their amount, and then it is called "The iniquity of the Amorite is full." In other words, it is evident that the land of Israel and the glory of the Creator, being the holy Divinity, do not belong to them.

Then they break that *Klipa* called "Amorite," and raise Divinity from the dust, and not a moment sooner, as in the verse. This is the meaning of the explicit number, four hundred years, which shows the great precision in that matter, that there are no concessions here at all. As our sages said, the matter of skipping over the end, which was mandatory and obligatory for Israel, that skipping caused all the exiles to this day.

It is also known that the general and particular are equal. That is, in each one from Israel, concerning the soul, there is the matter of coming to the land, and all that is said in the whole of Israel, and that in his awakening from below there is that number, 400 years, which is 400 of death, and 400 of life. Our sages said ASEH [do], for the meaning of 400 years of enslavement refers to the place in which he is permitted to pay back the measure of his labor precisely, for in that there are no concessions, not even as a hairsbreadth.

This is why our sages said, "I did not labor and found, do not believe," and also, "The Torah exists only in one who puts himself to death over it," as well as, "He who wishes to live shall put himself to death," and many others that are similar.

In contrast, they said, "I labored and did not find? Do not believe," for they knew that that wicked SAM, his lore is in his hand to show that it is possible to find the Creator's salvation *without labor beyond human capability*, by which one is made to let go of one's grip in the awakening from below, and he is repelled each day into a great abyss.

Afterward, when he returns and recognizes his falsehood and finds his faith in the words of our sages, that the lack of labor and awakening from below had lowered him to the netherworld, he therefore wishes to strengthen himself and dedicate himself to worshipping the Creator. At that time he promptly returns to him with new heresy.

Thus, even labor does not help at all because He, God forbid, does not hear the prayer of every mouth. That is, he has pre-prepared proofs to show that there are those who exert but do not find at all. This is why they warned, "I labored and did not find, do not believe."

Thus, I have shown you the web in which the robbed souls that have no comfort are judged is that mistake in the meaning of the word, "labor." However, truthful is the verse, "They who seek Me shall find Me."

I still see much evil in the world, where those caught in the web of the *Sitra Achra* labor needlessly, which is only a depiction of punishment. That is, it does not join the count of 400 years whatsoever, and for that, my heart aches more than anything.

About the such, a person should brace himself with the prayer, "May He grant, etc., that we will not labor in vain," for it requires great success in that matter.

You should also know that the labor and exertion that appear in one's heart during the prayer is the most reliable and most guaranteed to reach its goal than any other matter in reality.

Yehuda Leib

Letter No. 57

1932, Jerusalem

To the famous and pious student ... may his candle burn:

I received your letter, and while you are sorry for what is not missing, you should be sorry for what *is* missing. This is the rule: Anything that depends on the Creator exists in abundance, but the vessels of reception can be impressed only by the lower ones, since it is their labor in *Kedusha* [holiness/sanctity] and purity for which He stands and waits. This is what we are concerned with—adding labor. One who adds to that and worries needlessly is only subtracting. Not only is it needless, it is also harmful.

Regarding the friend's question that you ask, at the moment, I have no objection, and "Anyone who is prudent acts with knowledge." Regarding the rest of the questions to which you seek my answers, I will give my one answer to all of them.

There is no happier situation in man's world than when he finds himself despaired with his own strength. That is, he has already labored and done all that he could possibly imagine he could do, but found no remedy. It is then that he is fit for wholehearted prayer for His help because he knows for certain that his own work will not help him.

As long as he feels some strength of his own, his prayer will not be whole because the evil inclination rushes first and tells him, "First you must do what you can, and then you will be worthy of the Creator."

It was said about it, "The Lord is high and the low will see." Once a person has labored in all kinds of work, and has become disillusioned, he comes into real lowliness, knowing that he is the lowest of all the people, and there is nothing good about his body. At that time his prayer is whole, and he is granted by His generous hand.

The writing says about that, "And the children of Israel sighed because of the work ... and their cry went up." It is so because at that time they came into a state of despair from the work. It is as one who pumps out in a punctured bucket. He pumps all day but does not have a drop of water to quench his thirst.

So were the children of Israel in Egypt: Whatever they built was promptly swallowed in its place in the ground, as our sages said.

Similarly, one who has not been rewarded with His love, all that he has done in his work on purifying the soul the day before is as though completely burned the next day. And each day and each moment he must start anew as though he hasn't done a thing in his entire life.

Then, "The children of Israel sighed because of the work," for they evidently saw that they were unfit to ever produce something by their own work. This is why their sigh and prayer were whole, as they should be, and this is why "Their cry went up," since the Creator hears the prayer, and only awaits a wholehearted prayer.

It follows from the above that anything, small or great, is only obtained by prayer. All our labor and work, to which we are obliged, are only to discover our lack of strength and our lowliness—that we are unfit for anything in and of ourselves—for then we can pour out a wholehearted prayer before Him.

We could argue about it, "So I can decide that I am unfit for anything, and why all the labor and exertion?" However, it is a natural law that there is none so wise as the experienced, and before a person tries to actually do all he can do, he is utterly incapable of arriving at true lowliness, to the real extent, as said above.

This is why we must toil in *Kedusha* and purity, as it is written, "Whatsoever you find that you are able to do by your strength, that do," and understand that for it is true and profound.

I have not revealed this truth to you so you would not weaken and give up on the mercy. And although you do not see anything, for even when the measure of labor is complete, it is the time of prayer. But until then, believe in our sages: "I did not labor and found, do not believe."

When the measure is full, your prayer will be complete, and the Creator will grant generously, as our sages instructed us, "I labored and found, believe," for one is unfit for a prayer prior to it, and the Creator hears a prayer.

Yehuda Leib

Letter No. 58

1932, Jerusalem

To the holy rav whose light will shine forever...:

... The question was, "What does 'Haman from the Torah, wherefrom?' imply," from the verse, "Have you eaten from the tree of which I commanded you not to eat?" He said that the question was, "Where do we find in the Torah that the Creator will summon a messenger to reform a person against his will, as was with Haman?" and as it is written, "I will place over you a king such as Haman, and you will repent against your will."

This is what our sages showed about the verse, "Have you eaten from the tree," etc., for then the evil inclination—the angel of death—was created, forcing the man to engage in Torah, as it is written, "I have created the evil inclination, I have created the Torah as a spice." If one is not to engage in Torah, the evil inclination will put him to death.

It follows that the disclosure of the sin of the tree of knowledge that puts to death—explained in the words, "from the tree," etc., —is the messenger that compels a person to reform against his will. This is similar to "I will place over you a king such as Haman, and you will repent against your will."

Had he not been trapped in the serpent's net and had waited for the Sabbath, and ate from the tree of life prior to eating from the tree of knowledge, he would have been granted the *Tikkun* [correction] of the evil inclination being a spice for the Torah. He would not need a forcing messenger such as Haman, as in, "I have created the evil inclination, I have created the Torah as a spice." On the contrary, the evil inclination would have become a spice for the Torah, and now that he sinned, he needs a forcing messenger.

I added to it according to a higher source that there is in the sanctity of the Sabbath, that the evil inclination becoming a spice for the Torah is the meal on the Sabbath evening. This is what is implied in the songs of the ARI, "To enter the openings in the field of apples," as in, "This is the gate to the Lord," and as is explained through the rest of those songs.

On the Sabbath, at the meal of holy *Atik*, it is possible to receive from the highest place, for the Torah needs no spice, as in, "The Torah and the Creator are one," by ascending to the world of *Atzilut*, where it is said, "No harm shall come to you." It therefore follows that if *Adam HaRishon* had waited with his *Zivug* for the Sabbath, he would have been rewarded with the wonderful degree, "The Torah and the Creator are one," for at the time of *Adam HaRishon* the worlds were very high, as stated in Rashbi's essay, *Kedoshim* [holy ones].

Indeed, even after the sin he could have risen to *Atzilut*, through the ascent of the Sabbath, and not come down from there. This is the meaning of what is written, "lest he stretch out his hand and take also from the tree of life, and eat, and live forever." There it was in the form of "The Torah and the Creator are one." But the Creator drove him out from there, as it is written, "And He drove out the man." We should ask, "Why should the Creator mind if he ate from the tree of life and lived forever?"

The answer is that all the wonderful *Kedusha* [holiness] of "the Torah and the Creator are one" that was revealed on the Sabbath was only as a loan. The Sabbath is an awakening from above, without any awakening from below. But the Torah is completed only through an awakening from below, by observing Torah and *Mitzvot*. We should therefore wonder why he was rewarded wholeness on the part of the Creator if his Torah was still incomplete.

This is what our sages answered regarding what the Creator said, "They borrowed on My guarantee, and I collect." That is, "I can lend them the wholeness of Torah to the fullest, until it is enough for 'The Torah and the Creator are one' because 'I collect.' That is, I have no fear at all of 'Lend to the wicked and he will not pay,' for I can place over you a king such as Haman, and you will repent against your will and observe the Torah from love.

"'All that is destined to be collected is deemed collected.' Therefore, I am lending you on the Sabbath day, as it is written, 'and a righteous pardons and gives.'" This is why the Creator did not want him to "stretch out his hand and take also from the tree of life," since then *Adam HaRishon* would not be paying and revealing the Torah as an awakening from below, and it would have remained as a loan.

This would make it groundless from the start because a Torah that is not completed does not merit being "The Torah and the Creator are one." However, the Creator considers the loan as though it was already paid back, since He can force it, and "All that is destined to be collected is deemed collected." Hence, He really did force him: "And He drove out the man," to pay back the loan.

In truth, the suspension also extends from the eating of the tree of knowledge, and this is the meaning of what our sages said about the verse, "Libel is terrible to people," the sin of the tree of knowledge, "You came unto him with libel." With the above-said, we understand that it is to force him to pay for his loan.

With these words we also understand his holy words when he said that the intimation that Haman is from the Torah, since the tree of knowledge is the discernment of "I place over you a king such as Haman," etc. Just as Haman wished to destroy, to kill, and to annihilate all the Jews, women, and children in a single day, so is the tree of knowledge, "for in the day that you eat from it you will surely die."

And just as He forced them to repent from love through the fear of death through Haman's decree, so the abovementioned disclosure of the sin, as it is written, "Have you eaten from the tree of which I commanded you?," etc., will compel man to repent from love, as in, "I have created the evil inclination, I have created the Torah as a spice." It is so because if he does not engage in Torah, he will promptly die because of the serpent.

May the Creator help us pay for what we have borrowed, and may we be granted complete redemption.

About the Author

Rav Yehuda Leib HaLevi Ashlag (1884-1954) is known as Baal HaSulam (Owner of the Ladder) for his *Sulam* (ladder) commentary on *The Book of Zohar*. He was born in Warsaw, Poland, and at age nineteen was ordained as a rabbi in Warsaw. For sixteen years, he served as a *Dayan* (Jewish orthodox judge) and a teacher in Warsaw. In 1921, Baal HaSulam immigrated to Israel and settled in the Old City of Jerusalem.

Baal HaSulam dedicated his life to the dissemination of Kabbalah in Israel and throughout the world. He developed the Ari's method of teaching Kabbalah, making it possible for any person to delve into the depth of reality and reveal its roots and the purpose of existence.

The most famous of his numerous publications are The Sulam Commentary on *The Book of Zohar*—a contemporary explanation of the spiritual processes described in *The Zohar*, and *The Study of the Ten Sefirot*—explicating the Ari's *Tree of Life*. Baal HaSulam is regarded by many as the foremost Kabbalist of the 20th century.

Further Reading

The Secrets of the Eternal Book

The Five Books of Moses (The Torah) are part of the all-time bestselling book, The Bible. Ironically, the Bible is an encoded text. Beneath it lies another level, a hidden subtext that describes the ascent of humanity toward its highest level—the attainment of the Creator.

The Secrets of the Eternal Book decodes some of the Bible's most enigmatic, yet oft-cited epochs, such as the story of Creation, and the Children of Israel's exodus from Egypt.

The author's lively and easygoing style makes for a smooth entrance into the deepest level of reality, where one changes one's world simply by contemplation and desire.

Unlocking the Zohar

The greatest Kabbalist of the 20th century, Rav Yehuda Ashlag (1884-1954) paved a new way for us by which we can reveal the secrets of *The Book of Zohar*. He wrote the *Sulam* [Ladder] commentary and four introductions to the book, in order to help us understand the forces that govern our lives, and to teach us how we can assume control over our destinies.

Unlocking the Zohar is an invitation to a wondrous journey to a higher world. The author, Kabbalist Dr. Michael Laitman, wisely ushers us into the revelations of the *Sulam* commentary. In so doing, Laitman helps us fine-tune our thoughts as we read in *The Zohar*, to maximize the spiritual benefit derived from reading it.

Unlocking the Zohar is an invitation to a wondrous journey to a higher world. The author, Kabbalist Dr. Michael Laitman, wisely ushers us into the revelations of the Sulam commentary. In so doing, Laitman helps us fine-tune our thoughts as we read in *The Zohar*, to maximize the spiritual benefit derived from reading it.

The Kabbalah Experience

The depth of the wisdom revealed in the questions and answers within this book will inspire readers to reflect and contemplate. This is not a book to race through, but rather one that should be read thoughtfully and carefully. With this approach, readers will begin to experience a growing sense of enlightenment while simply absorbing the answers to the questions every Kabbalah student asks along the way.

The Kabbalah Experience is a guide from the past to the future, revealing situations that all students of Kabbalah will experience at some point along their journeys. For those who cherish every moment in life, this book offers unparalleled insights into the timeless wisdom of Kabbalah.

The Path of Kabbalah

This unique book combines beginners' material with more advanced concepts and teachings. If you have read a book or two of Laitman's, you will find this book very easy to relate to.

While touching upon basic concepts such as perception of reality and Freedom of Choice, *The Path of Kabbalah* goes deeper and expands beyond the scope of beginners' books. The structure of the worlds, for example, is explained in greater detail here than in the "pure" beginners' books. Also described is the spiritual root of mundane matters such as the Hebrew calendar and the holidays.

The Book of Zohar: annotations to the Ashlag commentary

The Book of Zohar is an age-old source of wisdom and the basis for all Kabbalistic literature. Since its appearance, it has been the primary, and often only source used by Kabbalists.

Written in a unique and metaphorical language, The Book of Zohar enriches our understanding of reality and widens our worldview. Rav Yehuda Ashlag's unique Sulam (Ladder) commentary allows us to grasp the hidden meanings of the text and "climb" toward the lucid perceptions and insights that the book holds for those who study it.

Attaining the Worlds Beyond

From the introduction to Attaining the Worlds Beyond: "...Not feeling well on the Jewish New Year's Eve of September 1991, my teacher called me to his bedside and handed me his notebook, saying, 'Take it and learn from it.' The following morning, he perished in my arms, leaving me and many of his other disciples without guidance in this world.

"He used to say, 'I want to teach you to turn to the Creator, rather than to me, because He is the only strength, the only Source of all that exists, the only one who can really help you, and He awaits your prayers for help. When you seek help in your search for freedom from the bondage of this world, help in elevating yourself above this world, help in finding the self, and help in determining your purpose in life, you must turn to the Creator, who sends you all those aspirations in order to compel you to turn to Him.'"

Attaining the Worlds Beyond holds within it the content of that notebook, as well as other inspiring texts. This book reaches out to all those seekers who want to find a logical, reliable way to understand the world we live in. This fascinating introduction to the wisdom of Kabbalah will enlighten the mind, invigorate the heart, and move readers to the depths of their souls.

The Wise Heart: Tales and allegories by three contemporary sages

Kabbalah students and enthusiasts in Kabbalah often wonder what the spiritual world actually feels like to a Kabbalist. *The Wise Heart* is a lovingly crafted anthology comprised of tales and allegories by Kabbalist Dr. Michael Laitman, his mentor, Rav Baruch Ashlag (Rabash), and Rabash's father and mentor, Rav Yehuda Ashlag, author of the acclaimed *Sulam* (Ladder) commentary on *The Book of Zohar*. The poems herein offer surprising and often amusing depictions of human nature, with a loving and tender touch that is truly unique to Kabbalists.

Shamati (I Heard)

Rav Michael Laitman's words on the book: "Among all the texts and notes that were used by my teacher, Rav Baruch Shalom Halevi Ashlag (the Rabash), there was one special notebook he always carried. This notebook contained transcripts of his conversations with his father, Rav Yehuda Leib Halevi Ashlag (Baal HaSulam), author of the *Sulam* (Ladder) commentary on *The Book of Zohar*, *The Study of the Ten Sefirot* (a commentary on the texts of the Kabbalist, Ari), and many other works on Kabbalah.

"Not feeling well on the Jewish New Year's Eve of September 1991, the Rabash summoned me to his bedside and handed me a notebook, whose cover contained only one word, *Shamati*

(I Heard). As he handed the notebook, he said, 'Take it and learn from it.' The following morning, my teacher perished in my arms, leaving me and many of his other disciples without guidance in this world.

Committed to Rabash's legacy to disseminate the wisdom of Kabbalah, I published the notebook just as it was written, thus retaining the text's transforming powers. Among all the books of Kabbalah, *Shamati* is a unique and compelling creation."

Kabbalah for the Student

Kabbalah for the Student offers authentic texts by Rav Yehuda Ashlag, author of the *Sulam* (Ladder) commentary on *The Book of Zohar*, his son and successor, Rav Baruch Ashlag, as well as other great Kabbalists. It also offers illustrations that accurately depict the evolution of the Upper Worlds as Kabbalists experience them. The book also contains several explanatory essays that help us understand the texts within.

In *Kabbalah for the Student*, Rav Michael Laitman, PhD, Rav Baruch Ashlag's personal assistant and prime student, compiled all the texts a Kabbalah student would need in order to attain the spiritual worlds. In his daily lessons, Rav Laitman bases his teaching on these inspiring texts, thus helping novices and veterans alike to better understand the spiritual path we undertake on our fascinating journey to the Higher Realms.

Rabash—the Social Writings

Rav Baruch Shalom HaLevi Ashlag (Rabash) played a remarkable role in the history of Kabbalah. He provided us with the necessary final link connecting the wisdom of Kabbalah to our human experience. His father and teacher was the great Kabbalist, Rav Yehuda Leib HaLevi Ashlag, known as Baal HaSulam for his *Sulam* (Ladder) commentary on *The Book of Zohar.* Yet, if not for the essays of Rabash, his father's efforts to disclose the wisdom of Kabbalah to all would have been in vain. Without those essays, few would be able to achieve the spiritual attainment that Baal HaSulam so desperately wanted us to obtain.

The writings in this book aren't just for reading. They are more like an experiential user's guide. It is very important to work with them in order to see what they truly contain. The reader should try to put them into practice by living out the emotions Rabash so masterfully describes. He always advised his students to summarize the articles, to work with the texts, and those who attempt it discover that it always yields new insights. Thus, readers are advised to work with the texts, summarize them, translate them, and implement them in the group. Those who do so will discover the power in the writings of Rabash.

Gems of Wisdom: words of the great Kabbalists from all generations

Through the millennia, Kabbalists have bequeathed us with numerous writings. In their compositions, they have laid out a structured method that can lead, step by step, unto a world of eternity and wholeness.

Gems of Wisdom is a collection of selected excerpts from the writings of the greatest Kabbalists from all generations, with particular emphasis on the writings of Rav Yehuda Leib HaLevi Ashlag (Baal HaSulam), author of the *Sulam* [Ladder] commentary of *The Book of Zohar.*

The sections have been arranged by topics, to provide the broadest view possible on each topic. This book is a useful guide to any person desiring spiritual advancement.

Let There Be Light: selected excerpts from The Book of Zohar

The Zohar contains all the secrets of Creation, but until recently the wisdom of Kabbalah was locked under a thousand locks. Thanks to the work of Rav Yehuda Ashlag (1884-1954), the last of the great Kabbalists, *The Zohar* is revealed today in order to propel humanity to its next degree.

Let There Be Light contains selected excerpts from the series *Zohar for All*, a refined edition of *The Book of Zohar* with the *Sulam* commentary. Each piece was carefully chosen for its beauty and depth as well as its capacity to draw the reader into *The Zohar* and get the most out of the reading experience. As *The Zohar* speaks of nothing but the intricate web that connects all souls, diving into its words attracts the special force that exists in that state of oneness, where we are all connected.

The Science of Kabbalah

Kabbalist and scientist Rav Michael Laitman, PhD, designed this book to introduce readers to the special language and terminology of the authentic wisdom of Kabbalah. Here, Rav Laitman reveals authentic Kabbalah in a manner both rational and mature. Readers are gradually led to understand the logical design of the Universe and the life that exists in it.

The Science of Kabbalah, a revolutionary work unmatched in its clarity, depth, and appeal to the intellect, will enable readers to approach the more technical works of Baal HaSulam (Rabbi Yehuda Ashlag), such as *The Study of the Ten Sefirot* and *The Book of Zohar*. Readers of this book will enjoy the satisfying answers to the riddles of life that only authentic Kabbalah provides. Travel through the pages and prepare for an astonishing journey into the Upper Worlds.

Introduction to the Book of Zohar

This volume, along with *The Science of Kabbalah*, is a required preparation for those who wish to understand the hidden message of *The Book of Zohar*. Among the many helpful topics dealt with in this text is an introduction to the "language of roots and branches," without which the stories in *The Zohar* are mere fable and legend. Introduction to *The Book of Zohar* will provide readers with the necessary tools to understand authentic Kabbalah as it was originally meant to be—as a means to attain the Upper Worlds.

The Kabbalist: a cinematic novel

At the dawn of the deadliest era in human history, the 20th century, a mysterious man appeared carrying a stern warning for humanity and an unlikely solution to its suffering. In his writings, Kabbalist Yehuda Ashlag described in clarity and great detail the wars and upheavals he foresaw, and even more strikingly, the current economic, political, and social crises we are facing today. His deep yearning for a united humanity has driven him to unlock *The Book of Zohar* and make it—and the unique force contained therein—accessible to all.

The Kabbalist is a cinematic novel that will turn on its head everything you thought you knew about Kabbalah, spirituality, freedom of will, and our perception of reality. The book carries a message of unity with scientific clarity and poetic depth. It transcends religion, nationality, mysticism, and the fabric of space and time to show us that the only miracle is the one taking place within, when we begin to act in harmony with Nature and with the entire humanity.

CONTACT INFORMATION

1057 Steeles Avenue West, Suite 532
Toronto, ON, M2R 3X1
Canada

Bnei Baruch USA,
2009 85th street, #51,
Brooklyn, New York, 11214
USA

E-mail: info@kabbalah.info
Web site: www.kabbalah.info

Toll free in USA and Canada:
1-866-LAITMAN
Fax: 1-905 886 9697